PORCHES, DECKS & FENCES

Other Publications:

THE TIME-LIFE GARDENER'S GUIDE

MYSTERIES OF THE UNKNOWN

TIME FRAME

FIX IT YOURSELF

FITNESS, HEALTH & NUTRITION

SUCCESSFUL PARENTING

HEALTHY HOME COOKING

UNDERSTANDING COMPUTERS

LIBRARY OF NATIONS

THE ENCHANTED WORLD

THE KODAK LIBRARY OF CREATIVE PHOTOGRAPHY

GREAT MEALS IN MINUTES

THE CIVIL WAR

PLANET EARTH

COLLECTOR'S LIBRARY OF THE CIVIL WAR

THE EPIC OF FLIGHT

THE GOOD COOK

WORLD WAR II

HOME REPAIR AND IMPROVEMENT

THE OLD WEST

PORCHES, DECKS & FENCES

TIME-LIFE BOOKS
ALEXANDRIA, VIRGINIA

Fix It Yourself was produced by
ST. REMY PRESS

MANAGING EDITOR	Kenneth Winchester
MANAGING ART DIRECTOR	Pierre Léveillé

Staff for *Porches, Decks & Fences*

Series Editor	Kathleen M. Kiely
Editor	Brian Parsons
Series Art Director	Diane Denoncourt
Art Director	Francine Lemieux
Research Editor	Elizabeth Cameron
Designers	Maryse Doray, Solange Pelland
Editorial Assistant	Fiona Gilsenan
Contributing Writers	Edward Earle, James Fehr, Stephen Jones, Grant Loewen
Electronic Designer	Daniel Bazinet
Contributing Illustrators	Gérard Mariscalchi, Jacques Proulx
Technical Illustrators	Nicolas Moumouris, Robert Paquet
Cover	Robert Monté
Index	Christine M. Jacobs
Administrator	Denise Rainville
Coordinator	Michelle Turbide
Systems Manager	Shirley Grynspan
Systems Analyst	Simon Lapierre
Studio Director	Maryo Proulx
Photographer	Julie Léger

Time-Life Books Inc. is a wholly owned subsidiary of
TIME INCORPORATED

FOUNDER	Henry R. Luce 1898-1967
Editor-in-Chief	Jason McManus
Chairman and Chief Executive Officer	J. Richard Munro
President and Chief Operating Officer	N. J. Nicholas Jr.
Editorial Director	Ray Cave
Executive Vice President, Books	Kelso F. Sutton
Vice President, Books	George Artandi

TIME-LIFE BOOKS INC.

EDITOR	George Constable
Executive Editor	Ellen Phillips
Director of Design	Louis Klein
Director of Editorial Resources	Phyllis K. Wise
Editorial Board	Russell B. Adams Jr., Dale M. Brown, Roberta Conlan, Thomas H. Flaherty, Lee Hassig, Donia Ann Steele, Rosalind Stubenberg, Henry Woodhead
Director of Photography and Research	John Conrad Weiser
Asst. Director of Editorial Resources	Elise Ritter Gibson
PRESIDENT	Christopher T. Linen
Chief Operating Officer	John M. Fahey Jr.
Senior Vice Presidents	Robert M. DeSena, James L. Mercer
Vice Presidents	Stephen L. Bair, Ralph J. Cuomo, Neal Goff, Stephen L. Goldstein, Juanita T. James, Hallett Johnson III, Carol Kaplan, Susan J. Maruyama, Robert H. Smith, Joseph J. Ward
Director of Production Services	Robert J. Passantino

Editorial Operations

Copy Chief	Diane Ullius
Production	Celia Beattie
Library	Louise D. Forstall
Correspondents	Elizabeth Kraemer-Singh (Bonn); Maria Vincenza Aloisi (Paris); Ann Natanson (Rome).

THE CONSULTANTS

Consulting Editor **David L. Harrison** served as an editor for several Time-Life Books do-it-yourself series, including *Home Repair and Improvement, The Encyclopedia of Gardening* and *The Art of Sewing.*

Joseph Truini is Shop and Tools Editor of Popular Mechanics magazine and specializes in how-to articles for do-it-yourselfers. He worked for many years as a home improvement contractor and carpenter, and has remodeled numerous homes.

Alfred W. Lees has been a home workshop editor for five national publications, including a 28-year association with Popular Science magazine. He has written several do-it-yourself books and has constructed numerous decks.

Karl Marcuse, special consultant for Canada, is a self-employed carpenter and contractor. He has worked as a home renovator in many countries and is now completing restoration of his century-old home.

Richard Day, a do-it-yourself writer for nearly a quarter century, is a founder of the National Association of Home and Workshop Writers and is the author of several home repair books.

Library of Congress Cataloging-in-Publication Data
Porches, decks & fences.
    p. cm. – (Fix it yourself)
  Includes index.
  ISBN 0-8094-6260-5.
  ISBN 0-8094-6261-3 (lib. bdg.)
1. Porches—Maintenance and repair—Amateurs' manuals.
2. Decks (Architecture, Domestic)— Maintenance and repair—Amateurs' manuals. 3. Fences—Maintenance and repair—Amateurs' manuals. I. Time-Life Books. II. Title: Porches, decks, and fences. III. Series.
TH4970.P67   1988
643' .55—dc19   88-24835
                             CIP

For information about any Time-Life book, please write:
Reader Information
Time-Life Customer Service
P.O. Box C-32068
Richmond, Virginia
23261-2068

CONTENTS

HOW TO USE THIS BOOK

Porches, Decks & Fences is divided into three sections. The Emergency Guide on pages 8-11 provides information that can be indispensable, even lifesaving, in the event of a household emergency. Take the time to study this section *before* you need the important advice it contains.

The Repairs section — the heart of the book — is a comprehensive approach to troubleshooting and repairing porches, decks and fences. Shown below are four sample pages from the chapter on fences, with captions describing the various features of the book and how they work.

For example, if the gate on your chain link fence is crooked or sagging, the Troubleshooting Guide on page 78 will suggest possible causes; if the problem is a damaged hinge, you will be directed to page 92 for detailed instructions on how to replace it. Or, if the surface of your wood fence is stained or discolored, the Troubleshooting Guide on page 77 will offer a number of causes, such as resins from trees or plants, mildew, or chalking paint; it will then direct you to page 79 for step-by-step cleaning and refinishing procedures. Each job has been rated by degree of difficulty and by the average time it

---

Introductory text
Describes the construction of porches, decks or fences, their most common problems and basic repair approaches.

Tools and techniques
General information on carpentry techniques, including sanding, is covered in the Tools & Techniques section *(page 102)*. When a specific tool or method is required for a job, it is described within the step-by-step repair.

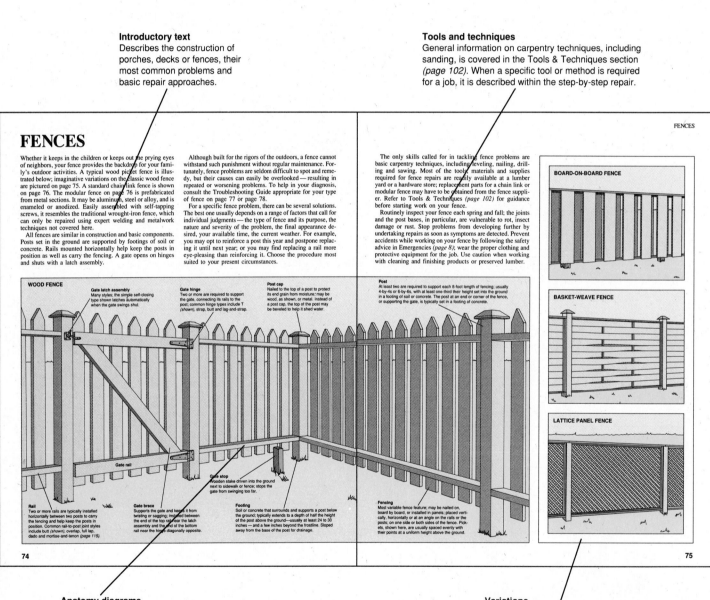

Anatomy diagrams
Locate and describe the various components of a porch, deck or fence.

Variations
Differences in porch, deck and fence construction are described throughout the book, particularly if a repair procedure varies from one type or situation to another.

will take for a do-it-yourselfer to complete. Keep in mind that this rating is only a suggestion. Before deciding whether you should attempt a repair, first read all the instructions carefully. Then be guided by your own confidence, and the tools and time available to you. For more complex or time-consuming repairs, such as rebuilding a concrete footing or replacing a post and concrete footing, you may wish to call for professional help. You will still have saved time and money by diagnosing the problem yourself. Most of the repairs in *Porches, Decks & Fences* can be made with carpentry tools such as hammers, screwdrivers, wrenches, saws, chisels, planes, drills and levels. Any special tool required is indicated in the Troubleshooting Guide. Basic tools — and the proper way to use them — along with information on fasteners and hardware, finishes, concrete and lumber is presented in the Tools & Techniques section starting on page 102. If you are a novice at home repair, read this chapter first in preparation for a job. Repairing a porch, deck or fence can be simple and worry-free if you work logically and systematically, and follow all safety tips and precautions.

Troubleshooting Guide
To use this chart, locate the symptom that most closely resembles your porch, deck or fence problem, review the possible causes in column 2, then follow the recommended procedures in column 3. Simple fixes may be explained on the chart; in most cases you will be directed to an illustrated, step-by-step repair sequence.

Name of repair
You will be referred by the Troubleshooting Guide to the first page of a specific repair job.

Step-by-step procedures
Bold lead-ins summarize each step or highlight the key action pictured. Follow the numbered repair sequence carefully. Depending on the result of each step, you may be directed to a later step, or to another part of the book, to complete the repair.

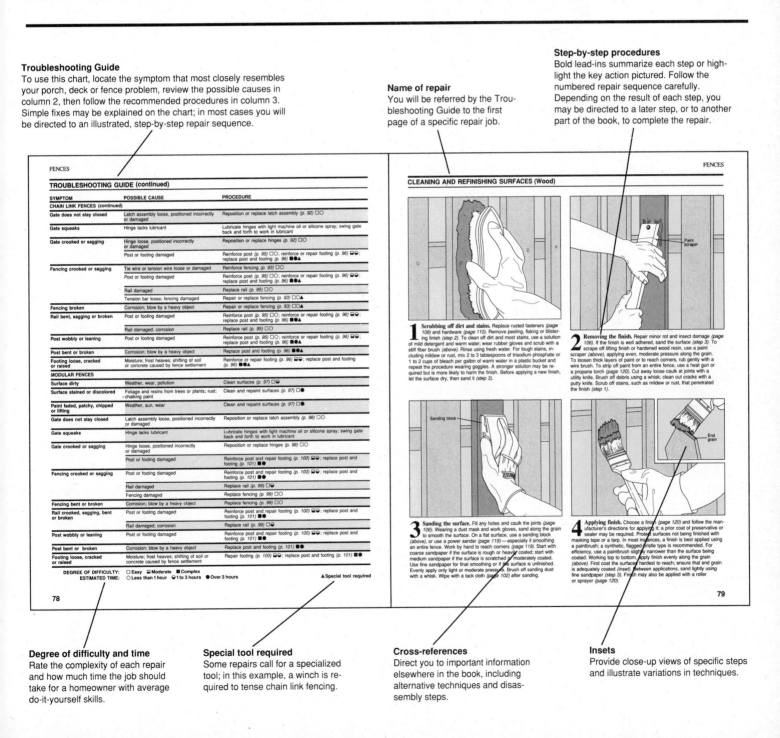

Degree of difficulty and time
Rate the complexity of each repair and how much time the job should take for a homeowner with average do-it-yourself skills.

Special tool required
Some repairs call for a specialized tool; in this example, a winch is required to tense chain link fencing.

Cross-references
Direct you to important information elsewhere in the book, including alternative techniques and disassembly steps.

Insets
Provide close-up views of specific steps and illustrate variations in techniques.

EMERGENCY GUIDE

Preventing problems in porch, deck and fence repair. Whether rustic or formal, your porch, deck or fence defines the quality of living outside your home. Designed for ruggedness, a porch, deck or fence nevertheless requires special care and maintenance to help it withstand the rigors of the outdoors.

The repair of a porch, a deck or a fence need not be any more dangerous than the uses for which it was built. Most work accidents arise from carelessness: improper use of tools, mishandling of toxic materials and misuse of electricity outdoors. The list of safety tips at right covers basic guidelines for the repair of any porch, deck or fence; consult the particular chapter for more specific advice. Also follow the precautions given for handling toxic materials and using electrical tools outdoors *(page 9)*.

Accidents can befall even the most careful worker. Prepare yourself to handle emergencies before they occur by reading the Troubleshooting Guide on page 9, which places emergency procedures at your fingertips. It provides quick-action steps to take and refers you to the procedures on pages 10 and 11 for detailed instructions. Also review Tools & Techniques *(page 102)*; it provides valuable information on repair procedures and the safe use of tools.

Fire and electrical shock are life-threatening emergencies. Deprive fire of its sneak attack by installing smoke detectors judiciously throughout your home. Have the correct fire extinguisher ready to snuff out a blaze before it gets the upper hand; learn how to use the extinguisher before you need it *(page 10)*. If you must rescue someone who is experiencing an electrical shock, do not touch him; use a wood stick, a wooden board or a wooden broom handle to knock the victim free of the power source *(page 10)*.

Keep people away from the work area and do not let anyone walk on a porch or a deck if you are working underneath it. Alert others to a potential hazard by setting up a temporary barrier *(page 11)*, and ensure that any dangerous area is well lit at night. If you suspect that your porch, deck or fence is unsound, use temporary barriers to block access to it, then undertake repairs as soon as possible.

Post emergency fire and medical numbers by the telephone and do not hesitate to use them; in most areas, dial 911 in the event of a life-threatening emergency. Also seek technical help when you need it. If you are in doubt about the nature or safety of a repair, have it checked by a professional builder. Even in non-emergency situations, a building inspector from your municipality can answer questions concerning the condition of your porch, deck or fence.

SAFETY TIPS

1. Before beginning any repair in this book, read the entire procedure. Familiarize yourself with the specific safety information presented in each chapter.

2. Always use the proper tool for the job. Refer to Tools & Techniques *(page 102)* for instructions on the correct use and maintenance of tools. When they are not in use, store tools in a dry location well out of the reach of children.

3. To guard against electrical shock, plug power tools into only GFCI-protected outlets. Never splice a power cord or remove the grounding prong from a three-prong plug. Do not use power tools outdoors during inclement weather, and never use them in a damp area.

4. When working outdoors with power tools, use only heavy-duty, three-prong extension cords rated for outdoor use. Inspect the cord closely; if it is damaged, replace it. Secure the connection between power tool and extension cord by looping the cords together loosely before plugging in the tool.

5. Wear a long-sleeved shirt, long pants, safety boots and work gloves when working with wood, sharp metal or concrete. Wear chemical-resistant rubber gloves when using cleaning solvents, preservatives or finishes. Change after you leave the work area and launder work clothes separately.

6. Use the proper protective gear for the job: a dust mask when sawing or sanding wood that is treated with a preservative or finish; a dust mask and goggles when operating a power saw or a demolition hammer; goggles when working above your head. Remove watches and jewelry before starting a repair.

7. Never undertake repairs when you are tired. If taking any medication, consult your physician. When thirsty, drink a non-alcoholic beverage — alcohol combined with sun or fumes from cleaning and refinishing products can cause illness.

8. Before applying a cleaning or refinishing product, carefully read the label. Follow the manufacturer's instructions for safe use and storage; observe all hazard warnings. Wipe up spills immediately using rags; hang the rags outdoors to dry. Store cleaning and refinishing products out of sunlight, away from heat and well out of the reach of children.

9. Consult your municipal authorities on safe disposal of scrap wood and sawdust, cleaning and refinishing products, and paint chips. Do not burn wood treated with a preservative or finish in a fireplace. Never pour a cleaning or refinishing product down a house drain or into a septic system.

10. Keep people away from the work area. Set up a temporary barrier *(page 11)* when stopping for a break and when working under a porch or deck. Light the work area at night.

11. Keep a first aid kit on hand. Stock it with mild antiseptic, sterile gauze dressings and bandages, adhesive tape and bandages, scissors, tweezers and a packet of needles.

12. Keep a portable ABC-rated fire extinguisher nearby and learn how to use it before you begin work *(page 10)*. Have the extinguisher charged professionally each time it is used. Install smoke detectors inside your home.

13. Post the telephone numbers of your local fire department, hospital and poison control center near the telephone.

TROUBLESHOOTING GUIDE

SYMPTOM	PROCEDURE
Fire in wood, in power tool or outlet, or in cleaning or refinishing product	Call fire department; then use ABC-rated fire extinguisher *(p. 10)*
Electrical shock	Knock person free from source using a wood stick, wooden board or wooden broom handle *(p. 10)*
	Check whether victim is breathing and has pulse. If not, have someone call for medical help, and begin artificial resuscitation or cardiopulmonary resuscitation (CPR) if you are qualified. Otherwise, place victim in recovery position *(p. 10)* and seek medical attention
Spark or shock from power tool	Unplug tool power cord at outlet or shut off power at main service panel; locate and repair cause of spark or shock before using tool again
Extension cord sparks or is hot to touch	Shut off power at main service panel; inspect extension cord and replace it with one rated for power tool being used
Head injury	Check whether victim is breathing and has pulse. If not, have someone call for medical help, and begin artificial resuscitation or cardiopulmonary resuscitation (CPR) if you are qualified. Otherwise, place victim in recovery position *(p. 10)* and seek medical attention
	If victim loses consciousness, even for only one second, seek medical attention
Splinter	Use sterilized needle and tweezers to open wound and pull out splinter *(p. 11)*; if splinter is lodged deeply or if wound becomes infected, seek medical attention
Cut or minor wound	Apply pressure with a clean cloth to stop the bleeding *(p. 11)*; if bleeding persists or if wound is deep or gaping, seek medical attention
Skin scratch or puncture from rusted or dirty fastener or hardware	Wash wound using soap and water; seek medical attention concerning need for a tetanus shot
Wet concrete on skin or clothing	Wash concrete off skin immediately using soap and water; if skin becomes irritated, seek medical attention
	Remove and wash clothing before rewearing; rinse off concrete in basin of water before putting clothing in washing machine
Large object embedded under skin	Support object in place with loose bandages and seek medical attention; removing object can cause hemorrhage
Sawdust, particle, or cleaning or refinishing product in eye	Do not rub eye; flush eye with water *(p. 11)* and seek medical attention
Cleaning or refinishing product swallowed	Call local poison control center or seek medical attention; follow emergency instructions on label and take product with you to hospital
Faintness, dizziness, nausea or blurred vision when working in hot sun	Lie down in shade with feet elevated; apply cool, wet cloth to forehead and drink non-alcoholic beverages; if symptoms persist, seek medical attention
Porch, deck or fence unsound or under repair	Set up a temporary barrier *(p. 11)*
Porch, deck or fence collapsed	Set up a temporary barrier *(p. 11)*; repair porch *(p. 12)*, deck *(p. 46)* or fence *(p. 74)* or consult a professional

HANDLING TOXIC MATERIALS

Wood that is treated with a preservative or finish, and the chemicals in cleaning and refinishing products, can be toxic; when handling them, exercise caution. Preserved lumber, also referred to as pressure-treated or wolmanized lumber, may contain inorganic arsenic-related compounds, pentachlorophenol or creosote. Particles of this wood are harmful if they are inhaled or come into prolonged contact with skin. Until the 1960s, lead was a major ingredient in paints. Lead paint is dangerous if chips of it are eaten or if dust from sanding or fumes from heat stripping are inhaled. Solvents used in cleaning and refinishing products may include petroleum distillates, acetone and methanol; these are harmful if their fumes are inhaled or if they contact your skin. Work with all of these chemicals in a well-ventilated area, and wear the proper safety gear described at left.

USING POWER TOOLS OUTDOORS

To prevent electrical hazards, extra precautions are required when using power tools outdoors. An electrical outlet protected by a ground-fault circuit interrupter (GFCI) is now mandatory in the United States for any new outdoor installation. The GFCI measures the electrical current entering and leaving an appliance plugged into the outlet. It instantly interrupts power if the difference is more than .005 amperes, protecting you from serious shock.

If your outdoor outlet is not GFCI-protected, consult an electrician to change it, or purchase a portable GFCI adapter. Also use a portable GFCI adapter when running an extension cord outdoors from an outlet inside the house that is not GFCI-protected at the main service panel.

CONTROLLING A FIRE

Class ABC extinguisher

Using a fire extinguisher. Call the fire department immediately. If flames or smoke obstruct the doorway, do not attempt to enter the house; call for help using a neighbor's telephone. To snuff a small fire in wood, in a power tool or outlet, or in cleaning or refinishing products, use a dry-chemical fire extinguisher rated ABC.

To use the extinguisher, stand 6 to 10 feet from the fire, with a clear, unobstructed route away from it. Pull the lock pin out of the extinguisher handle and, holding the extinguisher upright, aim the nozzle directly at the base of the flames. Squeeze together the two levers of the handle, spraying in a quick side-to-side motion until the fire is completely extinguished *(left)*. Watch closely for "flashback," or rekindling, and be prepared to spray again. Have the fire department examine the area even if the fire is out. Determine the cause of the fire and remedy it as soon as possible.

RESCUING A VICTIM OF ELECTRICAL SHOCK

Wooden board

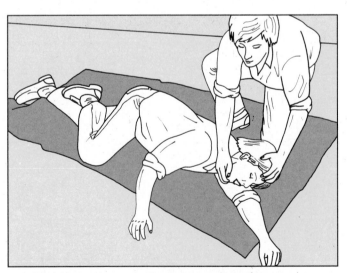

Freeing someone from the source of shock. Do not touch the victim or the power tool. Electrical shock usually throws a person back, but sometimes muscles contract involuntarily around the source of shock. Disconnect a power tool by pulling the power cord plug from the outlet, or shut off power at the main service panel. If power cannot be cut off immediately, use a length of wood such as a board or a wooden broom handle to knock the victim free *(above)*.

Handling a victim of electrical shock. Call for medical help immediately. Check the victim's breathing and heartbeat. If there is none, give mouth-to-mouth resuscitation or cardiopulmonary resuscitation (CPR) only if you are qualified. If an unconscious victim is breathing and has no back or neck injuries, place him in the recovery position *(above)*. Tilt the head back with the face to one side and the tongue forward to maintain an open airway. Keep the victim calm until help arrives.

PROVIDING FIRST AID

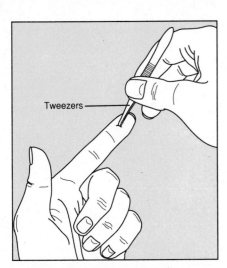

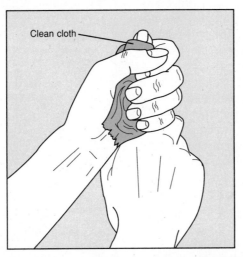

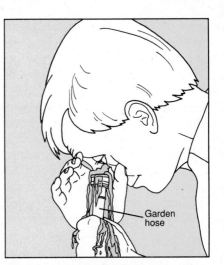

Pulling out a splinter. Wash the skin around the splinter using soap and water. Sterilize a needle and tweezers in alcohol or over a match flame. Ease out the splinter from under the skin using the needle, then pull the splinter out with the tweezers *(above)*. Wash the wound with soap and water. If the splinter cannot be removed, or if the wound becomes infected, seek medical attention.

Treating a cut. To stop a wound from bleeding, wrap it in a clean cloth and apply direct pressure with your hand, elevating the injured limb *(above)*, until the bleeding subsides. Add another clean cloth over the first one if it becomes blood-soaked. If the wound is minor, wash it using soap and water and bandage it with sterile gauze. Seek medical attention if the wound is deep or gaping or if bleeding persists.

Flushing particles and chemicals from the eye. Immediately wash out particles or chemicals that accidently enter the eye; do not rub the affected eye. Holding the eyelids apart with your fingers, flush the eye for 15 minutes using a steady, gentle flow of cool water from a garden hose *(above)* or faucet. Then cover the eye with a sterile gauze dressing and seek medical attention immediately.

SETTING UP A TEMPORARY BARRIER

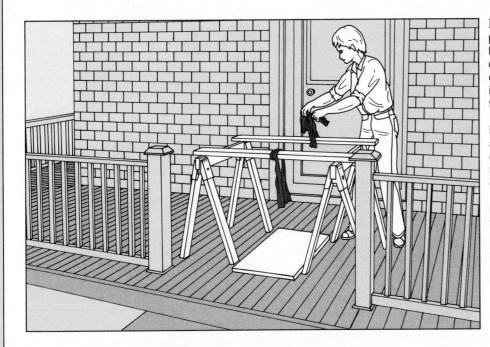

Blocking access with barricades. To prevent an accident, set up a temporary barrier on each accessible side of a porch, deck or fence hazard. Post warning signs for others and ensure that the dangerous area is well lit at night. Undertake or complete the repairs as soon as possible.

Use a sheet of plywood to cover an opening in flooring, or a hole in the ground from a post or a footing. Position sawhorses on opposite sides of the hazardous area and nail boards to them to enclose it. Tie bright-colored rags or ribbons on each side *(left)*.

Remove damaged flooring, stairs or railing—a visible hazard is a less serious risk than an unseen danger. If you suspect the soundness of your porch, deck or fence, or if you cannot identify the cause of its problem, block access to it completely and consult a professional.

PORCHES

The porch is an enduring American architectural feature that dates back to the 1800s. Perhaps no other structure better satisfies our contradictory needs for both shelter and communion with the out-of-doors. An example of the still-popular traditional porch is shown at right. Although the porches standing today vary in design and construction, and are governed by local building codes, they share considerable similarities in their structure and basic components.

Usually built at an entrance to the house, a porch is typically roofed; for any roofing problem that calls for structural repairs above the ceiling, consult a professional. Columns supporting the roof can be of several types: solid, box or round. A box or round column may have an interior solid column. A round column constructed of specially-milled tongue-and-groove lumber may have historical value; consult a professional before undertaking a major repair on it.

The standard porch flooring and ceiling consist of tongue-and-groove boards installed across joists. So the flooring can drain, it usually runs away from the house at a slight angle; its joists, therefore, are typically parallel to the house and supported at each end by a beam, although they can be perpendicular to the house with short spacer joists between them. A ledger fastened to the house supports one end of the beams or joists; the other end is carried by a header — doubled joists or a beam, sometimes called a band beam. Piers, usually of brick, carry the headers and any beams.

Depending on its height above the ground, a porch may have a railing assembly comprising a handrail, a rail and balusters, mounted on the columns or, at intermediate points, on a newel post. The common stair assembly consists of notched stringers, treads and often risers. A stringer is mounted on a header at the top and rests on a footing at the bottom; the notches hold horizontal treads and vertical risers.

The causes of some porch problems can be easily overlooked — resulting in repeated or worsening problems. A cracked joist, for example, can be repaired, but it may be a warning of a hidden problem with a beam or pier. To help in your diagnosis, consult the Troubleshooting Guide on pages 14 and 15. The best repair depends on the type of porch, the nature and severity of the problem, the final appearance desired, your available time and the weather. For example, you may opt to repair a column this year and postpone replacing it until next year; or you may find replacing a handrail more eye-pleasing than reinforcing or repairing it. All of the tools, materials and supplies required for porch repair are readily available at a lumber yard or a building supply center.

Whenever you are working below a porch, install a temporary barrier to keep others off it *(page 11)*. Always support the roof if you are working on a column *(page 33)*; before undertaking a repair on a joist, a beam, the ledger or a pier, ensure that beams and joists are adequately supported on jacks *(page 124)*. Refer to Tools & Techniques *(page 102)* and Emergencies *(page 8)* for guidance before starting a job. Inspect your porch each season. Wood joints and spots where water can collect are especially vulnerable to rot and insect damage.

PORCH ANATOMY

Column
One required every 8 to 10 feet to support the roof. Can be a solid 4-by-4, 4-by-6 or 6-by-6; a box made of four 1-by-6s, 1-by-8s *(shown)* or 1-by-10s nailed together; or a round pillar of specially-milled tongue-and-groove boards. A box or round column may have an interior solid column; air circulation is typically provided by a hole in the ceiling near it.

Handrail
Installed horizontally between columns or newel posts, usually with butt joints *(page 115)*; 30 to 40 inches above the flooring or as specified by local building codes.

Rail
Installed horizontally between columns or newel posts, usually with butt joints at each end *(page 115)*; height above flooring specified by local building codes.

Baluster
Installed vertically between the handrail and rail, 4 to 8 inches apart per local building codes.

Fascia
Trim board of 1-by-10 or 1-by-12 installed on the header for appearance; a miter joint *(page 115)* is commonly used at a corner.

Newel post
Supports a handrail and rail where there is no column; can be a solid 4-by-4, 4-by-6 or 6-by-6, or a box made of four 1-by-6s, 1-by-8s *(shown)* or 1-by-10s nailed together. Cap helps post shed water.

Riser
Optional board installed vertically on a notched stringer to close the space between two treads.

Tread
At least one, 10 3/4 inches wide, required for every 7 1/4 inches of porch height; typically supported at each end by a notched stringer.

Stringer
Two or more support the treads and risers; typically a notched 2-by-12 fastened at the top to the header behind the fascia board, and resting at the bottom on a footing.

Stair assembly footing
Supports the bottom of each stringer of the stair assembly; commonly concrete *(shown)*, 4 to 8 inches deep, or patio blocks.

Flooring
Typically 1-by-4 tongue-and-groove boards installed across joists; perpendicular to the house at a slight slope for drainage. The ceiling is of similar boards running parallel to the house.

Ledger
Supports beams or joists at the side of the house; installed on brick or masonry walls with expansion bolts, on wood walls with lag bolts or carriage bolts. May have a sill on which beams or joists rest (shown).

Molding
To trim bottom of a column, typically of 1-by-6 and quarter-round (shown) with miter joints (page 115) at the corners. A round column often has a separate piece at the bottom called a plinth, and at the top called a capital.

Joist
One required for every 16 or 24 inches of flooring; typically run parallel to the house, supported at each end by a beam, but can run perpendicular from the ledger to the header and carry short spacer joists. A full lap joint (page 115) commonly connects two joists on a beam (shown). Short joists called jack joists (shown) run to doubled corner joists.

Doubled corner joists
Support the flooring at a corner of the house; ends of each joist are beveled in opposite directions and installed at the ledger and header corners.

Header
Carries beams or joists at the perimeter; supported every 8 to 10 feet by at least one pier. Can be doubled joists or a beam, also known as a doubled band beam.

Pier
Can support a column, the end of a header, the end of a beam, a joist, or doubled corner joists. At least one required for each column; at least two required every 8 to 10 feet for a header, a beam, a joist and doubled corner joists. Often constructed of brick (shown); typically 12 inches by 16 inches — 16 inches by 16 inches at a corner. Supported by a concrete footing that usually extends to a depth of at least 24 to 30 inches and a few inches below the frostline.

Beam
One required every 8 to 10 feet to carry the joists; typically 2-by-12, supported at one end by a ledger and fastened at the other end to a header and supported by a pier.

Skirting panel
Installed on furring strips on the piers, and along the fascia board between piers, for appearance; lattice type (shown) allows air to circulate.

TROUBLESHOOTING GUIDE

SYMPTOM	POSSIBLE CAUSE	PROCEDURE
Surface dirty	Weather, wear, pollution	Clean surfaces (p. 16) □◑
Surface stained or discolored	Fasteners or hardware rusted	Replace fasteners (p. 108) □○ and hardware (p. 110) □○
	Plant foliage and resins; mildew caused by humidity; chalking paint	Clean and refinish surfaces (p. 16) □●
Finish faded, patchy, chipped, or lifting	Weather, sun, wear	Clean and refinish surfaces (p. 16) □●
Lattice skirting split or crooked; or wood spongy	Rot or insect damage	Repair minor rot and insect damage (p. 106) □○
	Skirting fasteners loose	Replace fasteners (p. 108) □○
	Wood shrinkage; porch settlement	Repair or replace lattice skirting panel (p. 17) □○
Flooring board sagging or lifted; or ceiling board sagging	Flooring or ceiling board fasteners loose	Replace fasteners (p. 108) □○
	Flooring or ceiling board, or joist under it, warped; board cupping or damaged	Reinforce flooring (p. 18) □○; repair or replace flooring or ceiling (p. 18) ◪◑
Baluster crooked or cracked; or wood spongy	Baluster fasteners loose	Replace fasteners (p. 108) □○
	Rot or insect damage	Repair minor rot and insect damage (p. 106) □○
	Wood shrinkage; porch settlement	Repair or replace baluster (p. 20) □○
Handrail or rail split or cracked; or wood spongy	Rot or insect damage	Repair minor rot and insect damage (p. 106) □○
	Wood shrinkage; shifting of wood joints caused by porch settlement	Reinforce (p. 21) □○, repair (p. 22) □◑ or replace (p. 23) □◑ handrail or rail
Handrail or rail wobbly, crooked, twisted or sagging	Handrail or rail fasteners or hardware loose	Replace fasteners (p. 108) □○ and hardware (p. 110) □◑
	Newel post or column loose or damaged	Reinforce (p. 24) ◪◑ or repair (p. 25) ◪◑ solid newel post; reinforce (p. 25) □○ or repair (p. 26) ◪◑ hollow newel post; replace newel post (p. 26) ◪◑; repair (p. 34) ◼◑ or replace (p. 35) ◼◑ solid column; repair (p. 35) ◼◑ or replace (p. 36) ◼◑ box column; repair plinth or capital (p. 36) ◪◑; replace round column (p. 37) ◼◑
	Handrail or rail damaged	Reinforce (p. 21) □○, repair (p. 22) □◑ or replace (p. 23) □◑ handrail or rail
Newel post cap crooked or cracked; or wood spongy	Rot or insect damage	Repair minor rot and insect damage (p. 106) □○
	Newel post fasteners loose	Replace fasteners (p. 108) □○
	Wood shrinkage; weather	Replace newel post cap (p. 23) □○
Newel post split or cracked; or wood spongy	Rot or insect damage	Repair minor rot and insect damage (p. 106) □○
	Wood shrinkage; shifting of wood joints caused by porch settlement	Reinforce (p. 24) ◪◑ or repair (p. 25) ◪◑ solid newel post; reinforce (p. 25) □○ or repair (p. 26) ◪◑ hollow newel post; replace solid or hollow newel post (p. 26) ◪◑
Newel post wobbly, twisted or leaning	Header, stringer, handrail, or rail fasteners or hardware loose	Replace fasteners (p. 108) □○ and hardware (p. 110) □◑
	Header or stringer supporting newel post damaged	Repair header (p. 40) ◪◑; reinforce (p. 28) □○, repair (p. 29) □◑ or replace (p. 30) ◪◑ stringer
	Newel post damaged	Reinforce (p. 24) ◪◑ or repair (p. 25) ◪◑ solid newel post; reinforce (p. 25) □○ or repair (p. 26) ◪◑ hollow newel post; replace solid or hollow newel post (p. 26) ◪◑
Tread or riser split or cracked; or wood spongy	Rot or insect damage	Repair minor rot and insect damage (p. 106) □○
	Wood shrinkage; porch settlement	Replace tread (p. 27) □○ or riser (p. 28) □○
Tread or riser crooked, twisted or sagging	Tread fasteners loose	Replace fasteners (p. 108) □○
	Tread, or stringer under it, warped	Reinforce tread (p. 27) □○
	Stringer damaged	Reinforce (p. 28) □○, repair (p. 29) □◑ or replace (p. 30) ◪◑ stringer
	Tread or riser damaged	Replace tread (p. 27) □○ or riser (p. 28) □○
Stringer split or cracked; or wood spongy	Rot or insect damage	Repair minor rot and insect damage (p. 106) □○
	Wood shrinkage; shifting of wood joints caused by porch settlement	Reinforce (p. 28) □○, repair (p. 29) □◑ or replace (p. 30) ◪◑ stringer

DEGREE OF DIFFICULTY: □ Easy ◪ Moderate ◼ Complex
ESTIMATED TIME: ○ Less than 1 hour ◑ 1 to 3 hours ● Over 3 hours

SYMPTOM	POSSIBLE CAUSE	PROCEDURE
Stringer crooked, twisted or sagging	Stringer fasteners loose	Replace fasteners *(p. 108)* □○
	Beam, header or joist connected to stringer damaged	Repair beam or header *(p. 40)* ◨●; replace beam *(p. 41)* ■●; reinforce *(p. 38)* □○, repair *(p. 38)* □● or replace *(p. 39)* ◨● joist
	Stringer damaged	Reinforce *(p. 28)* □○, repair *(p. 29)* □● or replace *(p. 30)* ◨● stringer
Stair assembly footing loose, cracked or raised	Moisture, frost heaves; shifting of soil or concrete caused by porch settlement	Reinforce or repair *(p. 31)* □●, or replace *(p. 32)* □● stair assembly footing
Column split or cracked; or wood spongy	Rot or insect damage	Repair minor rot and insect damage *(p. 106)* □○
	Wood shrinkage; shifting of wood joints caused by porch settlement	Repair *(p. 34)* ■● or replace *(p. 35)* ■● solid column; repair *(p. 35)* ■● or replace *(p. 36)* ■● box column; repair column plinth or capital *(p. 36)* ◨●; replace round column *(p. 37)* ◨●
Column wobbly, twisted or leaning	Header fasteners loose	Replace fasteners *(p. 108)* □○
	Pier or footing supporting column damaged	Replace wood pier *(p. 42)* ◨●; repair brick pier *(p. 43)* ◨● or replace brick pier and footing *(p. 44)* ■●
	Beam or header supporting column damaged	Repair beam or header *(p. 40)* ◨●; replace beam *(p. 41)* ■●
	Column damaged	Repair *(p. 34)* ■● or replace *(p. 35)* ■● solid column; repair *(p. 35)* ■● or replace *(p. 36)* ■● box column; repair column plinth or capital *(p. 36)* ◨●; replace round column *(p. 37)* ◨●
Joist split or cracked; or wood spongy	Rot or insect damage	Repair minor rot and insect damage *(p. 106)* □○
	Wood shrinkage; porch settlement	Reinforce *(p. 38)* □○, repair *(p. 38)* □● or replace *(p. 39)* ◨● joist
Joist crooked, twisted or sagging	Joist fasteners or hardware loose	Replace fasteners *(p. 108)* □○ or hardware *(p. 110)* □●
	Beam or header supporting joist damaged	Repair beam or header *(p. 40)* ◨●; replace beam *(p. 41)* ■●
	Joist damaged	Reinforce *(p. 38)* □○, repair *(p. 38)* □● or replace *(p. 39)* ◨● joist
Ledger sagging or cracked; or wood spongy	Rot or insect damage	Repair minor rot and insect damage *(p. 106)* □○
	Wood shrinkage; shifting of wood joints caused by porch or house settlement	Reinforce *(p. 39)* □○ or repair *(p. 40)* ◨● ledger
Beam or header split or cracked; or wood spongy	Rot or insect damage	Repair minor rot and insect damage *(p. 106)* □○
	Wood shrinkage; porch settlement	Repair beam or header *(p. 40)* ◨●; replace beam *(p. 41)* ■●
Beam or header crooked, twisted or sagging	Beam fasteners or hardware loose	Replace fasteners *(p. 108)* □○ and hardware *(p. 110)* □●
	Pier or footing supporting beam or header damaged	Replace wood pier *(p. 42)* ◨●; repair brick pier *(p. 43)* ◨● or replace brick pier and footing *(p. 44)* ■●
	Beam or header damaged	Repair beam or header *(p. 40)* ◨●; replace beam *(p. 41)* ■●
Wood pier split or cracked; or wood spongy	Rot or insect damage	Repair minor rot and insect damage *(p. 106)* □○
	Wood shrinkage; porch settlement	Replace wood pier *(p. 42)* ◨●
Wood pier wobbly, twisted or leaning	Wood pier or footing damaged	Replace wood pier and footing *(p. 42)* ◨●
Brick pier cracked or leaning	Moisture, frost heaves; shifting of soil or concrete caused by porch settlement	Repair brick pier *(p. 43)* ◨● or replace pier and footing *(p. 44)* ■●
Porch sagging	Pier or footing damaged	Replace wood pier *(p. 42)* ◨●; repair brick pier *(p. 43)* ◨● or replace brick pier and footing *(p. 44)* ■●
	Beam or header damaged	Repair beam or header *(p. 40)* ◨●; replace beam *(p. 41)* ■●
	Ledger damaged	Reinforce *(p. 39)* □○ or repair *(p. 40)* ◨● ledger
	Joist damaged	Reinforce *(p. 38)* □○, repair *(p. 38)* □● or replace *(p. 39)* ◨● joist
	Flooring boards rotted or damaged	Reinforce *(p. 18)* □○, repair or replace *(p. 18)* ◨● flooring

DEGREE OF DIFFICULTY: □ **Easy** ◨ **Moderate** ■ **Complex**
ESTIMATED TIME: ○ **Less than 1 hour** ◐ **1 to 3 hours** ● **Over 3 hours**

CLEANING AND REFINISHING SURFACES

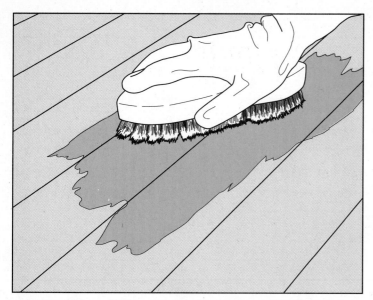

1 **Scrubbing off dirt and stains.** Replace rusted fasteners *(page 108)* and hardware *(page 110)*. Remove loose or lifting finish *(step 3)*. To clean off dirt and most stains, use a solution of mild detergent and warm water; wear rubber gloves and scrub with a stiff fiber brush *(above)*. Rinse using fresh water. On tough stains, such as mildew or rust, repeat the procedure wearing goggles, mixing 2 to 3 tablespoons of trisodium phosphate or 1 to 2 cups of bleach per gallon of warm water in a plastic bucket; higher concentrations, which may be required, are more likely to harm the finish.

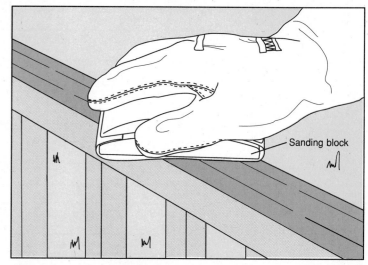

Sanding block

2 **Sanding the surface.** Repair minor rot and insect damage *(page 106)*. Fill holes and caulk joints *(page 106)*. Wearing a dust mask and work gloves, sand along the grain to smooth the surface. On a flat surface, use a sanding block *(above)* or a power sander *(page 119)*, especially if smoothing an entire porch. Work by hand to reach corners *(page 119)*. Start with coarse sandpaper if the surface is rough or heavily coated; start with medium-grit sandpaper if the surface is scratchy or moderately coated. Use fine sandpaper for final smoothing or if the surface is unfinished. Apply only light to moderate pressure. Brush off sanding dust with a whisk. Wipe using a tack cloth *(page 102)* after sanding is completed, then apply a finish *(step 4)*.

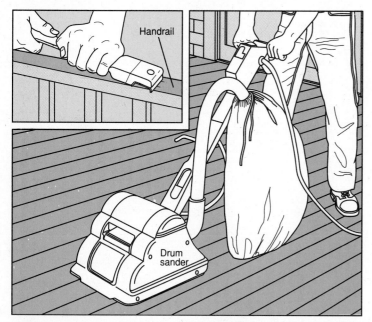

Handrail

Drum sander

3 **Removing the old finish.** To scrape off lifting finish or hardened wood resin, use a paint scraper *(inset)*; apply even pressure along the grain. To strip off paint, use a heat gun *(page 120)*. Scrub off stains that have penetrated the finish *(step 1)* and sand the surface *(step 2)* before applying a new finish. To strip paint off the entire floor, use a tilt-up drum sander, shown here, and a rotating-disk edger, available at a tool rental agency. Wear a dust mask and ear protection. Following the manufacturer's directions, sand along the grain *(above)*, overlapping each pass by 2 to 3 inches; start with coarse sandpaper and progress to medium and fine *(page 119)*. Use the edger on corners. Brush off debris using a broom, then wipe with a tack cloth *(page 102)*.

4 **Applying a finish.** Choose a finish *(page 120)* and follow the manufacturer's instructions for applying it; a primer coat of preservative or sealer may be required. Protect surfaces not to be finished with masking tape or a tarp. For large flat areas, use a roller, fitted with an extension pole to avoid bending or reaching *(above)*. In other instances, a finish is best applied using a paintbrush; a synthetic, flagged-bristle type is recommended. For efficiency, use a paintbrush slightly narrower than the surface width. Working top to bottom, apply finish evenly along the grain. Coat first the surfaces hardest to reach, and ensure that end grain is adequately coated. Between applications, sand lightly using fine sandpaper *(step 2)*. In the right conditions, apply finish with a paint sprayer *(page 120)*.

REPAIRING OR REPLACING THE FLOORING OR CEILING (continued)

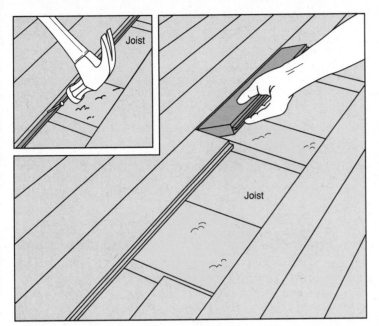

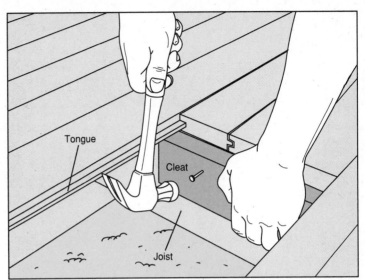

2 **Installing tongue-and-groove boards.** Purchase replacement boards at a lumber yard. If replacing a section of boards, add cleats *(step 3)*. If replacing a section of boards between joists, saw each new board to length *(page 112)*. Apply preservative or finish *(page 120)*. To install a board next to another board, fit its groove over the tongue on the other board and butt its end against the end of any undamaged board *(above)*; seat it with a rubber mallet. Drive a nail *(page 108)* into the tongue corner at each joist *(inset)* and cleat. To install a board between other boards, trim and insert it *(step 4)*.

3 **Adding support cleats.** To support new boards at the end of an undamaged section, add a cleat to the joist; use 2-by-4 or stronger wood. Saw each cleat to a length at least equal to the width of the open section at the joist *(page 112)* and apply preservative or finish *(page 120)*. Position the cleat at the top edge of the joist, bore pilot holes *(page 117)* and drive in nails *(above)* or screws *(page 108)*. For best results, install at least two fasteners, or space fasteners every 4 to 6 inches, offsetting them. Install each board next to another board *(step 2)* or between other boards *(step 4)*.

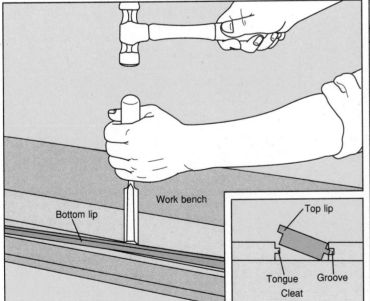

4 **Trimming and inserting tongue-and-groove boards.** If part of the length of a replacement board fits between other boards, trim off only the part of the bottom lip of its groove that fits the tongue of the board next to it; position the board to mark where they meet. If installing the entire length of a board between other boards, trim off the entire bottom lip. To trim off the bottom lip, use a utility knife and straight-edged wood block to score it, then cut it off with a wood chisel and ball-peen hammer *(above, left)* or mallet *(page 116)*. Apply preservative or finish to the cut edge *(page 120)*.

To install the board, fit its tongue in the groove of the board next to it *(inset)*; butting its end against the end of any undamaged board. Fit the top lip of its groove over the tongue on the other board *(above)* and seat it with a rubber mallet. Drive nails every 8 to 10 inches through the board into the boards next to it *(page 108)*. After installing boards all the way to the end of the floor or ceiling, mark the end of the boards with a chalkline *(page 112)*, saw them off *(page 112)* and apply preservative or finish to the end grain. Replace any nails removed from the molding. Fill holes *(page 106)* and refinish damaged surfaces *(page 16)*.

REPLACING A BALUSTER

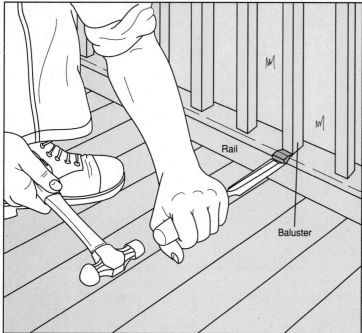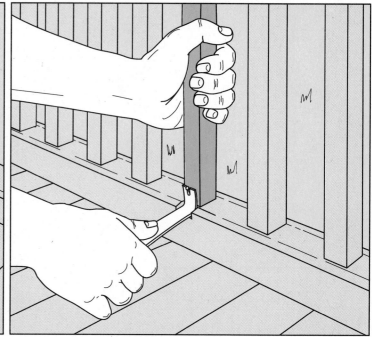

1 **Removing a baluster.** To remove a baluster from a channel, take off molding, cut an opening, or remove the handrail and rail *(page 23)*. To take off molding, pull the nails *(page 107)*; loosen them first by lifting up the molding with a pry bar. To cut an opening, saw into one side of the rail 3/4 to 1 inch deep on each side of the baluster *(page 112)*; chisel across the sawcuts with a wood chisel and ball-peen hammer *(above, left)* or mallet *(page 116)*; keep the block removed.

To remove the baluster, pull the nails using a pry bar *(above, right)*, hammer or nail puller *(page 107)*. First loosen the nails by hammering on the back of the baluster at the top near the handrail and at the bottom near the rail; cushion the blows with a wood block if the baluster will be reinstalled. If required, angle the baluster to slide it out. If the baluster is damaged, repair it *(step 2)*, especially if it is turned or ornate. Alternatively, install a new baluster *(step 3)*.

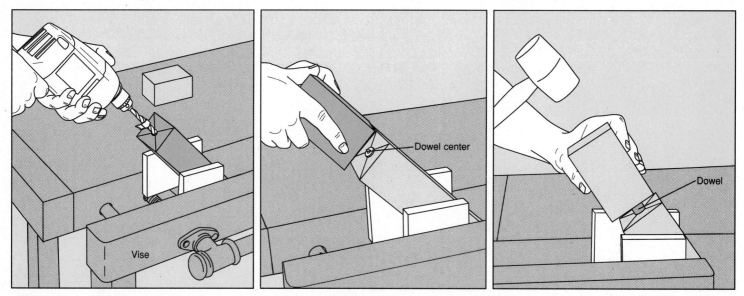

2 **Splicing a baluster.** If a baluster is split unevenly along its length, glue and clamp it *(page 116)*. If a baluster is broken cleanly across its width, splice it with a dowel. To splice the baluster, cut apart the sections at a 90-degree angle *(page 112)*; if a square section at the top or bottom of an ornate baluster is damaged, replace it. Purchase wood for the new section at a lumber yard; use a 1/4-inch dowel to join narrow sections, a 3/8-inch dowel for wide sections.

Saw the dowel about 1 1/2 inches long, beveling the ends with coarse sandpaper *(page 119)*. Saw any new section 1/16 inch longer than the old damaged section. Mark the center on the end of one section: if it is square, draw diagonal lines across opposite corners; if it is round, draw

two lines at about a 90-degree angle to each other, crossing at the center. Bore a hole 3/4 inch deep *(page 117)* using a bit the same width as the dowel; wrap tape around it to indicate when to stop *(above, left)*. Fit a dowel center into the hole. To mark the center of the other section, position it correctly and press it against the dowel center *(above, center)*. Bore a hole 3/4 inch deep in that section at the mark.

Apply preservative or finish *(page 120)*. Put glue in the holes and on the dowel, and join the sections: Use a rubber mallet to tap the dowel into the hole in one section, then tap the other section onto the dowel *(above, right)*. Clamp the splice *(page 116)*. Wipe off excess glue with a cloth. Allow the glue to set 24 hours.

3 Installing a baluster. If installing a new baluster, purchase wood for the replacement at a lumber yard and saw it to length *(page 112)*, positioning it against the handrail and rail to mark it. Apply preservative or finish *(page 120)*.

To install a new or repaired baluster, position it between the handrail and the rail; if required, slide it in at an angle and measure the distance between other balusters to space it evenly. To install a baluster in a channel, first fit it under the handrail and then slide it onto the rail *(far left)*.

Bore pilot holes *(page 117)* and drive two nails through the top into the handrail and through the bottom into the rail *(page 108)*. Nail on any block *(near left)* or molding removed, or reinstall the handrail and rail *(page 23)*. Fill holes *(page 106)* and refinish damaged surfaces *(page 16)*.

REINFORCING A RAIL OR HANDRAIL

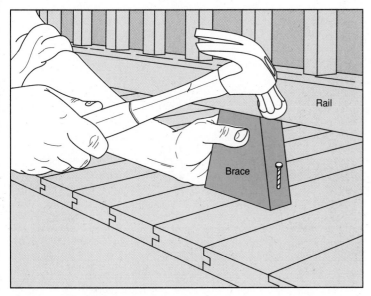

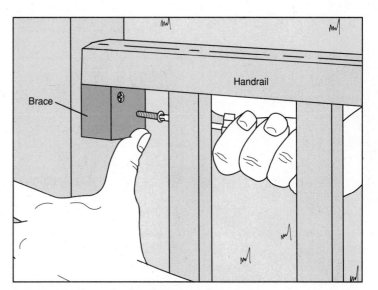

Bracing the length of a rail. To reinforce a rail along its length, install 2-by-4 or 2-by-6 braces under it. To mark a brace for size, position it on the flooring or tread against the rail; prop up the rail at its correct position or have a helper support it. Saw each brace to length *(page 112)*, angling the sides for drainage. Apply preservative or finish *(page 120)*. Position each brace under the rail, bore pilot holes *(page 117)* and drive nails *(page 108)* through each side of it into the flooring *(above)* or tread; also nail the rail onto the brace. Fill holes and caulk joints *(page 106)*. Refinish damaged surfaces *(page 16)*.

Bracing the end of a handrail or rail. To reinforce the end of a handrail or rail, install hardware *(page 110)* or a wood brace. Use lumber of the same dimensions as the handrail or rail and saw it to a length equal to the width of the handrail or rail *(page 112)*. Apply preservative or finish *(page 120)*. Position the brace under the handrail or rail and against the column or newel post. Bore pilot holes *(page 117)* and nail *(page 108)* or screw *(above)* the brace onto the newel post or column; also nail or screw the handrail or rail onto the brace. For best results, install two fasteners on each surface, offsetting them. Fill holes and caulk joints *(page 106)*. Refinish damaged surfaces *(page 16)*.

REPAIRING A RAIL OR HANDRAIL

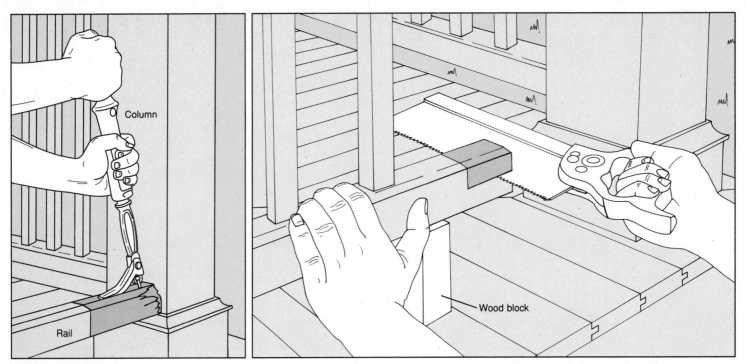

1 **Removing the damage.** Replace the damaged section of a handrail or a rail by splicing in a new section extending to the nearest column or post. Remove any molding in the way by pulling the nails *(page 107)*. Mark the end of the damaged section using a carpenter's square *(page 112)*. Have a helper support the undamaged section, brace it with pieces of wood or prop it on blocks, then saw it off with a handsaw *(page 112)*. Remove any balusters from the damaged section *(page 20)*. To take the end of the damaged section off the column or newel post, remove the fasteners *(page 107)* or hardware *(page 110)*; pull nails using a nail puller *(above, left)*, hammer or pry bar. At the cut end of the undamaged section, measure and mark one side of a half-lap joint 4 to 6 inches long: Using a tape measure and carpenter's square, mark the length of the half lap along the center of each side, and join their ends across one adjacent side. Saw the half lap *(page 115)* using a backsaw *(above, right)*; if required, temporarily nail on a straight-edged wood block as a saw guide *(page 108)*.

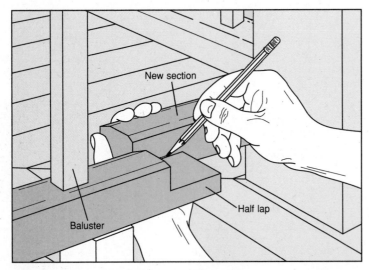

2 **Measuring and sawing a half-lap joint.** Purchase lumber for a splice of the same dimensions as the rail at a lumber yard. Saw the new section to length *(page 112)*, positioning it against the column or newel post and the end of the undamaged section to mark it. To mark the half lap, reposition the new section in turn against each side of the half lap on the undamaged section *(above)*. Saw the half lap using a backsaw *(page 115)*. If required, rout *(page 118)*, bore *(page 117)* or chisel *(page 116)* the new section to shape. Apply preservative or finish *(page 120)*.

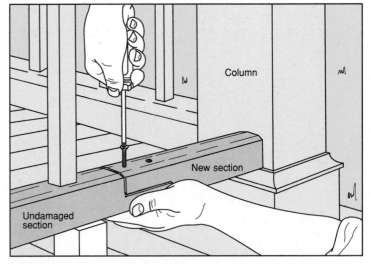

3 **Splicing a new section.** Position the new section against the undamaged section and clamp the half-lap joint *(page 116)*; if required, have a helper support the new section, brace it with pieces of wood or prop it on blocks. Bore pilot holes *(page 117)* and drive in screws *(above)* or nails *(page 108)*; for best results, install at least two fasteners, offsetting them. Drive screws or nails through the new section into the column or newel post, or install hardware *(page 110)*. Reinstall any baluster removed *(page 21)*; reinstall the balusters first if they fit into a channel. Nail on any molding removed. Fill holes and caulk joints *(page 106)*. Refinish damaged surfaces *(page 16)*.

REPLACING A RAIL OR HANDRAIL

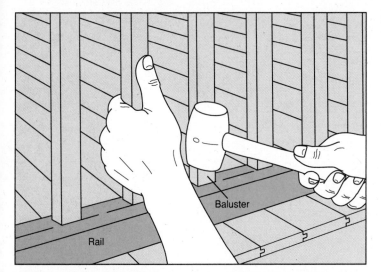

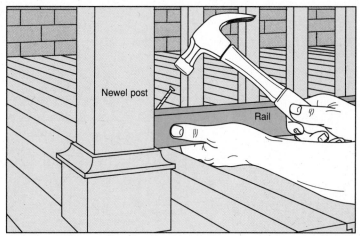

1 **Removing a rail or handrail.** To take off an entire railing assembly, remove the rail first and the handrail last. To remove a handrail or rail from a newel post or column, remove the fasteners *(page 107)* or hardware *(page 110)*; have a helper support it, brace it with pieces of wood or prop it on blocks. To loosen nails, hammer on the bottom of the handrail or rail near the newel post or column; cushion the blows with a wood block if it will be reinstalled. Using a rubber mallet, hammer on the bottom of the handrail or the top of the rail *(above)* to remove the balusters. Pull the nails with a hammer, pry bar or nail puller *(page 107)*.

2 **Installing a rail or handrail.** Purchase wood for a replacement handrail or rail at a lumber yard and saw it to length *(page 112)*; to position and mark it, have a helper support one end or temporarily nail it *(page 108)*. If required, rout *(page 118)*, bore *(page 117)* or chisel *(page 116)* it to shape. Apply preservative or finish *(page 120)*. To put up an entire railing assembly, install the handrail first and the rail last. To install a handrail or rail, position each end on the newel post or column with the balusters in the channel, if there is one. Bore pilot holes *(page 117)* and drive in nails *(above)* or screws *(page 108)* or install hardware *(page 110)*; use at least two fasteners at each end. Nail on the balusters. Fill holes and caulk joints *(page 106)*. Refinish damaged surfaces *(page 16)*.

REPLACING A NEWEL POST CAP

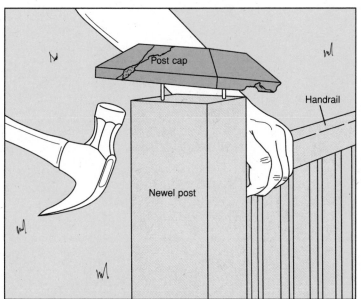

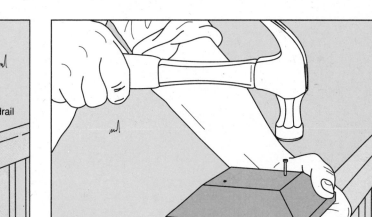

1 **Removing a newel post cap.** To take off a decorative post cap that is screwed on, turn it counterclockwise; first run a utility knife between it and the newel post to break the seal of any finish or caulk. To remove the double-ended screw, use pliers to twist it counterclockwise. To take off a standard post cap, pull the nails *(page 107)*. Loosen the nails by using a pry bar or hammering up on the bottom overhanging the newel post *(above)*; cushion the blows with a wood block if the post cap will be reinstalled.

2 **Installing a newel post cap.** Purchase a replacement post cap or wood for a standard post cap at a lumber yard. Saw a standard post cap to size *(page 112)*, measuring or tracing another to mark it; if required, rout *(page 118)*, plane *(page 117)* or chisel *(page 116)* it to shape. Apply preservative or finish *(page 120)*. To install a decorative post cap, twist a double-ended screw clockwise into the top of the newel post using pliers, then turn the post cap clockwise onto it; first bore a pilot hole *(page 117)*, marking diagonals across opposite corners to center it. To install a standard post cap, center it and drive at least two finishing nails *(page 108)* into opposite corners *(above)*. Fill holes and caulk joints *(page 106)*. Refinish damaged surfaces *(page 16)*.

REINFORCING A SOLID NEWEL POST

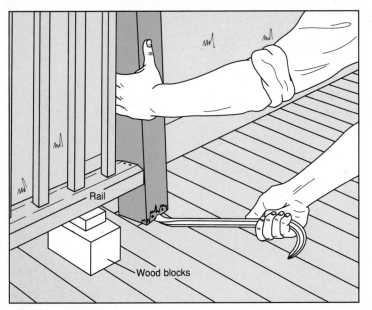

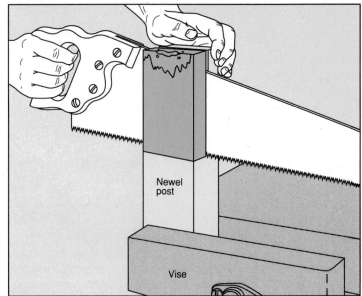

1 **Removing a newel post.** To reinforce a solid newel post, install hardware *(page 110)*; or splice a wooden brace called a tenon onto it, then install it through the flooring onto the side of the header or through the tread onto the side of the stringer. Remove any skirting panel in the way *(page 17)*. To splice on a tenon, take off the newel post. First remove any molding by pulling the nails *(page 107)* and take off any handrail and rail *(page 23)*. Mark the newel post's position on the flooring or tread and pull the nails out of the bottom, loosening them by lifting the newel post using a crowbar *(above)*.

2 **Measuring and sawing for a splice.** Bore *(page 117)*, chisel *(page 116)* and saw *(page 112)* an opening for a tenon in the flooring next to the header, or in the tread next to the stringer. Purchase lumber for a tenon of half the thickness of the newel post at a lumber yard; saw it 6 to 8 inches longer than the width of the header or stringer. Saw one side of a half-lap joint *(page 115)* 6 to 8 inches long at the bottom of the newel post *(above)* to fit the tenon; to mark the half lap, position the tenon against each side of the newel post, in turn. Apply preservative or finish *(page 120)*.

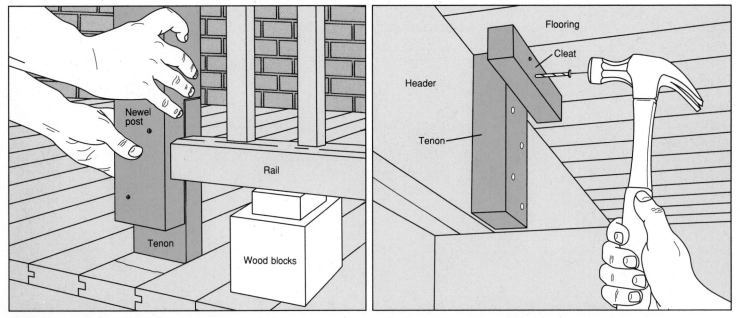

3 **Splicing a tenon and reinstalling the newel post.** To splice on the tenon, position it on the newel post, clamp the joint *(page 116)*, bore pilot holes *(page 117)* and install screws *(page 108)*; for best results, drive at least two screws into each side of the joint, off-setting them. To reinstall the newel post, slide the tenon through the opening in the flooring *(above, left)* and against the side of the header, or through the opening in the tread and against the side of the stringer. Position the newel post using a carpenter's level *(page 118)*, bore pilot holes and drive nails *(page 108)* at an angle through each side of it into

the header or stringer. From below, bore pilot holes through the tenon and nail or screw it onto the header or stringer. To support the flooring at the edge of the tenon, saw a 2-by-2 cleat to a length about twice the width of the tenon *(page 112)*. Apply preservative or finish *(page 120)*. Position the cleat against the flooring and tenon, bore pilot holes and drive nails *(above, right)* or screws through the cleat into the tenon, and through the flooring into the cleat. Reinstall any skirting panel *(page 17)*. Nail on any molding and reinstall any handrail and rail *(page 23)*. Fill holes and caulk joints *(page 106)*. Refinish damaged surfaces *(page 16)*.

REPAIRING A SOLID NEWEL POST

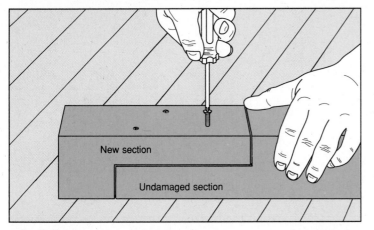

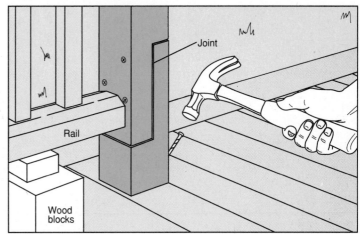

1 **Splicing a new section.** To repair a solid newel post, splice in a new section. Remove the newel post *(page 24)*. Saw off the damaged section *(page 112)* and saw one side of a half-lap joint 6 to 8 inches long at the cut end of the newel post *(page 115)*. Purchase lumber for a new section of the same dimensions as the newel post at a lumber yard. Saw it to length, with a half lap to fit the undamaged section. To mark it, position it against each side of the other half lap, in turn, and measure the height of another newel post. Apply preservative or finish *(page 120)*. Position the joint, bore pilot holes *(page 117)* and drive screws *(page 108)* into each side, offsetting them *(above)*.

2 **Reinstalling the newel post.** Position the newel post on the flooring or tread, using the marks left by the old one as a guide. Straighten the post using a carpenter's level *(page 118)*. Bore pilot holes *(page 117)* and drive nails *(page 108)* on each side of the newel post through the flooring into the header *(above)*, or through the tread into the stringer. Nail on any molding, and reinstall any handrail and rail removed *(page 23)*. Fill holes and caulk joints *(page 106)*. Refinish damaged surfaces *(page 16)*.

REINFORCING A HOLLOW NEWEL POST

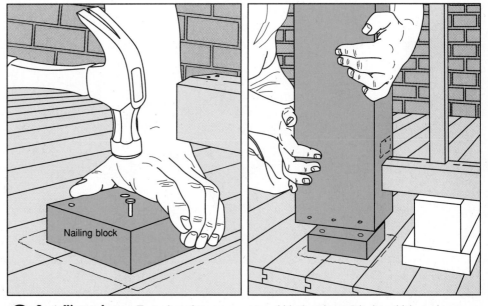

1 **Removing a newel post.** To reinforce a hollow newel post, install hardware on the outside *(page 110)* or a brace on the inside. To install a brace, take off the newel post. First, remove any molding by pulling the nails *(page 107)*, and take off any handrail and rail *(page 23)*. Mark the newel post position on the flooring or tread, pull the nails and lift off the newel post *(above)*.

2 **Installing a brace.** To make a brace, use a wood block at least 2 inches thick, and saw it to the length and width required to fit inside the newel post *(page 112)*. Apply preservative or finish *(page 120)*. Using the marks you made as a guide, position the brace on the flooring or tread, bore pilot holes *(page 117)* and drive nails *(above, left)* or screws *(page 108)*.
Position the newel post on the brace *(above, right)*, bore pilot holes and drive nails or screws through each side of it into the brace; also drive nails or screws through it into the flooring and header, or through it into the tread and stringer. Nail on any molding and reinstall any handrail and rail removed *(page 23)*. Fill holes and caulk joints *(page 106)*. Refinish damaged surfaces *(page 16)*.

REPAIRING A HOLLOW NEWEL POST

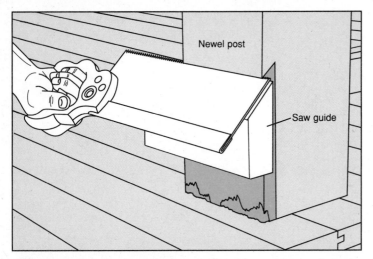

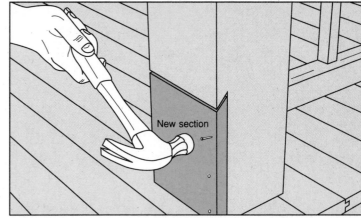

1 **Removing the damage.** To repair a hollow newel post, replace the damaged section. Remove any molding at the base of the newel post by pulling the nails *(page 107)*. Take off any handrail or rail in the way *(page 23)*. Mark a horizontal line across the post above the damaged section using a carpenter's level *(page 112)*. Temporarily nail on *(page 108)* a saw guide cut to a length equal to the width of the newel post, with one side beveled at a 45-degree angle *(page 112)*. To remove the damaged section, saw it off *(above)* and pull the nails out of the sides and bottom; loosen them by pulling out the sides of the section and lifting up its bottom with a pry bar.

2 **Installing a new section.** Purchase replacement wood for a new section at a lumber yard. Bevel the end using the saw guide as in step 1. Saw it to length *(page 112)*, measuring the distance from the top of the bevel on the post to the flooring or tread. Saw a tapered shape if required, fitting the new section under the undamaged section to mark it. If required, bevel the edges for miter joints *(page 115)*. Apply preservative or finish *(page 120)*. To install the new section, position it, bore pilot holes *(page 117)* and drive nails *(page 108)* every 2 to 3 inches into the sides *(above)*. Nail on any molding and reinstall any handrail or rail removed *(page 23)*. Fill holes and caulk joints *(page 106)*. Refinish damaged surfaces *(page 16)*.

REPLACING A SOLID OR HOLLOW NEWEL POST

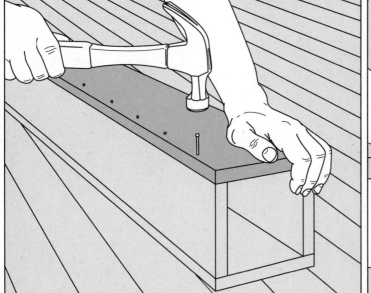

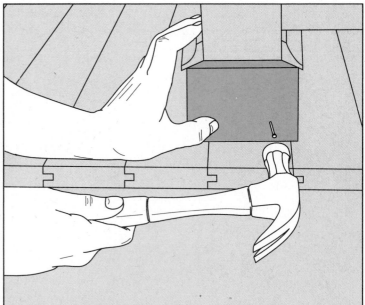

Removing and installing a newel post. Remove any molding by pulling the nails *(page 107)*. Take off any handrail, rail and post cap *(page 23)*. Mark the newel post position on the flooring or tread, pull the nails out of the bottom and remove it; loosen the nails by lifting the bottom using a crowbar. Purchase wood for a replacement newel post at a lumber yard and saw it to length *(page 112)*; to mark it, measure the height of another newel post. For a hollow newel post, saw a tapered shape if required, positioning each board against another newel post to mark it; if required, bevel the sides for miter joints *(page 115)*.

Apply preservative or finish *(page 120)*. For a hollow newel post, position the boards, bore pilot holes *(page 117)* and drive nails *(page 108)* every 4 to 6 inches into the sides *(above, left)*. To install a newel post, position it using the marks as a guide, and straighten the post using a carpenter's level *(page 118)*. Bore pilot holes and drive nails at an angle into each side through the flooring into the header, or through the tread into the stringer. Nail on any molding *(above, right)* and reinstall any handrail, rail and post cap removed *(page 23)*. Fill holes and caulk joints *(page 106)*. Refinish damaged surfaces *(page 16)*.

REINFORCING A TREAD

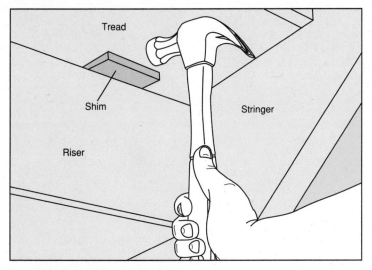

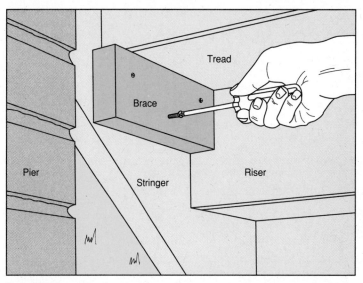

Bracing the length of a tread. To reinforce a tread along its length, install a wood shim every 4 to 6 inches along the top of the riser. To work above the stair assembly, remove any molding in the way by pulling the nails *(page 107)*; to work below, remove any skirting panel *(page 17)*. Saw *(page 112)*, chisel *(page 116)* or plane *(page 117)* each shim to a thickness of 1/4 to 1/2 inch, beveling one end into a point. Apply preservative or finish *(page 120)*. Use a hammer to tap each shim under the tread until it is level *(above)*; chisel off any end that can be seen protruding from the stair assembly. Nail on any molding *(page 108)* and reinstall any skirting panel removed *(page 17)*. Refinish damaged surfaces *(page 16)*.

Bracing the end of a tread. To reinforce the end of a tread, install hardware *(page 110)* or a wood brace. Remove any skirting panel required to work below the stair assembly *(page 17)*. For a brace, use a 2-by-2 or 2-by-4, and saw it to a length at least equal to the width of the tread *(page 112)*. Apply preservative or finish *(page 120)*. Position the brace under the tread and against the stringer. Bore pilot holes *(page 117)* and drive in screws *(page 108)*, offsetting them *(above)*; for best results, also nail through the tread into the brace *(page 108)*. Reinstall any skirting panel removed *(page 17)*. Fill holes *(page 106)* and refinish damaged surfaces *(page 16)*.

REPLACING A TREAD

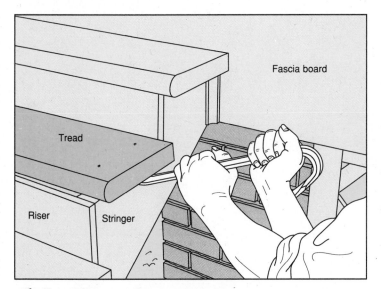

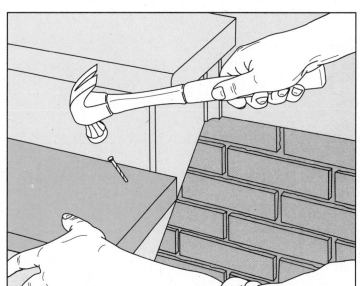

1 Removing a tread. To take off a tread, pull its nails out of each stringer and any riser *(page 107)*. First remove any molding by pulling the nails, and take off any newel post *(page 26)*. To loosen the nails in the tread, hammer up on the bottom overhanging the stringer, or use a crowbar to lift up the end *(above)*; protect undamaged surfaces with a wood block. From under the stair assembly, pull any nails in the tread driven through the back of a riser; to work under the stair assembly, remove any skirting panel in the way *(page 17)*. If the tread is damaged, replace it.

2 Installing a tread. Purchase wood for a replacement tread at a lumber yard, saw it to length *(page 112)* and apply preservative or finish *(page 120)*. To install a tread, position it on the stringers, butting it against any riser; bore pilot holes *(page 117)* and nail the tread *(page 108)* to each stringer *(above)*. For best results, also drive nails every 4 to 6 inches along the back of a riser into the tread. Nail on any molding and reinstall any newel post *(page 26)* and skirting panel removed *(page 17)*. Fill holes *(page 106)*. Refinish damaged surfaces *(page 16)*.

REPLACING A RISER

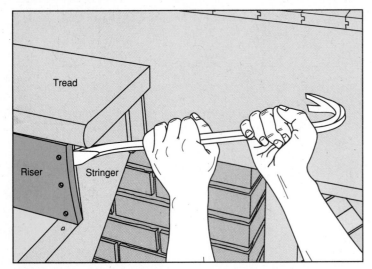

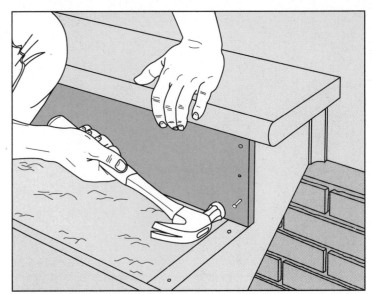

1 **Removing a riser.** To take off a riser, remove the tread in front of it *(page 27)* and pull the nails out of it along each stringer *(page 107)*. First loosen the nails by hammering on the back of the riser near the stringers, or use a crowbar to pull out the ends of the riser *(above)*. Protect undamaged surfaces with a wood block. Pull out nails with a hammer, a pry bar or a nail puller. If the riser is damaged, replace it.

2 **Installing a riser.** Purchase wood for a replacement riser at a lumber yard, saw it to length *(page 112)* and apply preservative or finish *(page 120)*. To install a riser, position it on the stringers, butting it against the tread above it; bore pilot holes *(page 117)* and nail it *(page 108)* to each stringer *(above)*. Reinstall the tread in front of the riser *(page 27)*. Fill holes *(page 106)* and refinish damaged surfaces *(page 16)*.

REINFORCING A STRINGER

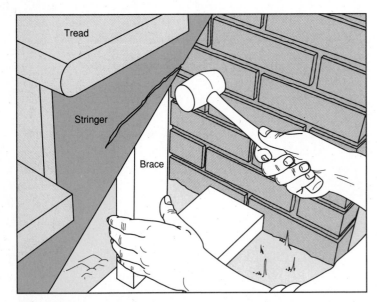

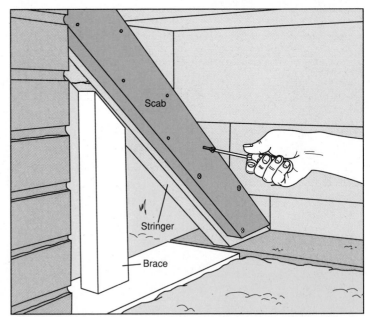

1 **Bracing a stringer.** To reinforce a stringer, support it in position with a wood brace, then install a scab: For best results, install the scab under the stair assembly. Remove any riser *(step 1, above)*, tread *(page 27)*, newel post *(page 26)* and skirting panel *(page 17)* in the way. For a brace, use 2-by-4 or stronger wood; saw it to the length required to support the stringer *(page 112)*, positioning it against the stringer to mark it. Set the brace on a wood pad and use a rubber mallet to tap the brace under the stringer until it is supported in position *(above)*. Temporarily nail *(page 108)* the brace to the stringer.

2 **Installing a scab.** Purchase lumber for a scab of the same dimensions as the stringer at a lumber yard. Saw it to a length at least 5 to 6 inches longer than the damaged section *(page 112)*. Apply preservative or finish *(page 120)*. Position the scab over the damaged section and bore pilot holes *(page 117)* through it into the stringer. Drive in screws *(page 108)* every 4 to 6 inches, offsetting them *(above)*. Reinstall any riser *(step 2, above)*, tread *(page 27)*, newel post *(page 26)* and skirting panel *(page 17)* removed. Fill holes *(page 106)* and refinish damaged surfaces *(page 16)*.

REPAIRING A STRINGER

Splicing a stringer run. To repair a stringer run, remove the damaged section and splice in a new section. Remove any riser *(page 28)*, tread *(page 27)* and newel post *(page 26)* in the way. Mark a horizontal line just below the damaged section using a carpenter's level *(page 112)*, then temporarily nail *(page 108)* a 2-by-2 along the line as a saw guide. Saw off the damaged section *(page 112)*, cutting across the stringer run *(above, left)* and down the stringer rise. Saw the new section to fit precisely the space left by the damaged section; this is easiest if you use a board of the same thickness as the stringer. Apply preservative or finish *(page 120)*. To install the new section, position it on the stringer run, butting it against the stringer rise; bore pilot holes *(page 117)* and nail *(above, right)* or screw *(page 108)* it to the stringer run. Reinstall any riser *(page 28)*, tread *(page 27)* and newel post *(page 26)* removed. Fill holes *(page 106)* and refinish damaged surfaces *(page 16)*.

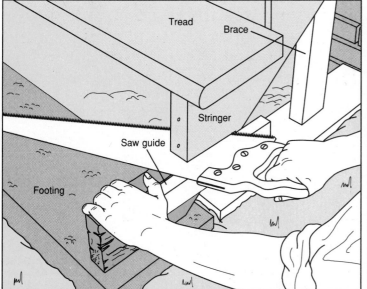

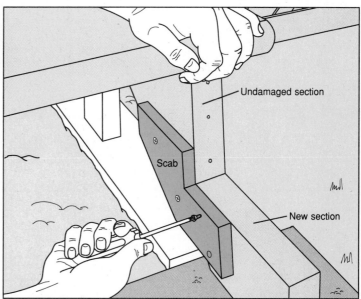

Splicing a stringer base. To repair a stringer base, support it in position with a wood brace and replace the damaged section. Remove any riser *(page 28)*, tread *(page 27)*, newel post *(page 26)* and skirting panel *(page 17)* in the way. For a brace, use 2-by-4 or stronger wood; saw it to the length required *(page 112)*, positioning it against the stringer to mark it. Set the brace on a wood pad and use a sledgehammer to tap the brace under the stringer; temporarily nail *(page 108)* the brace to the stringer. Just above the damaged section, mark a horizontal line using a carpenter's level *(page 112)*. Nail a 2-by-2 along the line as a saw guide and saw off the damaged section *(above, left)*. Purchase lumber for a new section of the same dimensions as the stringer at a lumber yard; also buy wood for a scab of at least half its thickness.

Support the wood for the new section against the undamaged section to mark its bottom edge; use the level to mark a horizontal line and saw along it. Sit the bottom on the footing, mark the top the same way and saw along it. To mark the bottom, rise and run lengths, measure another stringer; note the new section juts 1/16 to 1/8 inch above the run to allow for the saw kerf. Position the new section under the undamaged section. Position the scab over the joint to mark it and saw it 5 to 6 inches longer than the joint. Apply preservative or finish *(page 120)*. Position the new section and the scab, bore pilot holes *(page 117)* and screw on *(page 108)* the scab *(above, right)*. Reinstall any riser *(page 28)*, tread *(page 27)*, newel post *(page 26)* and skirting panel *(page 17)* removed. Fill holes *(page 106)* and refinish damaged surfaces *(page 16)*.

REPLACING A STRINGER

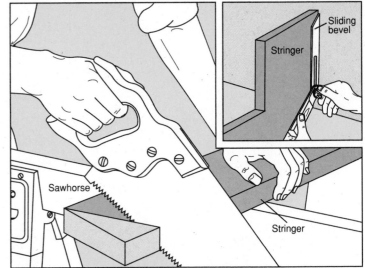

1 **Removing a stringer.** Remove any riser *(page 28)*, tread *(page 27)*, newel post *(page 26)* and skirting panel *(page 17)* in the way. To take off a stringer, remove the fasteners *(page 107)* or hardware *(page 110)* at the top from the header, under the fascia board; check also for fasteners at any wood block mounted on a joist to support the stair assembly. Use a screwdriver to take out screws *(above)*. If a stringer is damaged, replace it. Purchase wood for a replacement stringer at a lumber yard; or, if a damaged stringer is of a standard size, purchase a pre-notched stringer and install it *(step 4)*.

2 **Measuring and sawing a new stringer.** To mark the length of the new stringer, measure the length of the underside of another stringer, from the header to the footing. To mark each end of the new stringer, use a sliding bevel *(page 112)* to measure its angle on the underside of another stringer: at the top, the angle formed by the stringer and the header *(inset)*; at the bottom, the angle formed by the stringer and footing. Saw the new stringer to length *(page 112)*, with the required angle at each end *(above)*.

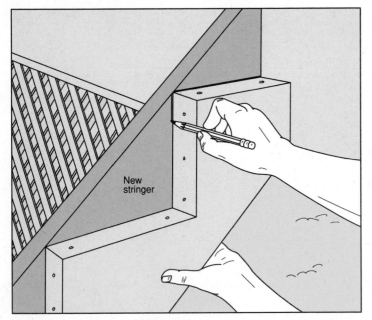

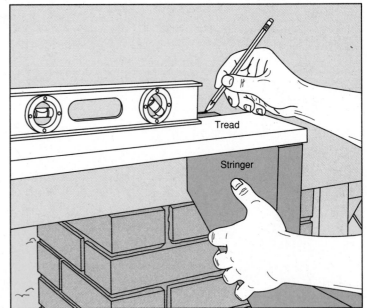

3 **Measuring and sawing stringer notches.** To mark notches on the new stringer, position it against another stringer; have a helper support it or temporarily nail it *(page 108)*. Trace the notches onto the new stringer using a pencil *(above)*. Take down the new stringer and saw the notches with a power saw, completing the ends of each cut using a handsaw *(page 112)*. If required, temporarily nail on a straight-edged wood block as a saw guide. Apply preservative or finish *(page 120)*.

4 **Installing a stringer.** To position a stringer, support the top against the header and sit the bottom on the footing. Reposition the stringer until a tread rests level on it; mark the stringer position on the header *(above)*. To install the stringer, bore pilot holes *(page 117)* and drive in screws *(page 108)* or install hardware *(page 110)* at the header; also drive screws into any wood block mounted on a joist to support the stair assembly. Reinstall any riser *(page 28)*, tread *(page 27)*, newel post *(page 26)*, fascia board and skirting panel *(page 17)* removed. Fill holes *(page 106)* and refinish damaged surfaces *(page 16)*.

REINFORCING OR REPAIRING A STAIR ASSEMBLY FOOTING

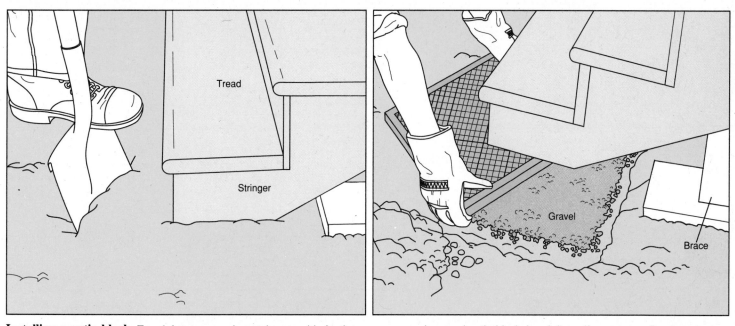

Installing a patio block. To reinforce or repair a stair assembly footing that is not concrete, install a patio block; if the stair assembly footing is a patio block, reposition or replace it. Support the bottom of each stringer in position with a wood brace; first remove any skirting panel in the way *(page 17)*. For braces, use 2-by-4 or stronger wood; saw each brace to the length required *(page 112)* by positioning it against the stringer to mark it. Set each brace on a wood pad and use a sledgehammer to tap each brace under the stringer until it is supported. Nail the braces to the stringers temporarily *(page 108)*. Wearing work gloves, remove a damaged patio block; break it up, if necessary. Purchase new patio blocks, 12 to 16 inches square, at a building supply center. To install a patio block, use a spade to dig a hole at the bottom of the stringer to a depth of 4 to 6 inches *(above, left)*. Tamp the bottom of the hole using your feet, line it with 2 to 4 inches of gravel and tamp again. Wearing work gloves, slide the patio block under the bottom of the stringer. Position the patio block, adding or removing gravel and tamping, until it sits level, with the stringer resting in position on it. Reinstall any skirting panel removed *(page 17)*.

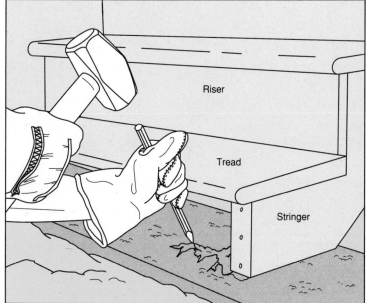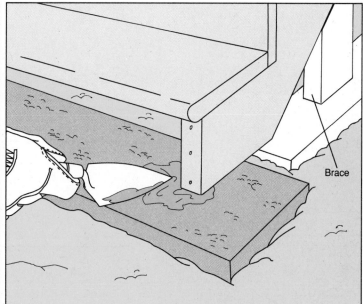

Breaking up and replacing concrete. To reinforce or repair a stair assembly footing made of concrete, break up the damaged section and replace it. Support the bottom of each stringer in position with a wood brace; first remove any skirting panel in the way *(page 17)*. For braces, use 2-by-4 or stronger wood; saw each brace to the length required *(page 112)* by positioning it against the stringer to mark it. Set each brace on a wood pad and use a sledgehammer to tap it under the stringer until it is supported. Temporarily nail the braces to the stringers *(page 108)*. Wearing work gloves and goggles, break up the damaged section of concrete using a bull-point chisel and a sledgehammer *(above, left)* or a demolition hammer *(page 122)*; first remove the bottom riser *(page 28)* or tread *(page 27)* if it is in the way. Clean off loose particles with a wire brush. Dampen undamaged concrete with water before repairing the footing. Mix and spread concrete patching compound *(page 122)* using a trowel *(above, right)*. Allow the footing to set. Reinstall any riser *(page 28)*, tread *(page 27)* and skirting panel *(page 17)* removed.

REPLACING A STAIR ASSEMBLY FOOTING

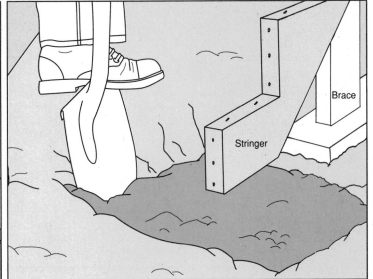

1 Removing a footing. Before replacing a stair assembly footing, support each stringer in position with a wood brace. First remove any riser *(page 28)*, tread *(page 27)*, newel post *(page 26)* and skirting panel *(page 17)* in the way. For braces, use 2-by-4 or stronger wood; saw each brace to the length required *(page 112)* by positioning it against the stringer to mark it. Set each brace on a wood pad, and use a sledgehammer to tap it under the stringer until it is supported. Temporarily nail the braces to the stringers *(page 108)*.

If the footing is concrete, wear work gloves and goggles and break it up using a bull-point chisel and a sledgehammer *(above, left)* or a demolition hammer *(page 122)*. Remove the pieces. If the footing is a patio block, lift it up with a crowbar and wear work gloves to remove it; if the patio block is damaged, replace it. To replace a footing, enlarge the hole at the bottom of the stringer 6 to 8 inches on each side using a spade *(above, right)* and install a patio block *(step 2)* or pour a concrete footing *(step 3)*.

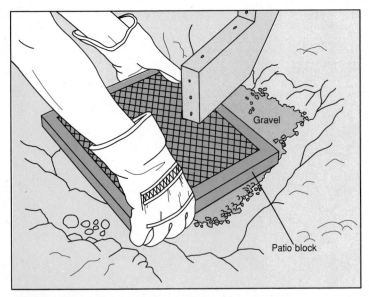

2 Installing a patio block. Purchase new patio blocks 12 to 16 inches square at a building supply center. To install a patio block, use a spade to dig the hole under the stringer to a depth of 4 to 6 inches. Tamp the bottom of the hole using your feet, line it with 2 to 4 inches of gravel and tamp again. Wearing work gloves, slide the patio block under the bottom of the stringer. Position the patio block, adding or removing gravel and tamping, until it sits level, with the stringer resting in position on it. Reinstall any riser *(page 28)*, tread *(page 27)*, newel post *(page 26)* and skirting panel *(page 17)* removed.

3 Pouring a concrete footing. Use a spade to dig the hole under the stringer to a depth of 10 to 12 inches. Tamp the bottom of the hole with your feet, line it with 2 to 4 inches of gravel and tamp again. Prepare a wood form *(page 123)*, setting the top of it even with the bottom of the stringer. Check that the form is level using a length of wood and a carpenter's level *(page 118)*; to reposition it, add or remove gravel and tamp. Wearing work gloves, use a spade to mix concrete *(page 122)* and fill the form *(above)*. Smooth the surface with a length of wood or a trowel. Allow the footing to set 48 hours before removing the form. Reinstall any riser *(page 28)*, tread *(page 27)*, newel post *(page 26)* and skirting panel *(page 17)* removed.

SHORING UP THE ROOF

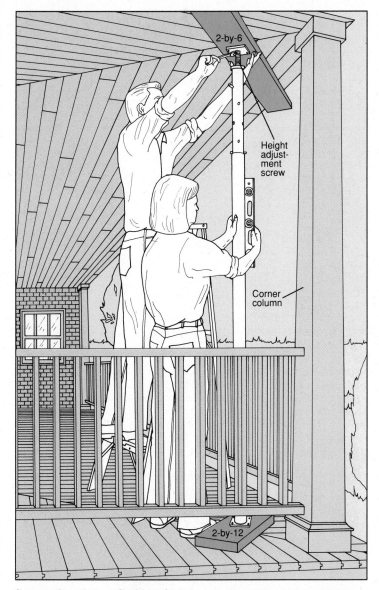

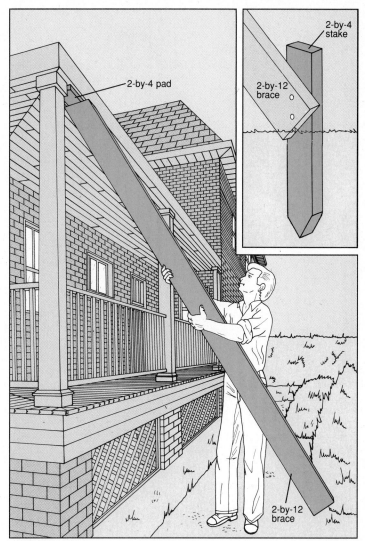

Supporting the roof with a jack. Use a telescoping jack, available at a tool rental agency. If repairing a column in position, or removing an end or corner column, set up at least one jack within 2 to 3 feet of it. If removing other than an end or corner column, set up jacks within 2 to 3 feet of each side of it. Position each jack plumb between the header under the flooring and the header above the ceiling; remove the rails *(page 23)* if they are in the way. At a corner column, shown here, position a jack plumb between the doubled joist under the flooring and the doubled joist above the ceiling. To locate headers or doubled joists, remove any skirting panel *(page 17)*, and bore holes *(page 117)* and chisel *(page 116)* an opening to help you find them, if necessary.

To set up a jack, saw a 2-by-10 or 2-by-12 pad 2 to 3 feet long *(page 112)* and nail the bottom plate of the jack onto it *(page 108)*. Use a 2-by-6 pad on the top plate of the jack: For under a header, saw it 2 to 3 feet long; for under a doubled joist, saw it long enough to reach the header on each side of the corner, as shown. With a helper supporting the jack, position it on the flooring with the pad centered over the header or joist. Raise the inner tube of the jack to within 2 to 3 inches of the ceiling and insert the pin through the holes to lock it. Have a helper plumb the jack with a carpenter's level *(page 118)* and position the top pad on the ceiling, centering it under the header or doubled joist. Turn the height adjustment screw clockwise until the top plate of the jack fits snugly against the pad *(above)*, supporting the roof without raising it.

Supporting the roof with a wood brace. For a brace, use a 2-by-12 about one-and-one-quarter times as long as the distance from the ceiling to the ground; use lengths of 2-by-4 for a pad, for cleats on the ceiling and for a stake in the ground. Purchase the 2-by-12 and 2-by-4 boards at a lumber yard. If repairing a column in position, or removing an end column, set up at least one brace within 2 to 3 feet of it. If removing any other column, such as the corner column shown here, set up a brace within 2 to 3 feet on each side of it. Position each brace between the header above the ceiling and the ground, at no more than a 60-degree angle. To locate headers, bore holes *(page 117)* and chisel *(page 116)* an opening to help you find them, if necessary.

To set up a wood brace, saw a 2-by-4 pad 3 to 4 feet long *(page 112)*. Position the pad on the ceiling, centering it under the header, and temporarily nail it *(page 108)*. Saw off one end of a 2-by-12 at about a 30-degree angle and fit it snugly under the pad *(above)*. Wedge the bottom of the 2-by-12 into the ground. Saw a 2-by-4 stake 3 to 4 feet long, angling the sides into a point at the bottom. Use a sledgehammer to drive the stake 2 feet into the ground next to the 2-by-12, and nail the 2-by-12 to it *(inset)*. At the top of the 2-by-12, drive nails through each side of it into the pad. For added support on each side of the 2-by-12, saw 2-by-4 cleats about 1 foot long and nail them to the pad and to the 2-by-12.

REPAIRING A SOLID COLUMN

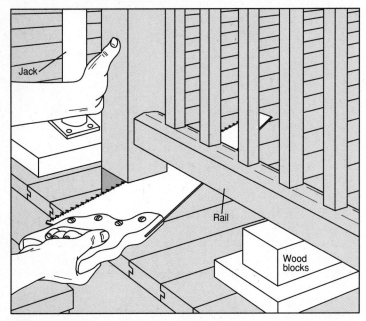

1 **Removing the damage.** To repair a solid column, above or below the rail, first support the roof *(page 33)*, remove any molding
by pulling the nails *(page 107)*, and mark the column position on
the flooring. To repair the column above the rail, measure and saw for
a half-lap splice *(step 2)*. To repair the column below the rail, as shown
here, prop the rail on blocks and saw off the damaged section horizontally *(page 112)* with a handsaw *(above)*; to disconnect it from the flooring, pull the nails or remove the hardware *(page 110)*. Saw a new
section from lumber of the same dimensions as the column, apply
preservative or finish *(page 120)* and splice it with a butt joint *(step 4)*.

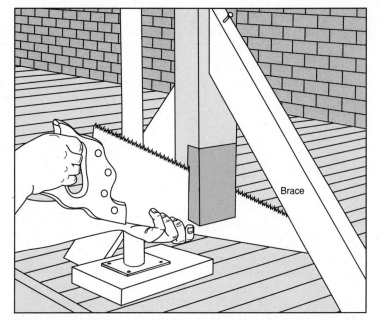

2 **Measuring and sawing for a half-lap splice.** Take off any handrail and rail attached to the column *(page 23)*. Mark the end of the
damaged section at least 8 inches above the base and saw it off
horizontally *(page 112)*. To disconnect it from the flooring, pull the nails
(page 107) or remove the hardware *(page 110)*. Temporarily install 2-by-4
braces on opposite sides of the undamaged section. Saw each brace
twice as long as the damaged section, cutting the ends at a 45-degree
angle, and nail it to the undamaged section and the flooring *(page 108)*.
At the end of the undamaged section, saw one side of a half-lap joint
(page 115) 6 to 8 inches long *(above)*.

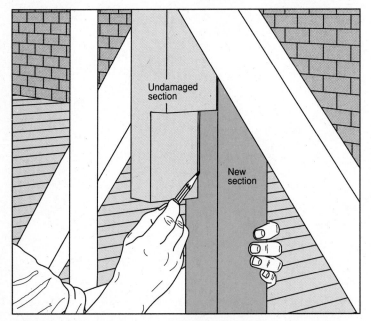

3 **Measuring and sawing a half-lap joint.** Purchase lumber for
a splice of the same dimensions as the column at a lumber yard.
To mark the half lap, position the end of the new section against
the flooring or hardware, and position the sides of the new section in
turn against each side of the half lap on the undamaged section
(above). Saw the half lap *(page 115)* using a handsaw or power saw.
Apply preservative or finish *(page 120)*.

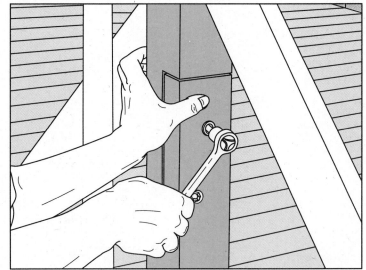

4 **Splicing a new section.** Position the new section on the undamaged section and on the flooring or hardware; use the marks as a
guide. For a half-lap splice, shown here, clamp the joint *(page
116)*, bore holes *(page 117)* and install at least two bolts *(page 108)*,
offsetting them *(above)*. For a butt splice, as in step 1, nail the joint
(page 108); bore pilot holes and drive nails on each side of the undamaged section at an angle into the new section. At the base of the new
section, drive nails on each side through the flooring into the header, or
install hardware *(page 110)*. Nail on any molding. Reinstall any handrail,
rail *(page 23)* and skirting panel *(page 17)* removed. Fill holes and caulk
joints *(page 106)*, and refinish damaged surfaces *(page 16)*.

REPLACING A SOLID COLUMN

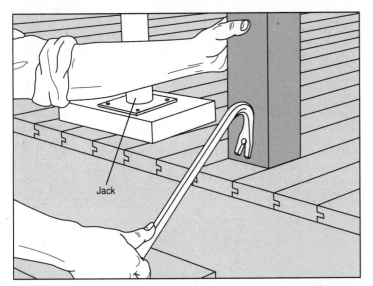

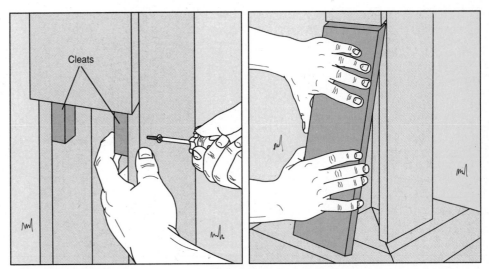

1 Removing a column. Support the roof *(page 33)*. Remove any molding from the column by pulling its nails *(page 107)* and take off any handrail and rail *(page 23)*. Mark the column position on the flooring and ceiling. To take out the column, pull the nails *(above)* or remove the hardware *(page 110)* at the bottom, then pull the nails at the top. First loosen the nails by knocking each side of the column near the flooring or ceiling using a sledgehammer; protect undamaged surfaces with a wood block. If required, remove the column by sawing it into sections *(page 112)*, then pulling off the ends using a crowbar.

2 Installing a column. Purchase wood for a replacement column at a lumber yard, saw it to length *(page 112)* and apply preservative or finish *(page 120)*. Position the column between the ceiling and the flooring or bottom hardware. If it is a tight fit, hammer on it, cushioning the blows with a wood block. Bore pilot holes *(page 117)* and drive nails *(page 108)* into the column on each side, through the ceiling into the header *(above)*. Also bore pilot holes and drive nails on each side at the bottom, through the flooring into the header; or reinstall the hardware *(page 110)*. Nail on any molding, and reinstall any handrail, rail *(page 23)* and skirting panel *(page 17)* removed. Fill holes and caulk joints *(page 106)*. Refinish damaged surfaces *(page 16)*.

REPAIRING A BOX COLUMN

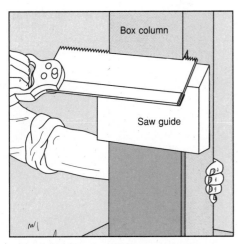

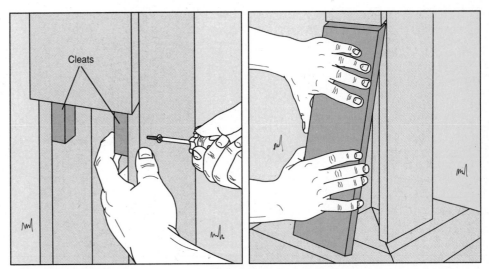

1 Removing the damage. To repair a box column, support the roof *(page 33)* and replace the damaged section. Remove any molding at the base by pulling the nails *(page 107)*. Take off any handrail and rail in the way *(page 23)*. At the end of the damaged section, temporarily nail on *(page 108)* a saw guide; cut it longer than the width of the column and bevel one edge at a 45-degree angle *(page 112)*. Saw off the damaged section *(above)*. Pull the nails out of the sides and bottom; first loosen them by using a pry bar to pull out the sides and lift up the bottom.

2 Installing a new section. Purchase replacement wood for a new section at a lumber yard. Bevel the end using the saw guide as in step 1 and saw it to length *(page 112)*, measuring from the top of the bevel on the undamaged section to the flooring. Taper the sides, if required, fitting the new section under the undamaged section to mark it. If required, bevel the edges for miter joints *(page 115)*. For added support, saw a 1-by-2 cleat 4 to 6 inches long for each side of the new section. Apply preservative or finish *(page 120)*. Position each cleat halfway under the undamaged section. Bore pilot holes *(page 117)* and drive screws *(page 108)* into it through each side of the column *(above, left)*. Position the new section *(above, right)*, bore pilot holes and drive nails *(page 108)* every 2 to 3 inches along its edges and into the cleats and along the bottom into the header. Nail on any molding, and reinstall any handrail, rail *(page 23)* and skirting panel *(page 17)* removed. Fill holes and caulk joints *(page 106)*. Refinish damaged surfaces *(page 16)*.

REPLACING A BOX COLUMN

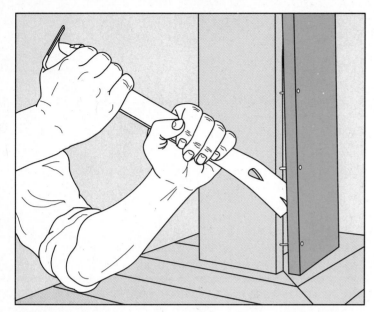

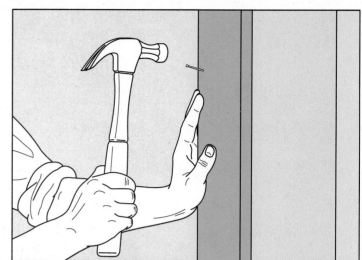

1 **Removing a box column.** Support the roof *(page 33)*. Remove any molding from the column by pulling the nails *(page 107)* and take off any handrail and rail *(page 23)*. Mark the column position on the flooring and ceiling. To take out the column, pull the nails at the bottom and top using a hammer, a pry bar or a nail puller. First loosen the nails by knocking the sides of the column near the flooring or ceiling with a sledgehammer; protect undamaged surfaces with a wood block. Bore holes *(page 117)* and chisel *(page 116)* an opening in the column to check for an interior solid column. Use a crowbar to pull out the sides of the column and lift up the bottom *(above)* to remove the column in sections. Repair *(page 34)* or replace *(page 35)* a solid column.

2 **Installing a box column.** Purchase wood for a replacement box column at a lumber yard and saw the boards to length *(page 112)*. Taper the boards if required, positioning each board against another column to mark it. If required, bevel the edges for miter joints *(page 115)*. Apply preservative or finish *(page 120)*. If there is no interior column, assemble the box column on the ground. Bore pilot holes *(page 117)* and drive nails *(page 108)* every 8 to 10 inches into the sides. If there is an interior column, nail three boards together, fit them around it, and nail on the fourth board *(above)*. Position the column using the marks as a guide, then drive nails into each side, through the ceiling into the header and through the flooring into the header. Nail on any molding and reinstall any handrail, rail *(page 23)* and skirting panel *(page 17)* removed. Fill holes and caulk joints *(page 106)*, and refinish damaged surfaces *(page 16)*.

REPAIRING A COLUMN PLINTH OR CAPITAL

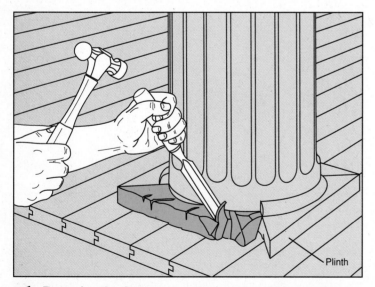

Plinth

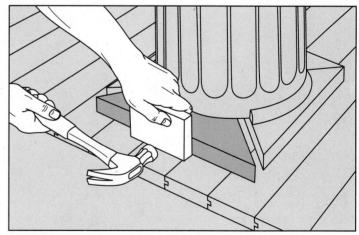

1 **Removing the damage.** To repair a column plinth or capital, support the roof *(page 33)* and replace the damaged section. Remove any molding in the way by pulling the nails *(page 107)*. Chip out the damaged section using a wood chisel and a ball-peen hammer *(above)* or a mallet *(page 116)*. Pull out nails using a hammer, a pry bar or a nail puller. Take out and replace no more than one-quarter section of the plinth or capital at a time.

2 **Installing a new section.** Purchase wood for a replacement section of the same dimensions at a lumber yard; saw *(page 112)*, chisel *(page 116)*, plane *(page 117)* or rout *(page 118)* it to the length, width and shape required, cutting 1 inch off the inside point for air circulation. Apply preservative or finish *(page 120)*. Tap in the new section using a hammer, cushioning the blows with a wood block *(above)*. Bore pilot holes *(page 117)* and nail the section *(page 108)* on the flooring. Nail on any molding. Reinstall any handrail, rail *(page 23)* and skirting panel *(page 17)* removed. Fill holes and caulk joints *(page 106)*, and refinish damaged surfaces *(page 16)*.

REPAIRING A ROUND COLUMN

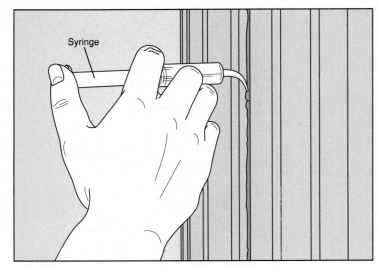

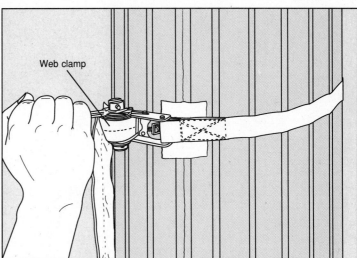

Gluing and clamping a joint. To repair a joint on a round column, glue and clamp it. Support the roof *(page 33)* to ease weight on the column. Clean the joint using a putty knife and sand inside the edges *(page 119)*. Brush off loose particles with a whisk and wipe the joint using a tack cloth *(page 102)*. Load a syringe with resorcinol or epoxy glue, fit the tip of the tube into the joint and press the plunger *(above, left)*. Use a toothpick or small wooden stick to help spread the glue evenly. Brace the joint with a web clamp every 10 to 12 inches; position waxed paper under it at the joint to keep it from adhering to the glue. To install a web clamp, wrap the web around the column and thread it through the ratchet; tighten the clamp by cranking the handle *(above, right)* or using a screwdriver. Wipe off excess glue with a cloth. For added reinforcement, bore pilot holes *(page 117)* and drive nails *(page 108)* through the joint every 2 to 3 inches. Let the glue set. Reinstall any handrail, rail *(page 23)* and skirting panel *(page 17)* removed. Fill holes and caulk joints *(page 106)*, and refinish damaged surfaces *(page 16)*.

REPLACING A ROUND COLUMN

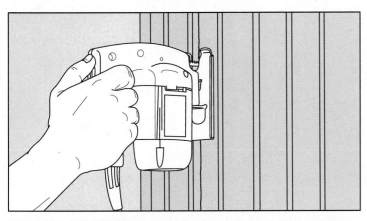

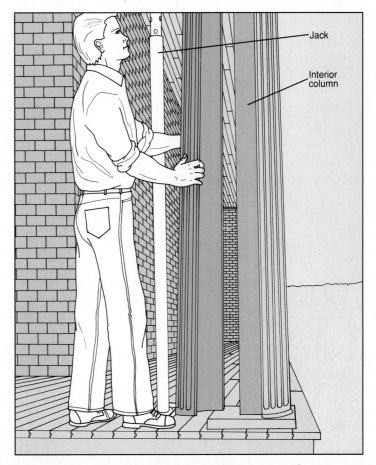

Removing and installing a round column. Support the roof *(page 33)*. Remove any molding from the column by pulling the nails *(page 107)*. Take off any handrail and rail *(page 23)*. Mark the column position on the flooring and ceiling. To remove the column, pull the nails at the bottom and top. Loosen them first by knocking the sides of the column near the flooring or ceiling with a sledgehammer, protecting undamaged surfaces with a wood block. Bore holes *(page 117)* and chisel *(page 116)* an opening to check for an interior solid column. If there is one, saw vertically along two opposite joints *(page 112)* using a saber saw *(above)* and remove the column in two sections *(right)*.

Repair *(page 34)* or replace *(page 35)* the solid column if necessary. Have a hollow round column repaired professionally, or replace it. To install a round column, position it using the marks as a guide, bore pilot holes and drive nails *(page 108)* into it, through the ceiling into any cut header and through the flooring into the header. Glue and clamp the joints *(step above)*. Nail on any molding and reinstall any handrail, rail *(page 23)* and skirting panel *(page 17)* removed. Fill holes and caulk joints *(page 106)*, and refinish damaged surfaces *(page 16)*.

REINFORCING A JOIST

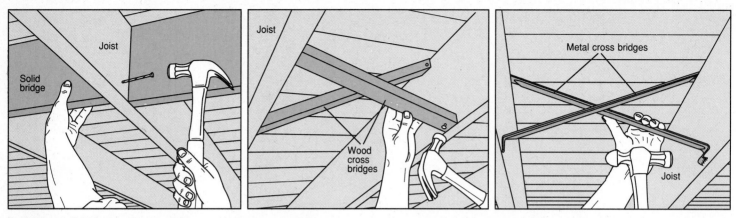

Installing bridges. To reinforce a joist, install a solid wood bridge, or two wood or metal cross bridges, every 6 to 8 feet between it and the joists on each side of it. Remove any skirting panel in the way *(page 17)*; if there is not enough room to work under the porch, remove flooring to work from above *(page 18)*. Purchase lumber of the same dimensions as a joist for solid bridges, or 1-by-2s or 1-by-3s for wood cross bridges, or metal cross bridges, at a lumber yard.

To make solid bridges, saw each to a length equal to the distance between the joists *(page 112)*. Apply preservative or finish *(page 120)*. Position the bridge between the joists, offset from any other bridge on the opposite side of the joist; drive in at least two nails *(page 108)* at each end of it *(above, left)*.

To make wood cross bridges, saw each to a length equal to the distance from the top of the joist to the bottom of the next joist, beveling the ends at opposite angles *(page 112)*; apply preservative or finish. To install a wood cross bridge, position a pair of bridges diagonally opposite to each other and drive in nails at each end *(above, center)*. For a metal cross bridge, position two bridges diagonally opposite to each other and hammer each end into the joist *(above, right)*. Reinstall any flooring *(page 19)* and skirting panel *(page 17)* removed.

REPAIRING A JOIST

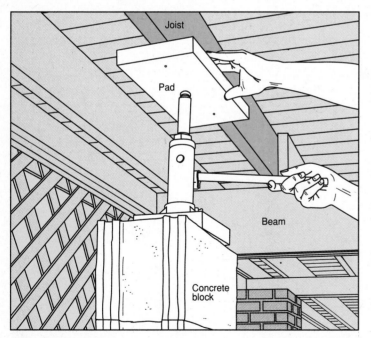

1 Supporting the joist. To repair a joist, support it in position with a jack *(page 124)* and install a scab on each side of it over the damaged section. Remove any skirting panel in the way *(page 17)*; if there is not enough room to work under the porch, remove flooring and work from above *(page 18)*. Remove any bridges from each side of the damaged section; pull nails using a hammer, pry bar or nail puller *(page 107)*. Set the jack on a level wood pad or concrete block, directly below the joist and at the center of the damaged section. Temporarily nail a 2-by-6 or 2-by-8 pad on the bottom of the damaged section *(page 108)*. Raise the jack until it fits snugly under the joist, supporting it in position but not lifting it *(above)*.

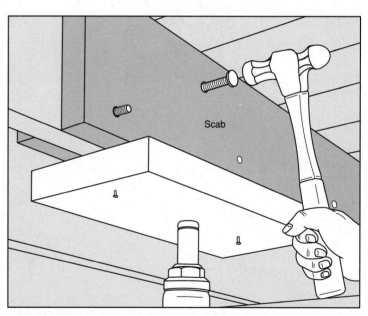

2 Installing scabs. Purchase lumber for a pair of scabs of the same dimensions as the joist at a lumber yard. Saw each scab to a length 4 to 6 feet longer than the damaged section *(page 112)*. Apply preservative or finish *(page 120)*. Position a scab on each side of the joist, centered over the damaged section; if required, have a helper support them or temporarily nail them *(page 108)*. Bore holes *(page 117)* through both scabs and the joist every 10 to 12 inches, offsetting them. Install carriage bolts *(page 108)*, using a ball-peen hammer to tap them into the holes *(above)*. Reinstall any bridges *(step above)*, flooring *(page 19)* and skirting panel *(page 17)* removed.

REPLACING A JOIST

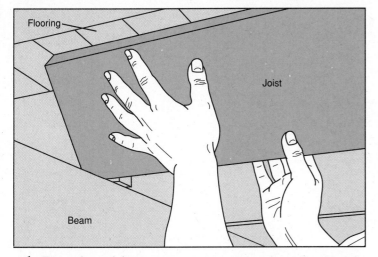

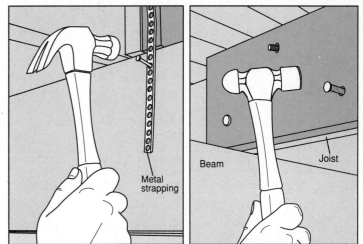

1 **Removing a joist.** To replace a joist, either remove it and install a new one, or install a sister joist alongside it. Remove any skirting panel in the way *(page 17)*; if there is not enough room under the porch, remove flooring to work from above *(page 18)*. Remove any bridges from both sides of the joist; pull nails using a hammer, a pry bar or a nail puller *(page 107)*. If a sister joist can be positioned against the joist, install it *(step 2)*. To remove the old joist, have a helper support it and remove its fasteners *(page 107)* or hardware *(page 110)* from the beams, the beam and header, or the ledger and header. To loosen the flooring nails from it, rap it with a sledgehammer. Bow or angle the joist to pull it off the beam *(above)*, header or ledger; if required, use the sledgehammer to knock it off, or saw it into sections *(page 112)*.

2 **Installing a joist.** Purchase wood for a new joist or sister joist at a lumber yard and saw it to length *(page 112)*. Apply preservative or finish *(page 120)*. With one or more helpers supporting the joist, raise it onto the beams, the beam and header, or the ledger and header. Bow or angle it, if required, or knock it into place using a sledgehammer, cushioning the blows with a wood block. Drive in nails *(page 108)* or install hardware *(page 110)* at each end of the joist; for reinforcement, nail metal strapping on the joist and the beam *(above, left)*, header or ledger. If installing a sister joist against the old joist, bore holes *(page 117)* through both joists, offset every 10 to 12 inches, and install carriage bolts *(page 108)*, using a ball-peen hammer to tap them into the holes *(above, right)*. Nail the flooring and reinstall any bridges *(page 38)*, flooring *(page 19)* and skirting panel *(page 17)* removed.

REINFORCING A LEDGER

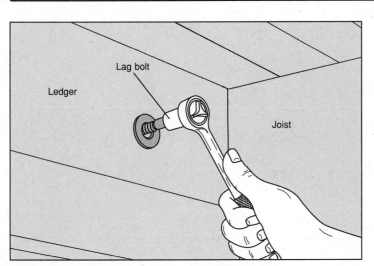

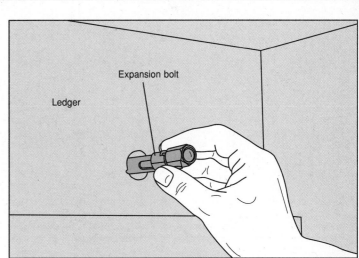

Installing lag bolts. To reinforce a ledger at other than a brick or masonry wall, install additional lag bolts every 3 to 4 feet along it. Remove any skirting panel in the way *(page 17)*; if there is not enough room to work under the porch, remove flooring to work from above *(page 18)*. Purchase lag bolts at a building supply center. To install a lag bolt, bore a hole through the ledger and any spacer behind it into the wall *(page 117)*. Stagger the bolt hole positions slightly. Fit a washer on the bolt and drive it into the hole with a socket wrench *(above)* or a nut driver. Reinstall any flooring *(page 19)* and skirting panel *(page 17)* removed.

Installing expansion bolts. To reinforce a ledger at a brick or masonry wall, install additional expansion bolts every 3 to 4 feet along it. Remove any skirting panel in the way *(page 17)*; if there is not enough room to work under the porch, remove flooring to work from above *(page 18)*. Purchase expansion bolts at a building supply center. To install an expansion bolt, bore a hole through the ledger and any spacer behind it, then change to a masonry bit and drill into the wall *(page 117)*. Stagger the bolt hole positions slightly. Fit an expansion bolt into the hole *(above)* and tap it flush with the ledger using a ball-peen hammer. Tighten the expansion bolt using a socket wrench or a nut driver. Reinstall any flooring *(page 19)* and skirting panel *(page 17)* removed.

REPAIRING A LEDGER

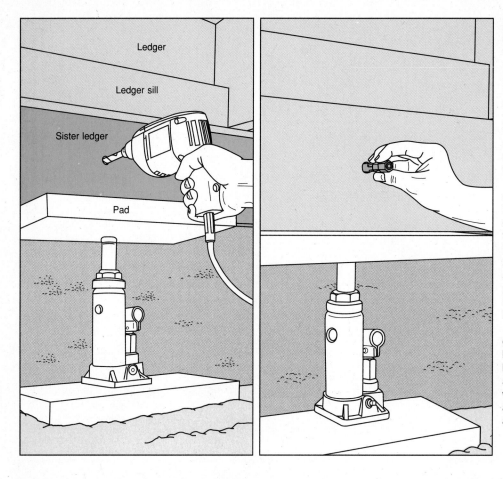

Installing a sister ledger. To reinforce a ledger, install a sister ledger under it. Remove any skirting panel in the way *(page 17)*; if there is not enough room to work under the porch, remove flooring to work from above *(page 18)*. Purchase lumber for a sister ledger of the same dimensions as the ledger at a lumber yard; saw it to a length 4 to 6 feet longer than the damaged section *(page 112)*. If required, saw wood blocks for spacers, apply preservative or finish *(page 120)* and nail them onto the back *(page 108)*.

To install the sister ledger, support it with one jack *(page 124)* for every 6 to 8 feet of its length. Set each jack on a level wood pad or concrete block directly below the ledger. Extend the jack's reach with a 4-by-4, or by lifting it on concrete blocks, if necessary. Position a 2-by-6 or 2-by-8 pad between the sister ledger and each jack. With one or more helpers supporting the sister ledger, raise each jack under it until it fits snugly against the ledger, supporting it in position but not lifting it.

Bore holes *(page 117)* through the sister ledger every 3 to 4 feet *(far left)* and install lag bolts or expansion bolts *(page 39)*. Drive a lag bolt using a socket wrench or a nut driver. Fit an expansion bolt into its hole *(near left)* flush with the ledger and tighten it using a wrench or a nut driver. Reinstall any flooring *(page 19)* and skirting panel *(page 17)* removed.

REPAIRING A BEAM OR HEADER

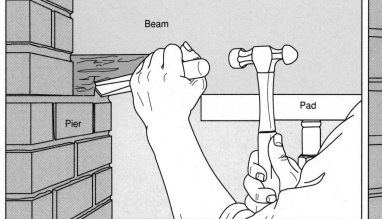
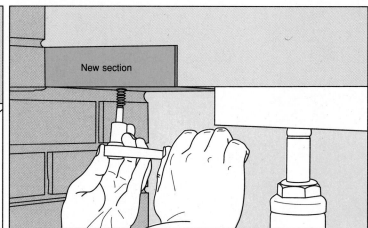

Splicing a new end section. To repair the end of a beam, header or doubled corner joist at a pier, support it in position with a jack *(page 124)* and splice in a new section. Remove any skirting panel in the way *(page 17)*; if there is not enough room to work under the porch, remove flooring to work from above *(page 18)*. Set the jack on a level wood pad or concrete block directly below the beam, header or doubled corner joist, within 2 to 4 feet of the damaged section. Temporarily nail *(page 108)* a 2-by-6 or 2-by-8 pad on the bottom of the damaged section. Raise the jack until it fits snugly under the beam, header or doubled corner joist, supporting it in position but not lifting it. Mark for a lap joint at the end of the damaged section on each side of the beam, header or doubled corner joist using a carpenter's level and a carpenter's square *(page 112)*. Saw *(page 112)* and chisel *(page 116)* the lap; make the vertical cut with a handsaw, then chip out the rest of the wood with a wood chisel and a ball-peen hammer *(above, left)* or mallet. Saw a new section to fit from wood of the same thickness as the beam or header; cut it 1 to 2 inches shorter than the old piece, if required for fit. Apply preservative or finish *(page 120)*. Position the new section, bore pilot holes *(page 117)* and install lag bolts *(page 108)* with a socket wrench *(above)* or a nut driver. Reinstall any flooring *(page 19)* and skirting panel *(page 17)* removed.

REPAIRING A BEAM OR HEADER (continued)

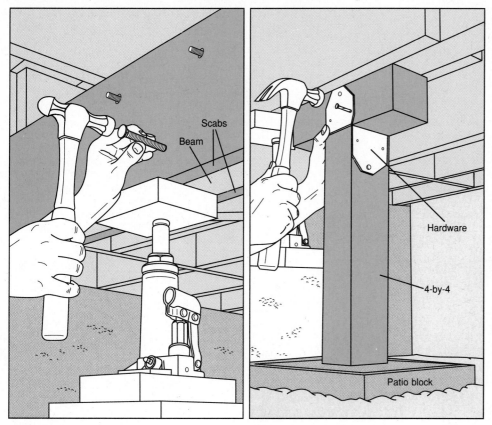

Installing scabs along the length. To repair a beam, support the damaged section with a jack *(page 124)* and install a scab on each side. To repair a header, pull the nails *(page 107)* to remove the fascia board and install a doubled scab on the opposite side. For reinforcement, also install 4-by-4s on a patio block under the damaged section. Remove any skirting panel in the way *(page 17)*; if there is not enough room to work under the porch, remove flooring to work from above *(page 18)*.

At a lumber yard, purchase wood for scabs of the same width and half the thickness of the beam or header, a 4-by-4 and a patio block 12 to 16 inches square. Saw each scab 4 to 6 feet longer than the damaged section *(page 112)*; cut it to fit around any joist or beam in the way. Apply preservative or finish *(page 120)*. Center the scabs over the damaged section and temporarily nail them *(page 108)*. Bore holes *(page 117)* every 10 to 12 inches and install bolts *(page 108)*, tapping them into the holes *(far left)*.

Remove the jack and center the patio block under the damaged section. Saw two lengths of 4-by-4 to fit between the damaged section and the patio block, as shown. Apply preservative or finish. Position the 4-by-4s, installing hardware *(page 110)* to connect them to each other *(near left)* and to the beam or header. Nail on any fascia board and reinstall any flooring *(page 19)* and skirting panel *(page 17)* removed.

REPLACING A BEAM

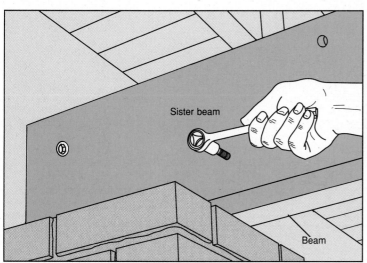

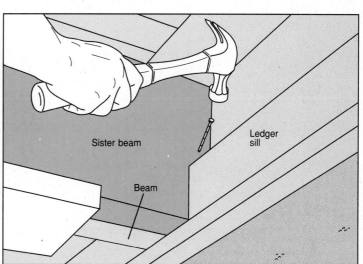

Installing a sister beam. Support the beam in position with one jack *(page 124)* for every 6 to 8 feet of its length, and install a sister beam along one side of it. Remove any skirting panel in the way *(page 17)*; if there is not enough room under the porch, remove flooring to work from above *(page 18)*. Set each jack on a level wood pad or concrete block, directly below the beam. Position a 2-by-6 or 2-by-8 pad between the beam and each jack. Raise each jack until it fits snugly under the beam, supporting it in position but not lifting it. Purchase lumber for a sister beam of the same dimensions as the beam at a lumber yard. Saw it to length *(page 112)* and apply preservative or finish *(page 120)*.

With one or more helpers supporting the sister beam, raise it into position. If the fit is tight at the ledger and the pier, carefully use a sledge-hammer to knock it into place, cushioning the blows with a wood block. Bore holes *(page 117)* through the beams every 3 to 4 feet and install carriage bolts *(page 108)*; tighten them using a socket wrench *(above, left)* or a nut driver. At the ledger, bore pilot holes *(page 117)* and install nails *(page 108)* or hardware *(page 110)*; drive at least two nails into each side *(above, right)*. Reinstall any flooring *(page 19)* and skirting panel *(page 17)* removed.

REPLACING A WOOD PIER

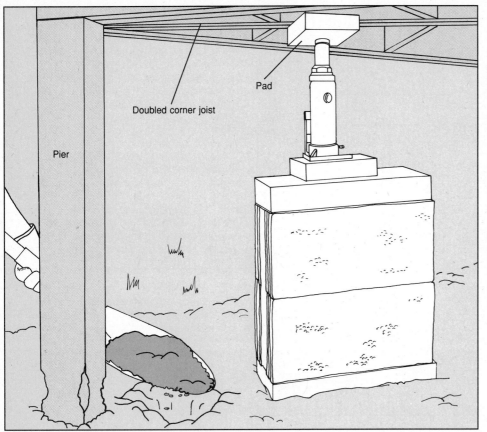

1 **Supporting the header, beam or doubled corner joist.** To replace a wood pier, first support the header, beam or doubled corner joist on each side of it using jacks *(page 124)*. Then install a 4-by-4 or 6-by-6 sister pier and concrete footing on one or both sides of the pier, within 2 to 4 feet of it. Remove any skirting panel in the way *(page 17)*; if there is not enough room to work under the porch, remove flooring to work from above *(page 18)*.

Set each jack on a level wood pad or concrete block 3 to 4 feet away from the pier, directly below the header, beam or doubled corner joist. Extend the jack's reach with a 4-by-4, or by lifting it on concrete blocks, if necessary. Position a 2-by-6 or 2-by-8 pad on each jack and raise it until it fits snugly against the header, beam or doubled corner joist, supporting it in position but not lifting it. Using a spade, dig a hole for each footing within 2 to 4 feet of the pier. Dig the hole 10 to 12 inches wide and 6 inches deeper than the frostline *(left)*—the minimum depth required is usually 24 to 30 inches.

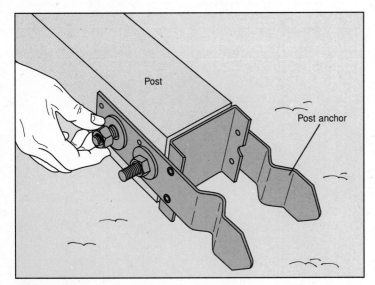

2 **Installing the sister pier.** Install a sister pier with a post anchor 2 to 4 inches above the ground. To determine the length of the sister pier, use a plumb bob *(page 118)* and tape measure to measure down from the sister pier's position at the header, beam or doubled corner joist. Purchase a 4-by-4 or 6-by-6 for a sister pier, and a post anchor to fit it, at a lumber yard. Saw the sister pier to length *(page 112)* and apply preservative or finish *(page 120)*. Position the post anchor on the bottom of the sister pier and install it *(page 110)*; twist a nut onto a bolt by hand *(above)* and tighten it using a wrench. With a helper supporting the sister pier in position, connect it to the header, beam or doubled corner joist with fasteners *(page 108)* or hardware *(page 110)*.

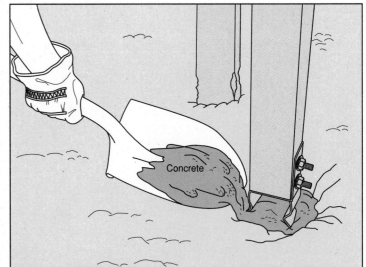

3 **Pouring a concrete footing.** Tamp the bottom of the hole using the end of a 2-by-4, use a spade to fill it with 6 inches of gravel and tamp again. Use a spade to mix concrete in a wheelbarrow or trough and, wearing work gloves, pour a concrete footing to a height at least 1 inch above the ground *(above)*. To settle the concrete, work a 2-by-4 up and down in it. Use a trowel to add concrete around the pier base, sloping the top away from the pier. Allow the concrete to set 48 hours before removing the jacks. To keep the concrete from drying out, dampen it with water until it has cured for one week, then caulk the pier base *(page 106)*. Reinstall any flooring *(page 19)* and skirting panel *(page 17)* removed.

REPAIRING A BRICK PIER

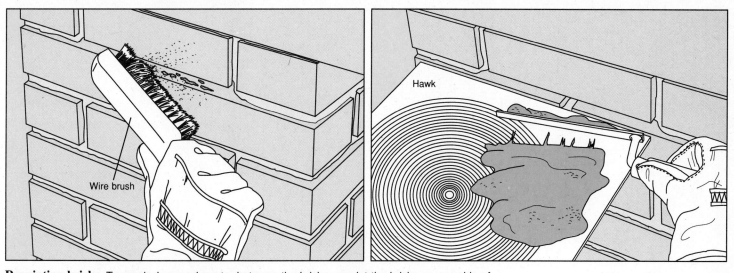

Repointing bricks. To repair damaged mortar between the bricks, repoint the bricks on one side of the pier at a time using mortar or concrete patching compound *(page 122)*. Remove any skirting panel in the way *(page 17)* to reach all sides of the pier. Wearing work gloves and goggles, chip out the damaged mortar using a cold chisel and a ball-peen hammer. Use a narrow wire brush to clean out loose particles between the bricks *(above, left)* and wipe the joint with a wet cloth.

Mix the mortar or concrete patching compound on a mason's hawk or a piece of plywood. Using a joint filler, pack the mortar or patching compound into the joints between the bricks *(above, right)*. Scrape excess off the bricks; for best results, discard the excess rather than reapplying it. Smooth each joint while it is still wet using a gloved finger, a rounded stick or a narrow pipe as a shaping tool. Reinstall any skirting panel removed *(page 17)*.

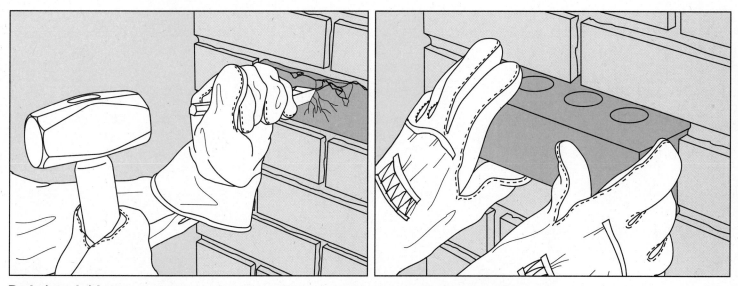

Replacing a brick. Replace damaged bricks one at a time on each side of the pier. Remove any skirting panel in the way *(page 17)* to reach all sides of the pier. Wearing work gloves and goggles, use a cold chisel and a ball-peen hammer to chip out the mortar around the brick and pry it out; if necessary, break the brick into pieces using the chisel or a brickset and a sledgehammer *(above, left)*. Chisel out all the mortar in the cavity, then use a narrow wire brush to clean out loose particles. Wipe the cavity with a wet cloth. Soak replacement bricks in water for half an hour and wet the cavity every 10 to 15 minutes.

Mix mortar or concrete patching compound on a mason's hawk or a piece of plywood. Using a trowel, apply a 1 inch layer of mortar or patching compound on all four sides of the cavity. Position a replacement brick level with the cavity and push it in *(above, right)* until its face is flush with the bricks around it; if necessary, tap it into place with the end of the trowel handle. Use the trowel to fill any gaps in the joints and scrape off any excess. Smooth the joints using a gloved finger, a rounded stick or a narrow length of pipe as a shaping tool. Reinstall any skirting panel removed *(page 17)*.

REPLACING A BRICK PIER AND FOOTING

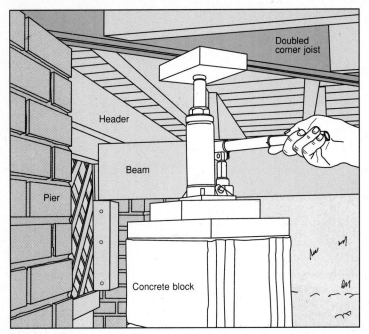

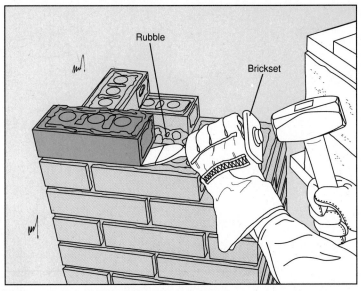

1 Supporting the header, beam or doubled corner joist. Support the header, beam or doubled corner joist on each side of the pier using jacks *(page 124)*; remove any skirting panel in the way *(page 17)*. Set each jack on a level wood pad or concrete block 3 to 4 feet from the pier, directly below the header, beam or doubled corner joist. Extend the jack's reach with a 4-by-4 or by lifting it on concrete blocks, if necessary. Position a 2-by-6 or 2-by-8 pad on each jack and raise it until it fits snugly against the header, beam or doubled corner joist, supporting it in position but not lifting it *(above)*.

2 Removing a pier. To reach the top course of bricks, pull the nails out of the fascia board *(page 107)* and remove it. Wearing work gloves and goggles, remove the first course of bricks. Chip out the mortar using a cold chisel and a ball-peen hammer and pull out the bricks; if necessary, break a brick into pieces using the chisel or a brickset and a sledgehammer. Use a similar procedure to remove each course of bricks; when there is enough clearance under the header, pry up the bottoms with the brickset *(above)* or knock them on the back with the sledgehammer. Chisel out mortar and rubble inside the pier after every few courses. If the footing is not damaged, rebuild the pier over it *(step 5)*; if the footing is damaged, remove it *(step 3)* and pour a new one *(step 4)*.

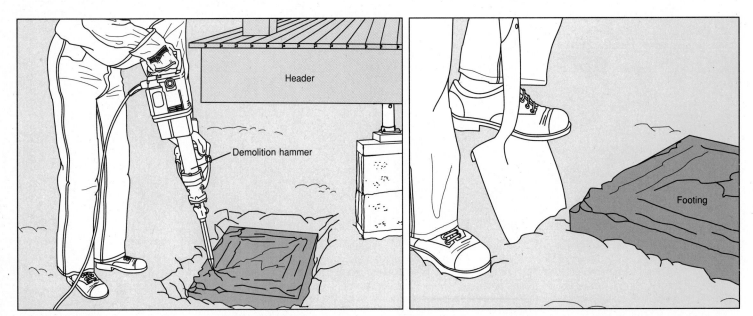

3 Removing the footing. If the footing is damaged, remove it. Wearing work gloves and safety goggles, use a demolition hammer *(above, left)* or a bull-point chisel and a sledgehammer *(page 122)* to break up the concrete. Chip holes 6 to 8 inches apart to crack the concrete, breaking it into pieces small enough to remove by hand or with a shovel. Dig up loose soil at the footing edges using a spade *(above, right)*. Continue breaking up concrete and digging until the footing is removed.

To position the center of the hole for a new footing, suspend a plumb bob *(page 118)* from the header. Use the spade to enlarge the hole and square the corners: for a corner pier, make it at least 20 inches by 20 inches; for other than a corner pier, make it at least 20 inches by 16 inches. Dig the hole 6 inches deeper than the frostline—24 to 30 inches is the minimum depth usually required. Tamp the bottom of the hole with the end of a 2-by-4, use the spade to fill the hole with 6 inches of gravel and tamp again.

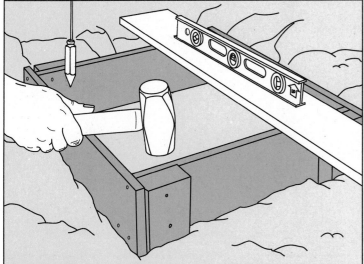

4 **Pouring a concrete footing.** Pour a concrete footing 1 to 2 inches below ground level. To shape the top of the footing, install a wood form of 1-by-10s with 2-by-4 stakes *(page 122)*. Build the form 16 inches by 20 inches; for a corner pier, build the form 20 inches by 20 inches. Set the form level, with its outside edge 2 inches beyond the outside edge of the header. To help position the form, suspend a plumb bob *(page 118)* from the outside edge of the header. To level the form, use a board and a carpenter's level; adjust the form by tapping the stakes farther into the ground with a sledgehammer *(above, left)*.

Wearing work gloves, use a spade to mix the concrete in a wheelbarrow or trough and fill the form up to the top. To settle the concrete, work a 2-by-4 up and down in it. Level the concrete using a 2-by-4, 3 to 4 feet long; pull it across the surface, shifting it from side to side to keep the concrete from adhering to it. Use a trowel to fill in depressions, remove excess concrete and smooth the surface *(above, right)*. Allow the concrete to set for 48 hours before removing the form or building the pier *(step 5)*. To keep the concrete from drying out, dampen it with water until it has cured for one week.

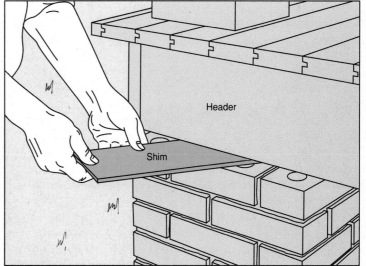

5 **Building a brick pier.** To determine the number of brick courses for the pier, use a mason's rule *(page 112)*; or, measure the distance from the bottom of the header to the footing and divide by the thickness of a brick, allowing about 1/2 inch between courses for mortar. To position the center of the pier, suspend a plumb bob *(page 118)* from the header. Using a carpenter's square or try square *(page 112)*, chalk the pier perimeter on the footing: For a corner pier, mark a 16-by-16 inch rectangle; for other than a corner pier, mark a 12-by-16 inch rectangle. Purchase replacement bricks at a lumber yard and soak them thoroughly using a garden hose.

Wearing work gloves, use a trowel to mix mortar on a mason's hawk or a piece of plywood. Apply a 1/2-inch layer on the bottom and ends of each brick and lay the first course, using the marks as a guide. Tap the bricks into place using the end of the trowel handle; check their

position with a carpenter's level *(page 118)* and the carpenter's square or try square. Apply a layer of mortar on the tops of the bricks and lay the second course, buttering the brick ends, as shown, and staggering their positions. Lay succeeding courses the same way *(above, left)*.

Scrape excess mortar off the bricks and discard it inside the pier. Smooth each joint while it is still wet using a gloved finger, a rounded stick or a narrow pipe as a shaping tool. Check the height of the pier every 3 to 4 courses using the mason's rule or the plumb bob and a tape measure; to end up with a top course of whole bricks, adjust the amount of mortar applied. Fill inside the pier with rubble to help reinforce it. Saw wood shims *(page 112)*, apply preservative or finish *(page 120)* and install them in any space between the header and the last course of bricks *(above, right)*. Nail on the fascia board *(page 108)*. Reinstall any skirting panel removed *(page 17)*.

DECKS

Since the 1950s, decks have become a popular feature of the American home: a graceful surround for a swimming pool or hot tub, or a lofty perch jutting out over a hillside. A typical deck is shown at right; your deck may vary in design, but is similar in structure and basic components.

Most decks are constructed of wood that is pressure-treated with preservatives, or of decay-resistant redwood or cedar. Deck boards are supported by joists and are spaced at least 1/4 inch apart for drainage. The joists are held up directly by posts, or supported by a beam on posts; if the deck is not freestanding, the joists are also supported by a ledger fastened to the side of the house. Railing posts, which carry the rails and the handrails, are fastened to a joist or beam; a railing post may end at the joist or beam, or extend into the ground. Each post is positioned in the ground by a footing, usually of concrete. The stair assembly consists of stringers, treads and usually cleats: stringers are mounted on a joist or beam of the deck at the top and rest on a footing at the bottom; cleats are fastened to the stringers and support the treads.

Although built for the rigors of the outdoors, a deck nonetheless can develop weaknesses caused by weather, settling of the house or shifting of the ground. A deck problem may be noticeable, but its root cause can be easily overlooked—resulting in worsening problems. A wobbly handrail, for example, while easily repaired, may be an early warning of a problem with a post or footing. To help in your diagnosis, consult the Troubleshooting Guide on pages 48 and 49.

A specific deck problem often has several solutions. The best one depends on a range of factors that call for individual judgments: the type of deck and its purpose, the nature and severity of the problem, the final appearance desired, your available time, the current weather. For example, you may opt to reinforce a stringer this year and postpone replacing it until next year; or you may find replacing a railing post more attractive than reinforcing it. Choose the procedure most suited to your present circumstances.

To tackle deck repair you need to know basic carpentry techniques, including leveling, nailing, drilling and sawing. All of the tools, materials and supplies required are readily available at a lumber yard or a building supply center. Whenever you are working beneath a deck, install a temporary barrier to keep others off it *(page 11)*; before undertaking a repair on a joist, beam, ledger or post, ensure that beams and joists are adequately supported on jacks *(page 124)*. Refer to Tools & Techniques *(page 102)* for guidance before starting a repair job.

Inspect your deck each spring and fall; the joints and the post bases, in particular, are vulnerable to rot, insect damage or rusted fasteners. Prevent accidents while working on the deck by following the basic safety advice in Emergencies *(page 8)*; wear the proper clothing and protective equipment for the job.

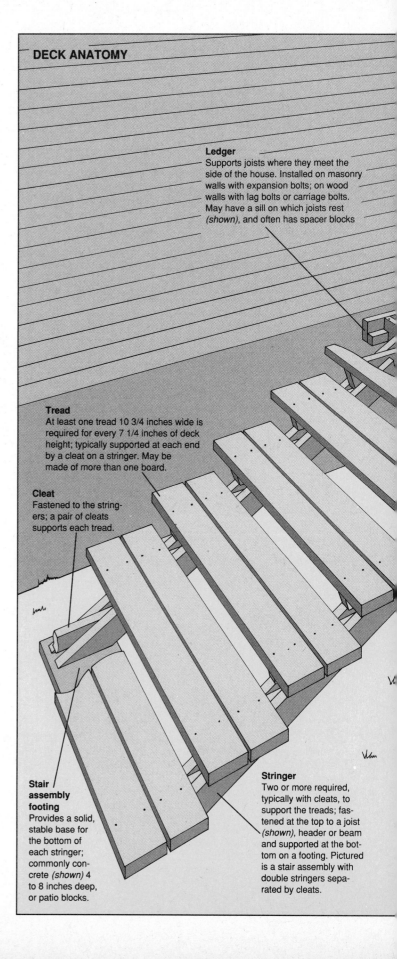

DECK ANATOMY

Ledger
Supports joists where they meet the side of the house. Installed on masonry walls with expansion bolts; on wood walls with lag bolts or carriage bolts. May have a sill on which joists rest *(shown)*, and often has spacer blocks

Tread
At least one tread 10 3/4 inches wide is required for every 7 1/4 inches of deck height; typically supported at each end by a cleat on a stringer. May be made of more than one board.

Cleat
Fastened to the stringers; a pair of cleats supports each tread.

Stair assembly footing
Provides a solid, stable base for the bottom of each stringer; commonly concrete *(shown)* 4 to 8 inches deep, or patio blocks.

Stringer
Two or more required, typically with cleats, to support the treads; fastened at the top to a joist *(shown)*, header or beam and supported at the bottom on a footing. Pictured is a stair assembly with double stringers separated by cleats.

Rail
One or more typically installed horizontally on the railing posts; common rail-to-post joints include overlap *(shown)*, butt, full lap and dado *(page 115)*. Balusters, if any, may be supported by the rails, or by a rail and a joist, header or beam, and are usually beveled *(page 112)* at the top for drainage. The spacing of rails and balusters is specified by local building codes.

Footing
Concrete that supports a post below the ground; typically at least 24 to 30 inches deep and a few inches beyond the frostline. May be poured in a cylindrical form. Top slopes away from the post for drainage. The post may extend to the bottom of the footing *(shown)* or be installed on top of it with a post anchor *(page 110)*.

Handrail
Installed across the tops of two or more posts to provide a ledge and protect posts and rails; usually mitered *(page 112)* at a corner. A board is fastened with the ends of the annular rings pointing down to keep it from cupping.

Deck board
Installed across joists, and positioned at least 1/4 inch apart for drainage. Typically 2-by-4 or 2-by-6 and placed perpendicular to joists *(shown)*, although they can be of other sizes and placed at other angles or in other patterns. A deck board is fastened with the ends of the annular rings pointing down to keep it from cupping.

Railing post
At least two are required for each length of a rail or handrail; typically 4-by-4s fastened to joists or a beam, and may extend to footings. The height of railing posts is specified by local building codes.

Joist
Usually evenly spaced every 16 or 24 inches under the deck boards, although the span may be greater; fastened on posts *(shown)* or supported by a beam on posts, and connected to the house by a ledger. A header may be fastened to the exposed ends of the joists to brace them, to protect the end grain, and for appearance. Pictured is a deck with double joists separated by posts.

Post
At least one is required to support the outer end of each joist or each end of a beam; typically 4-by-4 *(shown)*, although can be 4-by-6 or 6-by-6, and supported by a concrete footing. Posts may extend above joists or beam to carry rails and handrails.

TROUBLESHOOTING GUIDE

SYMPTOM	POSSIBLE CAUSE	PROCEDURE
Surface dirty	Weather, wear, pollution	Clean surfaces (p. 50) □◐
Surface stained or discolored	Fasteners or hardware rusted	Replace fasteners (p. 108) □○ and hardware (p. 110) □◐
	Foliage and resins from trees or plants; black, gray or colored mildew caused by humidity or poor circulation; water running off roof or splashing from pool	Clean and refinish surfaces (p. 50) □●
Finish faded, patchy, chipped or lifting	Weather, sun, wear	Clean and refinish surfaces (p. 50) □●
Deck board split or cracked; or wood spongy	Rot or insect damage	Repair minor rot and insect damage (p. 106) □○
	Wood shrinkage; shifting of wood joints caused by deck settlement	Repair or replace decking (p. 51) ◪○
Deck board crooked, twisted, sagging or lifted	Deck board fasteners loose	Replace fasteners (p. 108) □○
	Deck board or joist under it warped	Reinforce decking (p. 51) □○
	Deck board cupping or damaged	Repair or replace decking (p. 51) ◪○
Baluster crooked or cracked; or wood spongy	Baluster fasteners loose	Replace fasteners (p. 108) □○
	Rot or insect damage	Repair minor rot and insect damage (p. 106) □○
	Wood shrinkage; shifting of wood joints caused by deck settlement	Replace baluster (p. 52) □○
Rail or handrail split or cracked; or wood spongy	Rot or insect damage	Repair minor rot and insect damage (p. 106) □○
	Wood shrinkage; shifting of wood joints caused by deck settlement	Reinforce (p. 53) □○ or replace (p. 53) □◐ handrail; replace rail (p. 54) □◐
Rail or handrail wobbly, crooked, twisted or sagging	Rail or handrail fasteners or hardware loose	Replace fasteners (p. 108) □○ and hardware (p. 110) □◐
	Railing post loose or damaged	Reinforce (p. 55) □○, repair or replace (p. 55) ◪◐ railing post
	Rail or handrail cupping or damaged	Reinforce (p. 53) □○ or replace (p. 53) □◐ handrail; replace rail (p. 54) □◐
Railing post split or cracked; or wood spongy	Rot or insect damage	Repair minor rot and insect damage (p. 106) □○
	Wood shrinkage; shifting of wood joints caused by deck settlement	Reinforce (p. 55) □○, repair or replace (p. 55) ◪◐ railing post
Railing post wobbly, twisted or leaning	Beam, joist or stringer fasteners or hardware loose	Replace fasteners (p. 108) □○ and hardware (p. 110) □◐
	Beam, joist or stringer supporting railing post damaged	Repair (p. 64) ◪◐ or replace (p. 64) ■● beam; reinforce (p. 60) □○, repair (p. 60) □◐ or replace (p. 61) ◪◐ joist; reinforce (p. 57) □○, repair (p. 57) □◐ or replace (p. 58) ◪◐ stringer
	Railing post damaged	Reinforce (p. 55) □○, repair or replace (p. 55) ◪◐ railing post
Tread split or cracked; or wood spongy	Rot or insect damage	Repair minor rot and insect damage (p. 106) □○
	Wood shrinkage; shifting of wood joints caused by deck settlement	Replace tread (p. 56) □○
Tread crooked, twisted or sagging	Tread fasteners loose	Replace fasteners (p. 108) □○
	Stringer damaged	Reinforce (p. 57) □○, repair (p. 57) □◐ or replace (p. 58) ◪◐ stringer
	Cleat supporting tread damaged	Replace cleat (p. 56) □○
	Tread cupping or damaged	Replace tread (p. 56) □○
Cleat split or cracked; or wood spongy	Rot or insect damage	Repair minor rot and insect damage (p. 106) □○
	Wood shrinkage; shifting of wood joints caused by deck settlement	Replace cleat (p. 56) □○
Cleat crooked, twisted or sagging	Cleat fasteners loose	Replace fasteners (p. 108) □○
	Stringer supporting cleat damaged	Reinforce (p. 57) □○, repair (p. 57) □◐ or replace (p. 58) ◪◐ stringer
	Cleat damaged	Replace cleat (p. 56) □○

DEGREE OF DIFFICULTY: □ Easy ◪ Moderate ■ Complex
ESTIMATED TIME: ○ Less than 1 hour ◐ 1 to 3 hours ● Over 3 hours

SYMPTOM	POSSIBLE CAUSE	PROCEDURE
Stringer split or cracked; or wood spongy	Rot or insect damage	Repair minor rot and insect damage (p. 106) □○
	Wood shrinkage; shifting of wood joints caused by deck settlement	Reinforce (p. 57) □○, repair (p. 57) ◨◕ or replace (p. 58) ◨◕ stringer
Stringer crooked, twisted or sagging	Stringer fasteners loose	Replace fasteners (p. 108) □○
	Beam or joist connected to stringer damaged	Repair (p. 64) ◨◕ or replace (p. 64) ■● beam; reinforce (p. 60) □○, repair (p. 60) □◕ or replace (p. 61) ◨◕ joist
	Stair assembly footing damaged	Repair or replace stair assembly footing (p. 59) ◨◕
	Stringer damaged	Reinforce (p. 57) □○, repair (p. 57) □◕ or replace (p. 58) ◨◕ stringer
Stair assembly footing loose, cracked or raised	Moisture, frost heaves; shifting of soil or concrete caused by deck settlement	Repair or replace stair assembly footing (p. 59) ◨◕
Joist split or cracked; or wood spongy	Rot or insect damage	Repair minor rot and insect damage (p. 106) □○
	Wood shrinkage; shifting of wood joints caused by deck settlement	Reinforce (p. 60) □○, repair (p. 60) □◕ or replace (p. 61) ◨◕ joist
Joist crooked, twisted or sagging	Joist fasteners or hardware loose	Replace fasteners (p. 108) □○ and hardware (p. 110) □◕
	Post or footing damaged	Reinforce (p. 66) □○ or repair (p. 67) ◨◕ post; reinforce or repair footing (p. 69) ◨◕; repair (p. 69) ■◕ or replace (p. 71) ■● post and footing
	Beam supporting joist damaged	Repair (p. 64) ◨◕ or replace (p. 64) ■● beam
	Joist damaged	Reinforce (p. 60) □○, repair (p. 60) □◕ or replace (p. 61) ◨◕ joist
Ledger sagging or cracked; or wood spongy	Rot or insect damage	Repair minor rot and insect damage (p. 106) □○
	Wood shrinkage; shifting of joints caused by deck or house foundation settlement	Reinforce (p. 62) □○, repair (p. 63) ◨◕ or replace (p. 63) ■● ledger
Beam split or cracked; or wood spongy	Rot or insect damage	Repair minor rot and insect damage (p. 106) □○
	Wood shrinkage; shifting of wood joints caused by deck settlement	Repair (p. 64) ◨◕ or replace (p. 64) ■● beam
Beam crooked, twisted or sagging	Beam fasteners or hardware loose	Replace fasteners (p. 108) □○ and hardware (p. 110) □◕
	Post or footing supporting beam damaged	Reinforce (p. 66) □○ or repair (p. 67) ◨◕ post; reinforce or repair footing (p. 69) ◨◕; repair (p. 69) ■◕ or replace (p. 71) ■● post and footing
	Beam damaged	Repair (p. 64) ◨◕ or replace (p. 64) ■● beam
Post split or cracked; or wood spongy	Rot or insect damage	Repair minor rot and insect damage (p. 106) □○
	Wood shrinkage; shifting of wood joints caused by deck settlement	Reinforce (p. 66) □○ or repair (p. 67) ◨◕ post; repair (p. 69) ■◕ or replace (p. 71) ■● post and footing
Post wobbly, twisted or leaning	Post or footing damaged	Reinforce (p. 66) □○ or repair (p. 67) ◨◕ post; reinforce or repair footing (p. 69) ◨◕; repair (p. 69) ■◕ or replace (p. 71) ■● post and footing
Footing loose, cracked or raised	Moisture, frost heaves; shifting of soil or concrete caused by deck settlement	Reinforce or repair footing (p. 69) ◨◕; repair (p. 69) ■◕ or replace (p. 71) ■● post and footing
Deck sags, sways or bounces	Post or footing loose or damaged	Reinforce (p. 66) □○ or repair (p. 67) ◨◕ post; reinforce or repair footing (p. 69) ◨◕; repair (p. 69) ■◕ or replace (p. 71) ■● post and footing
	Beam damaged	Repair (p. 64) ◨◕ or replace (p. 64) ■● beam
	Ledger damaged or ledger fasteners loose	Reinforce (p. 62) □○, repair (p. 63) ◨◕ or replace (p. 63) ■● ledger
	Joist damaged	Reinforce (p. 60) □○, repair (p. 60) □◕ or replace (p. 61) ◨◕ joist
	Deck boards rotted or damaged	Reinforce (p. 51) □○, repair or replace (p. 51) ◨○ decking

DEGREE OF DIFFICULTY: □ **Easy** ◨ **Moderate** ■ **Complex**
ESTIMATED TIME: ○ **Less than 1 hour** ◕ **1 to 3 hours** ● **Over 3 hours**

CLEANING AND REFINISHING SURFACES

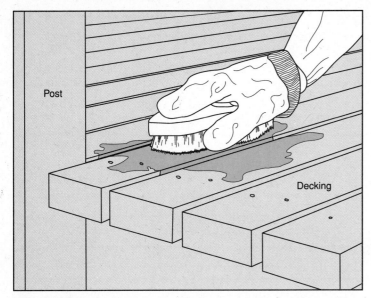

1 **Scrubbing off dirt and stains.** Replace rusted fasteners *(page 108)* and hardware *(page 110)*. Remove loose or lifting finish *(step 2)*. Clear debris out of cracks with a putty knife. To clean off dirt and most stains, use a solution of mild detergent and warm water; wear rubber gloves and scrub with a stiff fiber brush *(above)*. Rinse with fresh water. For tough stains, such as mildew or rust, mix 2 to 3 tablespoons of trisodium phosphate or 1 to 2 cups of bleach per gallon of warm water in a plastic bucket and repeat the procedure wearing goggles. A stronger solution is more likely to harm the finish. Before applying a new finish, sand the surface *(step 3)*.

2 **Removing old finish and wood resin.** Repair minor rot and insect damage *(page 106)*. If the finish is well adhered, sand the surface *(step 3)*. To scrape off lifting finish or hardened wood resin, wear goggles and use a paint scraper *(above)*, applying even, moderate pressure along the grain. To loosen thick layers or reach tight corners, rub gently with a wire brush. Cut away loose caulk at joints with a utility knife. Brush debris off the surface using a whisk; use a putty knife to clear debris from cracks. Scrub off stains such as mildew or rust that have penetrated the finish *(step 1)*.

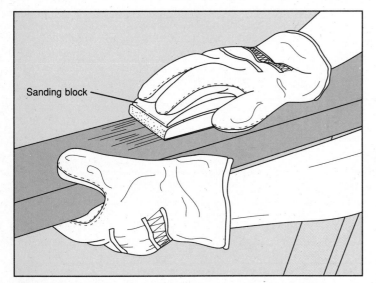

3 **Sanding the surface.** Fill holes and caulk joints *(page 106)*. Wearing a dust mask and work gloves, sand along the grain to smooth the surface. On a flat surface, use a sanding block *(above)*, or use a power sander *(page 119)*—especially if smoothing large areas. Work by hand to reach tight corners *(page 119)*. Start with coarse sandpaper if the surface is rough or heavily coated; start with medium-grade sandpaper if the surface is scratched or moderately coated. Use fine sandpaper for final smoothing or if the surface is unfinished. Apply light or moderate pressure evenly along the grain. Brush off dust with a whisk. Wipe using a tack cloth *(page 102)* after sanding.

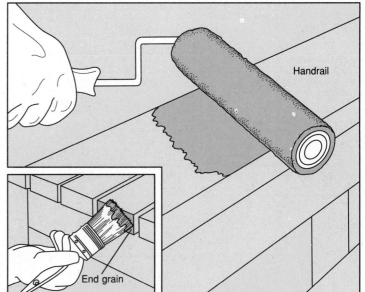

4 **Applying finish.** Choose a finish *(page 120)* and follow the manufacturer's directions for applying it; a primer coat of preservative or sealer may be required. Protect surfaces not being finished with masking tape or a tarp. Working top to bottom, apply finish evenly along the grain. Coat surfaces hardest to reach first, using a paintbrush; a synthetic, flagged-bristle type is recommended. Ensure that the end grain is adequately coated *(inset)*. To apply finish on a large, flat surface, use a roller *(above)*; fit it with an extension pole if needed. Work on a small area at a time. To spread a stain or penetrating finish evenly, backbrush the edges with a dry paintbrush.

REINFORCING THE DECKING

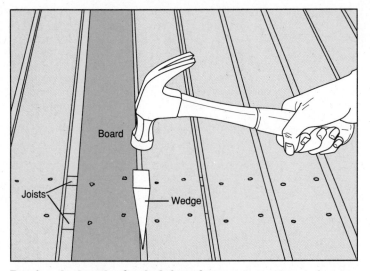

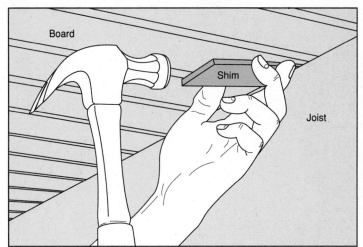

Bracing the length of a deck board. To reinforce a board along its length, remove the fasteners where required to reposition it *(page 107)*. Have a helper pull the board into place with a crowbar, or use one or more wedges. Saw each wedge from wood about 3/4 inch thick to a length of 6 to 8 inches, beveling it to a point at the end *(page 112)*. Use a hammer to tap each wedge into the narrowest space next to the board until the board is straight *(above)*. Bore pilot holes *(page 117)* and drive two screws into the board at each joist *(page 108)*. Fill holes *(page 106)* and refinish damaged surfaces *(page 50)*.

Bracing the underside of a deck board. To lift the surface of a board level with the boards around it, install a wood shim under it on each side of the joist; if required for access, remove nearby boards to work from above *(step below)*. Saw *(page 112)*, chisel *(page 116)* or plane *(page 117)* a shim to a thickness of 1/4 to 1/2 inch and equal in width to the board, beveling one side into a point at the bottom *(page 112)*; apply preservative or finish *(page 120)*. Use a hammer to tap each shim between the joist and the board *(above)* until the board is level with the boards beside it. Reinstall any deck boards removed *(page 52)* and refinish damaged surfaces *(page 50)*.

REPAIRING OR REPLACING THE DECKING

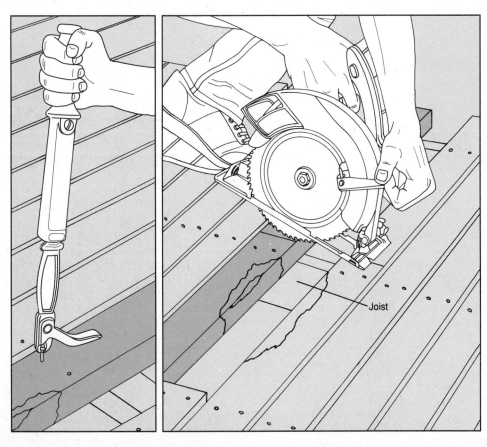

1 Removing deck boards. To repair the decking, replace only the section of each damaged board between joists or from a joist to the end of the decking. To replace the decking, take off the entire length of each damaged board.

To take off a section or the entire length of a board, remove the fasteners from it *(page 107)*; pull nails using a nail puller *(far left)*, pry bar or hammer. To loosen nails, lift the board at the joist with a crowbar; use a wood block to protect undamaged boards. Or, hammer on the bottom of the board near the joist; cushion the blows with a wood block if the board can be reinstalled.

To replace a section of a board, mark the end of the section on the board at the inside edge of a joist. To replace a section of adjacent boards, mark the end of the section on each board at the inside edge of the same joist; or, for best results, stagger the end of the section by marking each alternate board at the inside edge of different joists. Saw off the end of a board *(near left)* using a power saw set to the thickness of the board to make a plunge cut *(page 112)*; complete the sawcut ends using a handsaw *(page 112)* or a wood chisel *(page 116)*.

Purchase replacement deck boards at a lumber yard. If replacing only a section of each board, add cleats *(step 2)*. If replacing the entire length of each board, install new boards *(step 3)*.

REPAIRING OR REPLACING THE DECKING (continued)

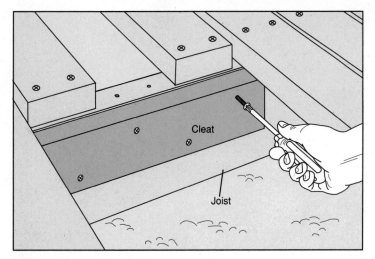

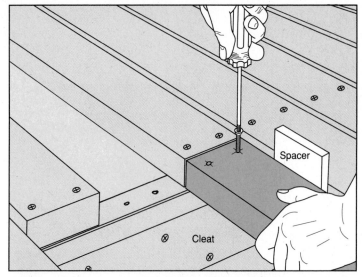

2 **Adding support cleats.** To support new boards at the end of an undamaged section, add a cleat on the joist; use 2-by-4 or stronger wood. Saw a cleat to a length at least equal to the distance of the undamaged section at the joist *(page 112)* and apply preservative or finish *(page 120)*. Position a cleat at the top of the joist, bore pilot holes *(page 117)* and drive in screws *(above)* or nails *(page 108)*; for best results, install at least two fasteners or space them every 4 to 6 inches, offsetting them *(above)*. If replacing a section of boards from one joist to another joist, saw each new board to length *(page 112)*, positioning it against each end of the undamaged section to mark it.

3 **Installing deck boards.** Apply preservative or finish *(page 120)*. To position a board on the joists, use wood blocks as spacers; at the end of an undamaged section, butt the end of a new board against it on the cleat. To install a board, bore pilot holes *(page 117)* and drive in two screws *(page 108)* at each joist and each cleat *(above)*. If installing new boards to the end of the decking, mark the end of the decking on the boards with a chalkline *(page 112)*, saw them off *(page 112)* and reapply preservative or finish on the end grain. Fill holes *(page 106)*. Refinish damaged surfaces *(page 50)*.

REPLACING A BALUSTER

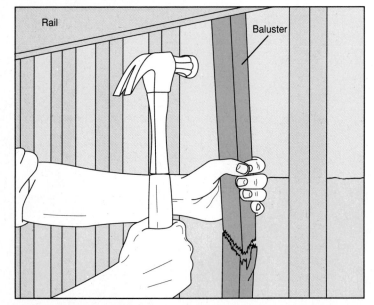

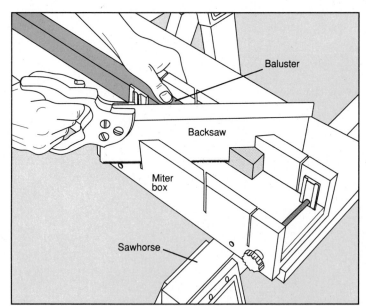

1 **Removing a baluster.** To remove a baluster, unscrew its screws, or pull its nails using a hammer, a pry bar or a nail puller *(page 107)*. To loosen the nails, hammer on the back of the baluster at the top near the rail *(above)* and at the bottom near the rail, joist, beam, or other part to which it is nailed. Cushion the blows with a wood block if the baluster will be reinstalled. If the baluster is damaged, replace it.

2 **Installing a baluster.** Purchase wood for a replacement baluster at a lumber yard and saw it to length *(page 112)*, measuring or tracing another baluster to mark it; use a backsaw and miter box to bevel the ends *(above)*. Apply preservative or finish *(page 120)*. Position the baluster and bore pilot holes *(page 117)*; to space the balusters evenly, hold a length of wood between them while boring the holes. Drive in two nails or screws at the top on the rail and at the bottom on the rail, joist, beam, or other part *(page 108)*. Fill holes *(page 106)* and refinish damaged surfaces *(page 50)*.

REINFORCING A HANDRAIL

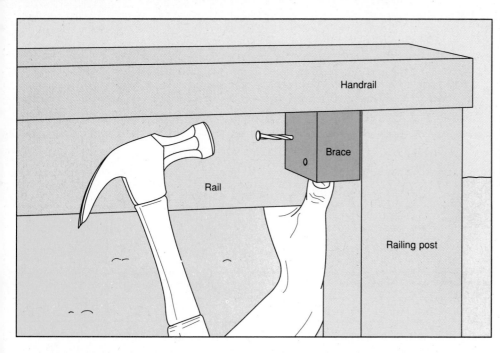

Bracing the end of a handrail. To reinforce the end of a handrail, install hardware *(page 110)* or a wood brace. Use lumber of the same dimensions as the handrail and saw it to a length equal to the width of the post *(page 112)*. Apply preservative or finish *(page 120)*.

Position the brace under the handrail and against the post. Bore pilot holes *(page 117)* and nail *(left)* or screw *(page 108)* the brace onto the post; also nail or screw the handrail and rail, if any, onto the brace. For best results, install two fasteners on each surface, offsetting them. Fill holes and caulk joints *(page 106)*. Refinish damaged surfaces *(page 50)*.

REPLACING A HANDRAIL

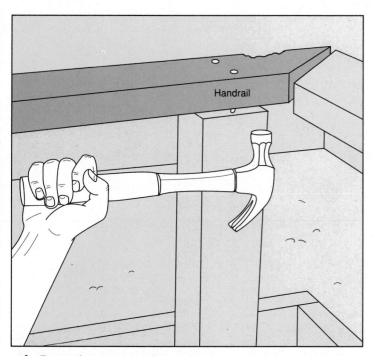

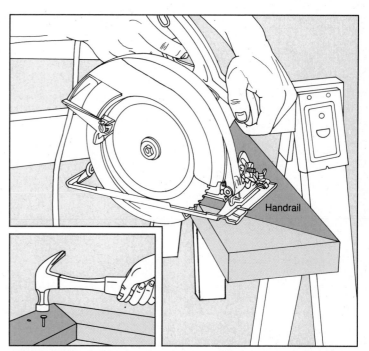

1 Removing a handrail. To take off a handrail, pull the nails or remove the screws *(page 107)* or hardware *(page 110)*. To loosen nails, hammer up on the bottom of the handrail *(above)*; cushion the blows with a wood block if the handrail will be reinstalled. If the handrail is damaged, replace its entire length, or just replace the section between two railing posts. To remove a section of the handrail that extends across the top of a post, mark it at the post's center and use a power saw set to the thickness of the handrail to cut it *(page 112)*. Remove the damaged section.

2 Installing a handrail. Purchase wood for a replacement handrail at a lumber yard and position it against the ends of the undamaged handrail to mark it. Using a power saw or a handsaw, cut the new handrail to length *(page 112)*, shaping the ends to match the existing joints *(above)*. Apply preservative or finish *(page 120)*. Position the handrail, bore pilot holes *(page 117)* and drive in two nails or screws *(page 108)* at each railing post *(inset)*; for best results, also drive nails through adjacent sides of handrails at a mitered corner. Rout the edges *(page 118)* to match the handrail, if necessary. Fill holes and caulk joints *(page 106)*. Refinish damaged surfaces *(page 50)*.

REPLACING A RAIL

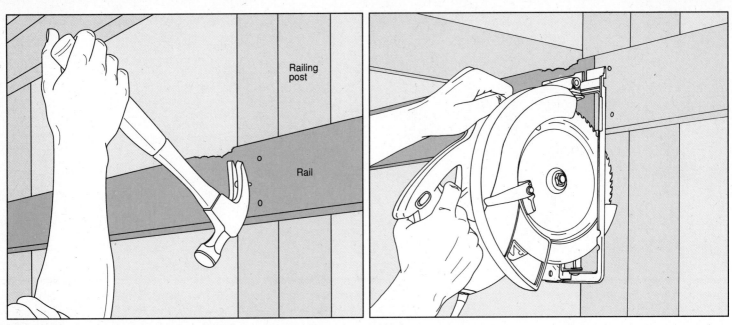

1 **Removing a rail.** Remove any balusters in the way *(page 52)*. To take off a rail, pull the nails *(page 107)* or remove the hardware *(page 110)*; pull nails using a hammer *(above, left)*, a pry bar or a nail puller. Loosen the nails first by hammering on the back of the rail near the railing post; cushion the blows with a wood block if the rail will be reinstalled.

If the rail is damaged, replace its entire length or only the section between railing posts. To remove a section of the rail that spans a post, mark the center line of the railing post across it and use a power saw set to the thickness of the rail *(page 112)* to cut it *(above, right)*. Remove the damaged section.

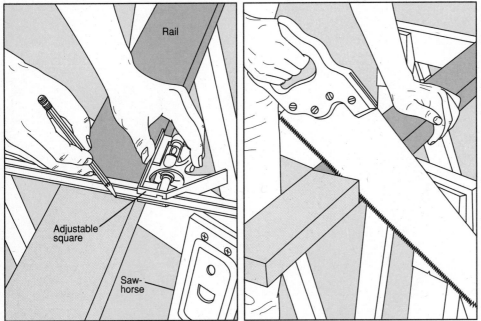

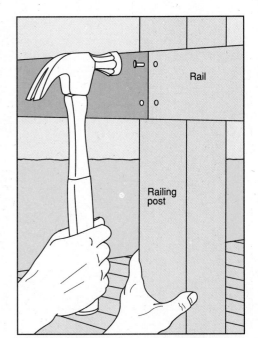

2 **Measuring and sawing a new rail.** Purchase wood for a replacement rail at a lumber yard. Position the new rail on the railing posts to mark it; have a helper support one end or temporarily nail it *(page 108)*. Take down the rail to mark the ends on each side of it *(above, left)*. Using a handsaw *(above, right)* or a power saw, cut the new rail to length *(page 112)*. Shape the ends to fit the existing rail joints *(page 115)*; if required, temporarily nail on a straight-edged wood block as a saw guide. Apply preservative or finish *(page 120)*.

3 **Installing a rail.** Position the rail, bore pilot holes *(page 117)* and drive in two nails *(page 108)* at each railing post *(above)* or install hardware at each end *(page 110)*; for best results, also drive nails through adjacent sides of rails that meet at an outside corner. Reinstall any balusters removed *(page 52)*. Fill holes and caulk joints *(page 106)*. Refinish damaged surfaces *(page 50)*.

REINFORCING A RAILING POST

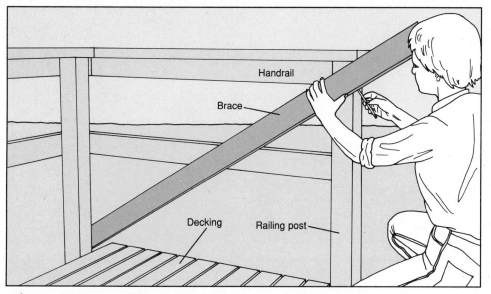

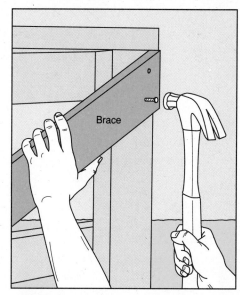

1 Measuring and sawing a brace. To reinforce a railing post, install a wood brace from the top of it, near the handrail or the top rail, to the bottom of the railing post next to it, near the decking. To remove a damaged brace, pull the nails *(page 107)*. Purchase lumber for a brace of the same dimensions as a rail at a lumber yard.

Remove any balusters *(page 52)* or rails *(page 54)* in the way. Position the brace against the railing posts to mark it *(above)*; have a helper support one end or temporarily nail it *(page 108)*. If the railing posts are offset, as shown, position the brace on opposite sides of them. Saw the brace to length *(page 112)*. Apply preservative or finish *(page 120)*.

2 Installing a brace. To install the brace, position it against the railing posts, bore pilot holes *(page 117)* and drive in two nails *(above)* or screws *(page 108)* at each end; for best results, also nail or screw any intermediate rail or balusters onto the brace. Fill holes and caulk joints *(page 106)*. Refinish damaged surfaces *(page 50)*.

REPAIRING OR REPLACING A RAILING POST

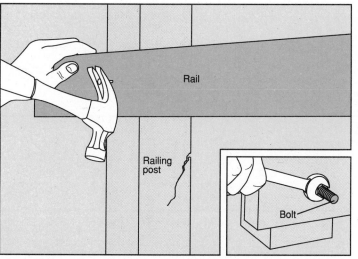

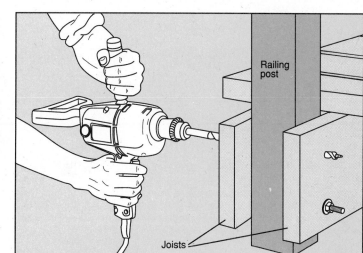

1 Removing a railing post. If a railing post set in a footing is damaged below a joist or beam, repair the post *(page 67)*. In other cases, first remove any rail *(page 54)* and handrail *(page 53)* by pulling the nails with a hammer *(above)*, a pry bar or a nail puller *(page 107)*. If a railing post set in a footing is damaged above a joist or beam, cut off the damaged part, sawing one side of a half-lap joint *(page 115)* just below the damaged area. If a railing post that does not extend to a footing is damaged, remove the fasteners *(page 107)* connecting it to the joist, beam or stringer and take it off; use a wrench to loosen the nuts on carriage bolts *(inset)*.

2 Installing a railing post. Purchase wood for a replacement railing post at a lumber yard. To install a railing post at a joist *(above)*, beam or stringer, position it, bore two holes all the way through *(page 117)* and install bolts *(page 108)*. If installing part of a post above a joist or beam, saw a half lap *(page 115)* to fit the undamaged section, clamp the joint *(page 116)* and install bolts. Saw the railing post to height *(page 112)*, measuring another. Rout *(page 118)*, bore or chisel *(page 116)* it to shape if required. Apply preservative or finish *(page 120)*. Reinstall any rail *(page 54)* and handrail *(page 53)* removed. Fill holes and caulk joints *(page 106)*. Refinish damaged surfaces *(page 50)*.

REPLACING A TREAD

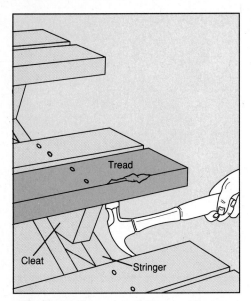

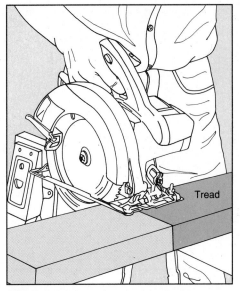

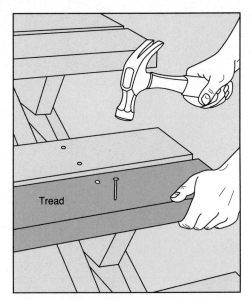

1 **Removing a tread.** To take off a tread, remove the fasteners *(page 107)*; pull nails using a hammer, a pry bar or a nail puller. To loosen nails, hammer up on the bottom of the tread near the cleat *(above)* or the stringer; cushion the blows with a wood block if the tread will be reinstalled. If the tread is damaged, replace it.

2 **Measuring and cutting a new tread.** Purchase wood for a replacement tread at a lumber yard. Using a power saw *(above)* or a handsaw, cut the new tread *(page 112)* to length, measuring other treads to mark it. To steady the saw, temporarily nail on a straight-edged wood block as a saw guide *(page 108)*. Apply preservative or finish *(page 120)*.

3 **Installing a tread.** Position the tread, bore pilot holes *(page 117)* and drive in two nails *(above)* or screws *(page 108)* at each cleat or stringer. To position double treads, use a wood block as a spacer between them. Fill holes *(page 106)* and refinish damaged surfaces *(page 50)*.

REPLACING A CLEAT

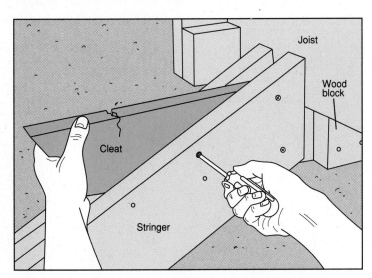

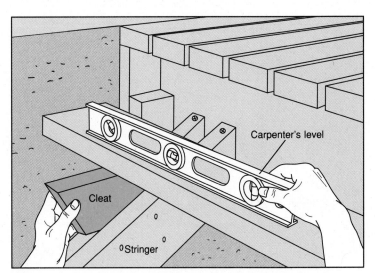

1 **Removing a cleat.** Remove any tread in the way *(step above, left)*. To take off a cleat, remove its fasteners on the stringer *(page 107)*; if taking off a top cleat, check for fasteners on a wood block mounted on the joist supporting the stair assembly. Use a screwdriver to take out screws *(above)*. Tap out a cleat between a double stringer, shown here, using a hammer; cushion the blows with a wood block if the cleat will be reinstalled. If a cleat is damaged, replace it. Purchase wood for a replacement cleat at a lumber yard and cut it to shape *(page 112)*, measuring or tracing another cleat to mark it. Apply preservative or finish *(page 120)*.

2 **Installing a cleat.** To position a cleat, support it at the stringer, resting a tread in position on it. If the cleat fits between double stringers tap it in with a hammer, cushioning the blows with a wood block. Reposition the cleat until the tread is level *(above)* and mark the cleat edges on the stringer. Bore pilot holes *(page 117)* and drive in at least two nails or screws *(page 108)*. If positioning a top cleat, also install fasteners at any wood block mounted on the joist to support the stair assembly. Reinstall the tread removed *(step above, right)*. Fill holes *(page 106)* and refinish damaged surfaces *(page 50)*.

REINFORCING A STRINGER

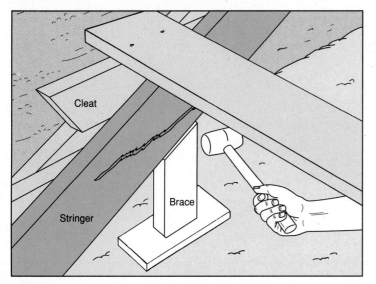

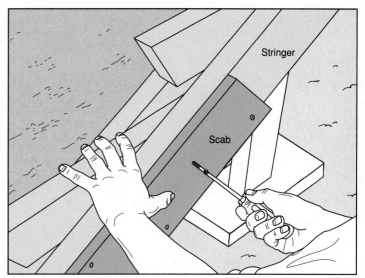

1 Bracing a stringer. To reinforce a stringer, support it in position with a wood brace and install a scab. Remove any tread *(page 56)*, railing post *(page 55)* and baluster *(page 52)* in the way. For a brace, use 2-by-4 or stronger wood. Saw it to the length required to support the damaged section *(page 112)*, positioning it against the stringer to mark it. Set the brace on a flat board and use a sledgehammer to tap it under the damaged section until the stringer is supported in the proper position *(above)*.

2 Installing a scab. Purchase lumber for a scab of the same width as the stringer at a lumber yard and cut it 6 inches longer than the damaged section *(page 112)*. Apply preservative or finish *(page 120)*. To install the scab, position it on the damaged section, bore pilot holes *(page 117)* and drive in screws *(page 108)* every 4 to 6 inches, offsetting them *(above)*. Reinstall any tread *(page 56)*, railing post *(page 55)* and baluster *(page 52)* removed. Fill holes *(page 106)* and refinish damaged surfaces *(page 50)*.

REPAIRING A STRINGER

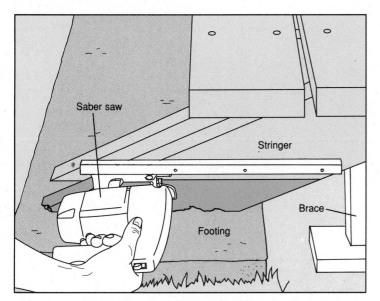

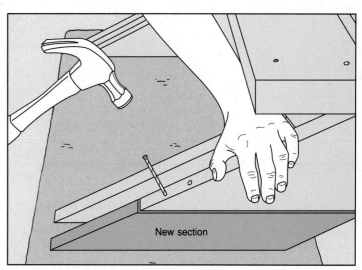

1 Removing the damage. To repair a stringer damaged near the footing, support it in position with a wood brace and cut off the damaged section. Remove any tread, cleat *(page 56)*, railing post *(page 55)* and baluster *(page 52)* in the way. For a brace, use 2-by-4 or stronger wood; saw it to the length required to support the stringer *(page 112)*, positioning it against the stringer to mark it. Use a sledge-hammer to tap the brace under the stringer until it is supported in the proper position. Using a carpenter's level, mark a horizontal line across the stringer just above the damaged section *(page 112)*. Cut it off *(above)* with a saber saw *(page 112)*; if required, temporarily nail on a wood block as a saw guide *(page 108)*. Remove the damaged section.

2 Splicing the stringer. Purchase lumber of the same dimensions as the stringer at a lumber yard. To cut the bottom end of the new section to rest on the footing, hold it flat against the stringer, align-ing their edges, and mark the end of the stringer on the new section. Cut the new section along the mark. Rest this cut end on the footing, align the edges again and mark the end of the stringer on the new sec-tion again. Cut along this mark to form a piece that fits precisely. Apply preservative or finish *(page 120)*. Position the new section under the stringer, bore pilot holes *(page 117)* and drive at least two nails *(above)*, or screws *(page 108)*, through each end of the splice. For reinforce-ment, install a scab *(step 2, above)*. Reinstall any cleat, tread *(page 56)*, railing post *(page 55)* and baluster *(page 52)* removed. Fill holes *(page 106)* and refinish damaged surfaces *(page 50)*.

REPLACING A STRINGER

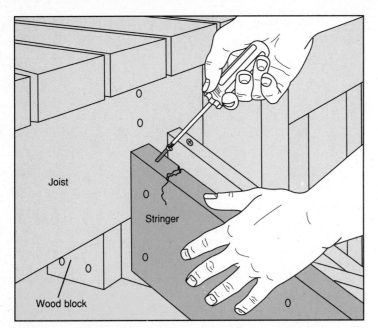

1 Removing a stringer. Remove any tread, cleat *(page 56)*, railing post *(page 55)* and baluster *(page 52)* in the way. To take off a stringer, remove the fasteners *(page 107)* or hardware *(page 110)*; check for fasteners in a wood block mounted on a joist that supports the stair assembly. Use a screwdriver to take out screws *(above)*. If a stringer is damaged, replace it. Purchase wood for a replacement stringer at a lumber yard. If a damaged stringer is a standard notched type, purchase a matching pre-notched stringer and install it *(step 4)*.

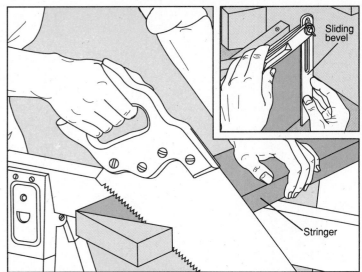

2 Measuring and sawing a new stringer. To mark the length of the new stringer, measure the length of the upper edge of the other stringer, from the joist, beam or header to the footing; if the stringer is notched, measure its lower edge. To mark each end of the new stringer, use a sliding bevel *(page 112)* to measure the angles of the ends of the other stringer: at the top, measure between the upper edge and the joist, beam or header *(inset)* and at the bottom, between the upper edge and the footing; if the stringer is notched, measure along the lower edge. Use the sliding bevel to mark these angles on the ends of the new stringer. Saw the new stringer to length *(page 112)* along the marks *(above)*. If the stringer does not require notches, apply preservative or finish *(page 120)* and install it *(step 4)*.

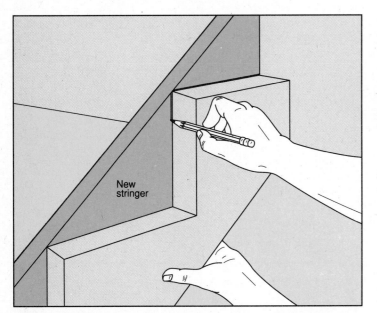

3 Measuring and cutting stringer notches. To mark notches on the new stringer, position it against the other stringer with their edges even; have a helper support it or temporarily nail it *(page 108)*. Trace the notches on the new stringer using a pencil *(above)*. Take down the new stringer and cut the notches with a power saw, completing the ends of each sawcut using a handsaw *(page 112)*; if required, temporarily nail on a straight-edged wood block as a saw guide. Apply preservative or finish *(page 120)*.

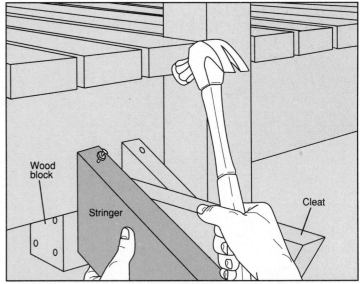

4 Installing a stringer. To position the new stringer, support the top end against the joist, beam or header and set the bottom end on the footing. Reposition the stringer until a tread rests level on it; have a helper support the tread or temporarily nail *(page 108)* the stringer *(above)*. For the correct spacing of double stringers, reposition the cleat. To install the stringer, bore pilot holes *(page 117)* and drive in screws *(page 108)* or install hardware *(page 110)* at the joist, beam or header; also drive screws into any wood block mounted on a joist that supports the stair assembly. Reinstall any cleat, tread *(page 56)*, railing post *(page 55)* and baluster *(page 52)* removed. Fill holes *(page 106)* and refinish damaged surfaces *(page 50)*.

REPAIRING OR REPLACING A STAIR ASSEMBLY FOOTING

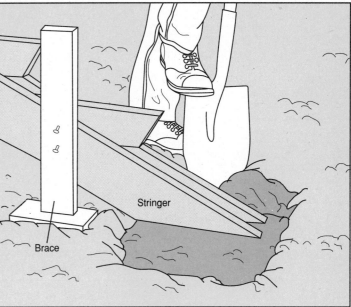

1 Removing a footing. To repair or replace a stair assembly footing, support the bottom of each stringer in position with a wood brace; remove any tread in the way *(page 56)*. For braces, use 2-by-4 or stronger boards 24 to 30 inches long *(page 112)*; nail a wood foot 8 to 10 inches long onto the bottom. Have a helper hold each stringer in position while you temporarily nail on a brace about 12 inches up from the bottom end. If the old footing is concrete, wear work gloves and goggles and break up the damaged area or the entire footing, using a bull-point chisel and a sledgehammer *(above, left)* or a demolition hammer *(page 122)*. If only part of the footing was damaged, repair it using concrete patching compound *(page 122)*. If the footing is a patio block, lift it up with a crowbar and remove it. To replace the footing, enlarge the hole 6 to 8 inches on each side of the stringer using a spade *(above, right)*; install a patio block *(step 2)* or pour a concrete footing *(step 3)*.

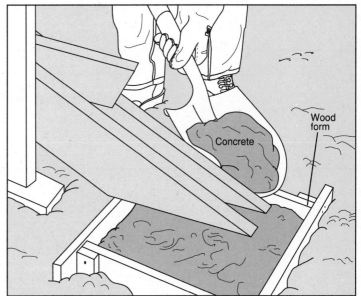

2 Installing a patio block. Purchase a patio block about 16 inches square at a building supply center. Using a spade, dig the hole at the bottom of the stringer to a depth of 4 to 6 inches. Tamp the bottom of the hole using your feet, line it with 2 to 4 inches of gravel and tamp again. Wearing work gloves, slide the patio block in position under the bottom end of the stringer. Reposition the patio block, adding or removing gravel and tamping, until it sits level, with the stringer resting on it in its proper position. Reinstall any tread removed *(page 56)* and take off the brace.

3 Pouring a concrete footing. To install a concrete footing, use a spade to dig the hole at the bottom of the stringer to a depth of 10 to 12 inches. Tamp the bottom of the hole using your feet, line it with 2 to 4 inches of gravel and tamp again. Prepare a wood form *(page 122)*, setting the top of it level and even with the bottom end of the stringer. Check the form position using a line level or a board and a carpenter's level *(page 118)*; to reposition the form, add or remove gravel and tamp. Wearing work gloves, use a spade to mix concrete *(page 122)* and fill the form *(above)*; smooth the surface with a board or a trowel. Allow the footing to set 48 hours before removing the form. Reinstall any tread removed *(page 56)* and take off the brace.

REINFORCING A JOIST

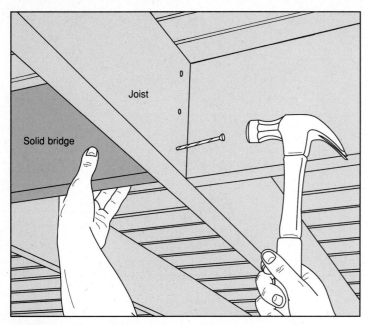

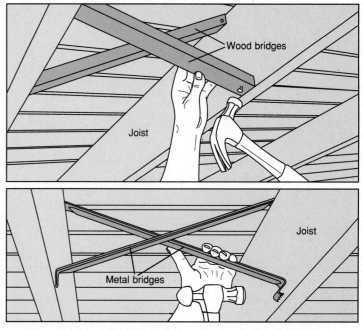

Installing solid bridges. To reinforce a joist with solid bridges, install a bridge every 6 to 8 feet between it and the joist on each side of it. If there is not enough clearance to work under the deck, remove deck boards to work from above *(page 51)*. Purchase lumber for bridges of the same dimensions as the joists at a lumber yard. Saw each bridge to a length equal to the distance between the joists *(page 112)*. Apply preservative or finish *(page 120)*. To install a bridge, position it between the joists, offset from any other bridge on the opposite side of a joist, and centered under a deck board. Drive in at least two nails *(page 108)* at each end of it *(above)*. Caulk joints *(page 106)* and reinstall any deck boards removed *(page 52)*.

Installing cross bridges. To reinforce a joist with cross bridges, install two bridges diagonally every 6 to 8 feet between it and the joist on each side of it; if there is not enough clearance to work under the deck, remove deck boards to work from above *(page 51)*. Purchase 1-by-2s or 1-by-3s, or metal bridges, at a lumber yard. Saw a wood bridge to fit from the top of the joist to the bottom of the next joist, beveling the ends at opposite angles *(page 112)*. Apply preservative or finish *(page 120)* and drive in nails *(page 108)* at each end *(above, top)*. To install a metal bridge, hammer each end into the joist *(above, bottom)*. Caulk joints *(page 106)* and reinstall any deck boards removed *(page 52)*.

REPAIRING A JOIST

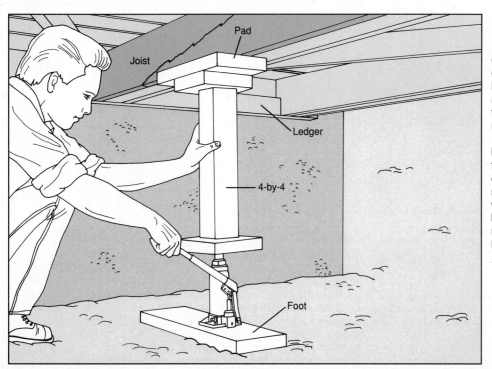

1 Supporting the joist. To repair a joist, support it in position with a jack *(page 124)* and install a scab on each side of it over the damaged section; if there is not enough clearance to work under the deck, remove deck boards to work from above *(page 51)*. Remove any bridges from each side of the damaged section; pull the nails using a hammer, pry bar or nail puller *(page 107)*.

Set the jack on a level wood pad or concrete block, directly below the joist and at the center of the damaged section. Temporarily nail a 2-by-6 or 2-by-8 pad onto the bottom of the damaged section. If required, add to the reach of the jack with a length of 4-by-4, or by stacking concrete blocks under it. Raise the jack until it fits snugly under the joist, supporting it in position but not lifting it *(left)*.

REPAIRING A JOIST (continued)

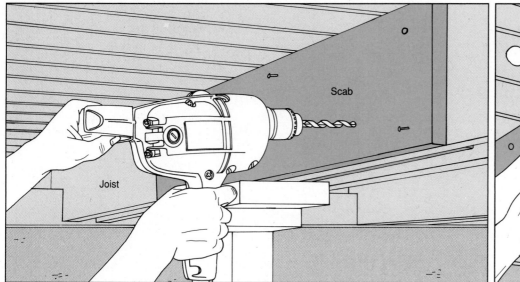
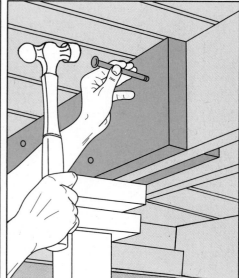

2 **Installing scabs.** Purchase lumber for a pair of scabs of the same dimensions as the joist at a lumber yard. Saw each scab to a length 4 to 6 feet longer than the damaged section *(page 112)*; if there is a stringer, railing post or baluster in the way, cut the scab to fit around it. Apply preservative or finish *(page 120)*.

To install the scabs, position one on each side of the joist, centered over the damaged section; if required, have a helper support them or temporarily nail them *(page 108)*. Bore holes *(page 117)* through both scabs and the joist every 10 to 12 inches, offsetting them *(above, left)*. Install carriage bolts *(page 108)*, using a ball-peen hammer to tap them into the holes *(above, right)*. Caulk joints *(page 106)*. Reinstall any bridges *(page 60)* and deck boards *(page 52)* removed.

REPLACING A JOIST

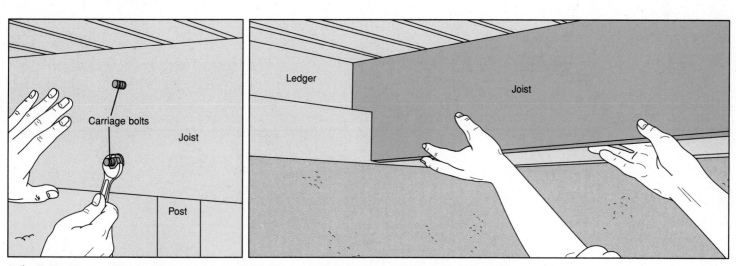

1 **Removing a joist.** To replace a joist, either remove it and install a new one, or install a sister joist alongside it. If there is not enough clearance to work under the deck, remove deck boards to work from above *(page 51)*. Remove any bridges from both sides of the joist; pull nails using a hammer, a pry bar or a nail puller *(page 107)*. If a sister joist can be positioned against the joist or within 4 to 6 inches of it, install one on the same ledger *(step 2)*, beams and header, if any, and post *(step 3)* occupied by the joist.

To take off the joist for replacement, remove its fasteners from the deck boards and any header *(page 107)*. Remove any stringer *(page 58)*, railing post *(page 55)* or baluster *(page 52)* attached to it . Having a helper support the joist, remove its fasteners or hardware *(page 110)* from the ledger, beams, if any, and each post; use a wrench to remove the nuts from bolts at a post *(above, left)*. Take off the end of the joist farthest from the ledger first; if required, use a sledgehammer carefully to knock it off, or saw the joist into sections *(page 112)*. Take off the joist *(above, right)*.

REPLACING A JOIST (continued)

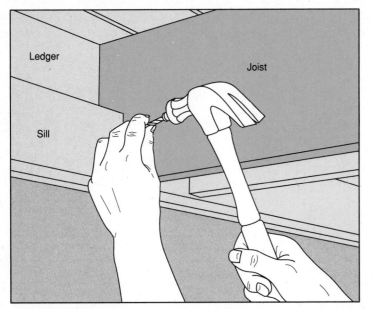

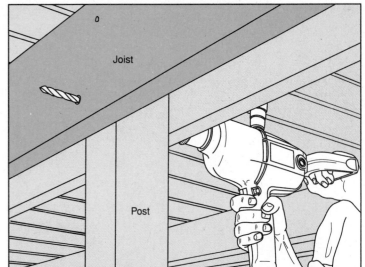

2 **Positioning a joist on a ledger.** Purchase lumber of the same dimensions as the old joist at a lumber yard. Mark the replacement by measuring another joist, and saw the joist to length *(page 112)*, with an overlap joint to fit the ledger sill *(page 115)*, if necessary. Apply preservative or finish *(page 120)*. With one or more helpers supporting the joist, raise it into position on the ledger and on any beam *(step 3)*. At the ledger, bore pilot holes *(page 117)* and install nails *(page 108)* or hardware *(page 110)*; drive at least two nails into each side of the joist at the ledger *(above)*.

3 **Positioning a joist on a beam and posts.** To position the joist between the decking and a beam, bow or angle it; if required, use a sledgehammer to knock it, cushioning the blows with a wood block. Or, position the joist directly on the posts, as shown; if required, temporarily nail it *(page 108)*. Drive in nails or install hardware *(page 110)* at the ledger *(step 2)* and at the beam, if any. At a post, install hardware or bore two holes *(page 117)*, offsetting them *(above)*, and install bolts *(page 108)*. Caulk joints *(page 106)*. Reinstall bridges *(page 60)* and any stringer *(page 58)*, railing post *(page 55)* or baluster *(page 52)* removed. Fasten the deck boards and any header to the joist. Reinstall any deck boards removed *(page 52)*.

REINFORCING A LEDGER

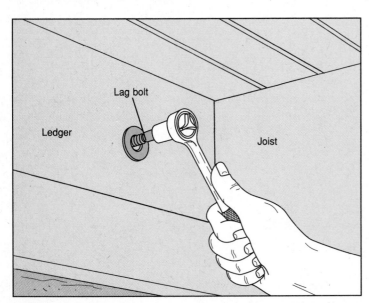

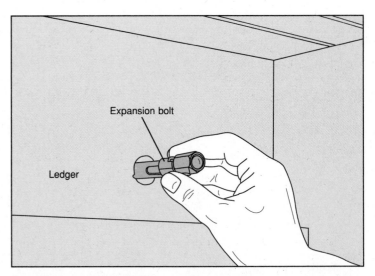

Installing lag bolts. To reinforce a ledger on other than a brick or masonry wall, install additional lag bolts every 3 to 4 feet along it; if there is not enough space to work under the deck, remove deck boards to work from above *(page 51)*. Purchase lag bolts at a building supply center. Bore pilot holes through the ledger and any spacers behind it into the wall *(page 117)*. Offset the bolt hole positions slightly. Fit a washer on the bolt and drive it into the hole with a socket wrench *(above)* or a nut driver. Reinstall any deck boards removed *(page 52)*.

Installing expansion bolts. To reinforce a ledger on a brick or masonry wall, install additional expansion bolts every 3 to 4 feet along it; if there is not enough space to work under the deck, remove deck boards to work from above *(page 51)*. Purchase expansion bolts at a building supply center. To install an expansion bolt, bore a hole through the ledger and any spacer behind it, then change to a masonry bit and drill into the wall *(page 117)*. Offset the bolt hole positions slightly. Fit an expansion bolt in the hole *(above)* and tap it flush with the ledger using a ball-peen hammer. Tighten the expansion bolt using a socket wrench or a nut driver. Reinstall any deck boards removed *(page 52)*.

REPAIRING A LEDGER

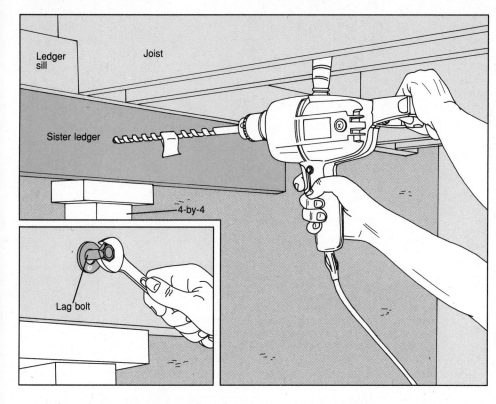

Installing a sister ledger. To repair a ledger, install a sister ledger. If there is not enough room to work under the deck, remove deck boards to work from above *(page 51)*. Purchase lumber for a sister ledger of the same dimensions as the ledger at a lumber yard; saw it to a length 4 to 6 feet longer than the damaged section *(page 112)*. If required, saw wood blocks for spacers and nail them on the back *(page 108)*. Apply preservative or finish *(page 120)*.

To support the sister ledger for installation, use one jack *(page 124)* for every 6 to 8 feet of its length. Set each jack on a level wood pad or concrete block directly below the ledger. Extend the jack's reach with a 4-by-4 or by lifting it on concrete blocks, if necessary. Position a 2-by-6 or 2-by-8 pad between the sister ledger and each jack. With one or more helpers supporting the sister ledger in place, raise each jack under it until it fits snugly under the ledger, supporting it in position but not lifting it.

Bore holes *(page 117)* through the sister ledger every 3 to 4 feet *(left)* and install lag bolts or expansion bolts *(page 62)*; tighten them using a wrench *(inset)* or nut driver. Caulk joints *(page 106)* and reinstall any deck boards removed *(page 52)*.

REPLACING A LEDGER

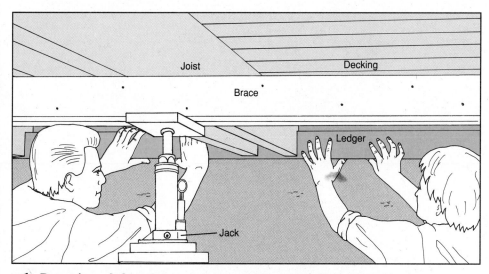

1 **Removing a ledger.** Before removing a ledger, support all the joists with a brace made of two 2-by-10s temporarily nailed together, supported by jacks *(page 124)* every 6 to 8 feet. If there is not enough room to work under the deck, remove deck boards to work from above *(page 51)*.

Set each jack 3 to 4 feet from the ledger on a level wood pad or concrete block, directly below a joist. Extend a jack's reach with a 4-by-4, or by lifting it on concrete blocks, if necessary. Position a 2-by-6 or 2-by-8 pad between the brace and each jack. With two or more helpers supporting the brace, raise each jack under it until the brace fits snugly against the joists, supporting them without lifting them.

To take off the ledger, remove the nails *(page 107)* or hardware *(page 110)* fastening the joists to it. With one or more helpers supporting the ledger *(above)*, remove the bolts connecting it to the wall *(page 107)* and take it down. Fill the holes in the wall *(page 106)*; for brick or masonry, use concrete patching compound *(page 122)*.

2 **Installing a ledger.** Purchase wood for a replacement ledger at a lumber yard. Saw it to length *(page 112)* and apply preservative or finish *(page 120)*. Nail on any required sill or spacer blocks *(page 108)*. To install the ledger, position it on the wall under the joists; have one or more helpers support it. Bore holes every 3 to 4 feet *(page 117)* and install lag bolts or expansion bolts *(page 62)*. Drive in nails or install hardware *(page 110)* to attach the joists to the ledger *(above)*. Caulk joints *(page 106)* and reinstall any deck boards removed *(page 52)*.

REPAIRING A BEAM

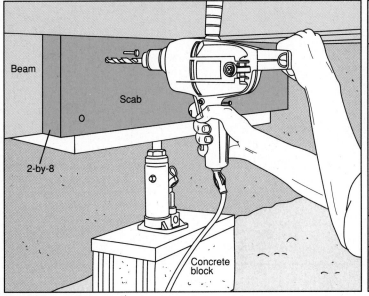

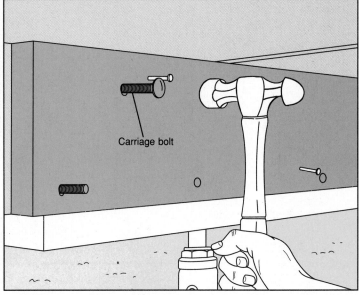

Installing scabs. To repair a beam, support it in position with a jack *(page 124)* and install a scab on each side of the damaged section; if there is not enough room to work under the deck, remove deck boards to work from above *(page 51)*. Set the jack on a level wood pad or concrete block directly below the beam at the center of the damaged section. If required, add to the reach of the jack with a 4-by-4, or by stacking concrete blocks under it. Temporarily nail *(page 108)* a 2-by-6 or 2-by-8 pad on the bottom of the damaged section. Raise the jack until it fits snugly under the beam, supporting it in position but not lifting it.

Purchase lumber for scabs, the same width as the beam and half its thickness, at a lumber yard. Saw each scab to a length 4 to 6 feet longer than the damaged section *(page 112)*; if required, cut a scab to fit around any joist, stringer, railing post or baluster. Apply preservative or finish *(page 120)*. Nail a scab on each side of the beam, centered over the damaged section. Bore holes for bolts through both scabs and the beam every 10 to 12 inches *(page 117)*, offsetting them *(above, left)*. Install bolts *(page 108)*, using a ball-peen hammer to tap them into the holes *(above, right)*. Caulk joints *(page 106)*, and reinstall any deck boards removed *(page 52)*.

REPLACING A BEAM

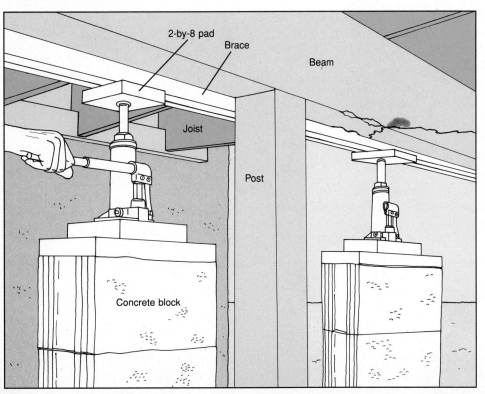

1 Supporting the joists. Before removing a beam, support all the joists on both sides of it with braces made of two 2-by-10s temporarily nailed together, supported by jacks *(page 124)* every 6 to 8 feet. If there is not enough room to work under the deck, remove if necessary some deck boards to work from above *(page 51)*.

Set each jack 3 to 4 feet from the beam, on a level wood pad or concrete block, directly below a joist. Extend a jack's reach with a 4-by-4, or by lifting it on concrete blocks, if necessary. Position a 2-by-6 or 2-by-8 pad between the brace and each jack. With helpers supporting the brace, raise each jack under it until the brace fits snugly against the joists, supporting them without lifting them. Install the second brace the same way.

REPLACING A BEAM (continued)

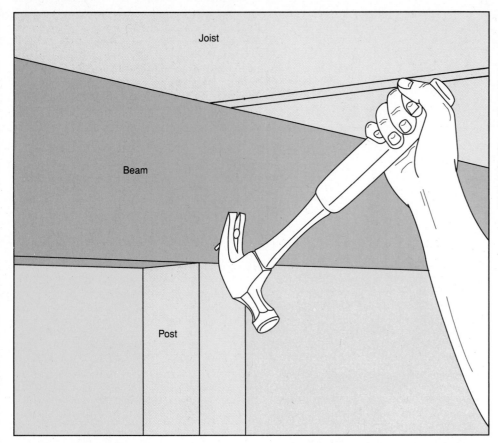

2 **Removing the beam.** To take down the beam, first remove any stringer *(page 58)*, railing post *(page 55)* or baluster *(page 52)* attached to it. Disconnect each joist from the beam by pulling the nails *(page 107)* or removing the hardware *(page 110)*. To loosen nails, hammer on the side of the joist near the beam, cushioning the blows with a wood block; pull the nails using a hammer, a pry bar or a nail puller.

With two or more helpers supporting the beam, remove the bolts *(page 107)* or hardware connecting the beam to each post. Lower the beam off the posts; if required, carefully use a sledgehammer to knock it out from between the joists and the posts, or saw it into sections *(page 112)*.

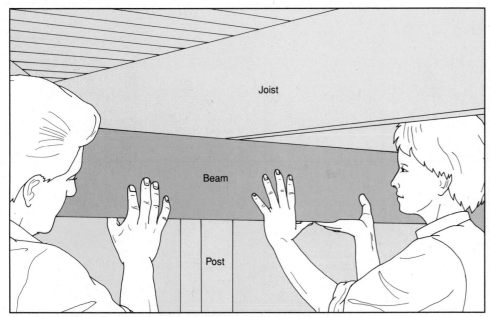

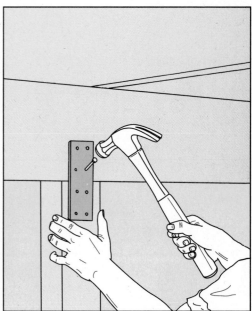

3 **Installing a new beam.** Purchase lumber for a replacement beam of the same dimensions as the old beam at a lumber yard, and saw it to length *(page 112)*. Apply preservative or finish *(page 120)*. To install the beam, position it on the posts and under the joists; have two or more helpers support it *(above, left)*. If the fit is tight, carefully use a sledgehammer to knock the beam between the joists and the posts, cushioning the blows with a wood block.

Connect the beam to each post *(above, right)* by installing bolts *(page 108)* or hardware *(page 110)*. Connect each joist to both sides of the beam by driving in nails or installing hardware. Caulk the joints *(page 106)*. Reinstall any stringer *(page 58)*, railing post *(page 55)* or baluster *(page 52)* removed. Reinstall any deck boards removed *(page 52)*.

REINFORCING A POST

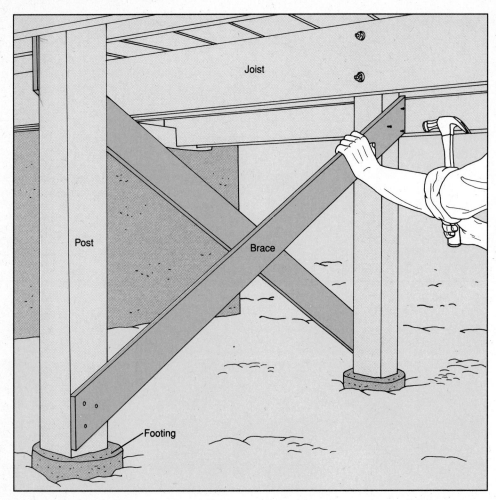

Installing post-to-post braces. To reinforce a post with cross braces, install a brace from the top of the weak post, near the joist or beam, to the bottom of a post next to it near the footing. For added reinforcement, also install a brace running diagonally opposite on the other side of the posts. To remove a damaged brace, pull the nails *(page 107)*. If there is no room to work under the deck, remove deck boards to work from above *(page 51)*.

Purchase 1-by-6 or 2-by-6 boards for braces at a lumber yard. Position each brace against the posts to mark it; have a helper support one end or temporarily nail it *(page 108)*. Saw each brace to length, with the required angle at each end *(page 112)*. Apply preservative or finish *(page 120)*.

To install a brace, position it against the posts, bore pilot holes *(page 117)* and drive in at least two nails *(left)* or screws *(page 108)* at each end. Caulk joints *(page 106)* and reinstall any deck boards removed *(page 52)*.

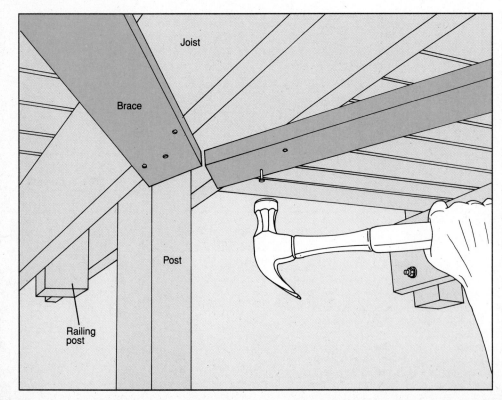

Installing post braces on joists or beams. To reinforce a post using horizontal braces, install a brace running from the joist or beam at the top of the weak post, to the joist or beam at the top of a post diagonally across from it. For added reinforcement, install a similar brace near an adjacent side of the post running to another post diagonally across from it. To remove a damaged brace, pull the nails *(page 107)*. If there is no room to work under the deck, remove deck boards to work from above *(page 51)* .

Purchase 1-by-6 or 2-by-6 boards for braces at a lumber yard. Position each brace against the joists or beams near the posts to mark it; have a helper support one end or temporarily nail it *(page 108)*. Saw each brace to length, angling the ends if required for fit *(page 112)*. Apply preservative or finish *(page 120)*.

To install a brace, position it on the joist or beam near each post, bore pilot holes *(page 117)* and drive in at least two nails *(left)* or screws *(page 108)* at each end. Caulk joints *(page 106)* and reinstall any deck boards removed *(page 52)*.

REPAIRING A POST

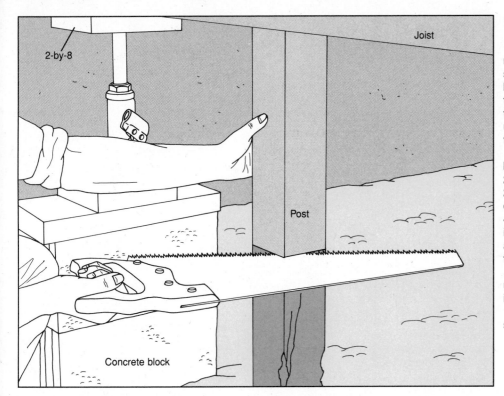

2-by-8

Joist

Post

Concrete block

1 **Supporting joists or a beam.** If a post set in a footing serves as a railing post and is damaged above the joist or beam, repair it as for a railing post *(page 55)*. If a post set in a footing is damaged below a joist or beam, support each joist or beam attached to the post using a jack *(page 124)* and replace the damaged section. If there is no room to work under the deck, remove deck boards to work from above *(page 51)*.

Set the jack on a level wood pad or concrete block, directly below the joist or beam and within 2 feet of the post. Temporarily nail *(page 108)* a 2-by-6 or 2-by-8 pad on the bottom of the joist or beam. Add to the reach of the jack with a 4-by-4, or by stacking concrete blocks under it, if necessary. Raise the jack until it fits snugly against the joist or beam, supporting it in position but not lifting it.

Mark the post just above the damaged section using a carpenter's square *(page 112)*, and saw it off with a handsaw *(left)* or a power saw *(page 112)*. To guide the saw, temporarily nail on a straight-edged wood block if necessary.

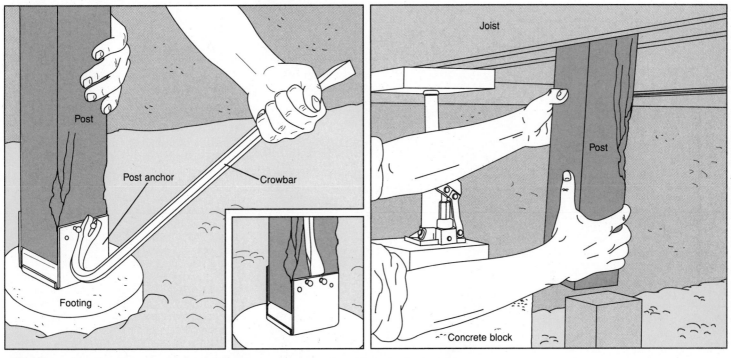

Post

Post anchor

Crowbar

Footing

Joist

Post

Concrete block

2 **Removing the damage.** To remove the damaged section of post from the footing, remove the hardware *(page 110)*. To loosen nails in a post anchor, pry out the plate *(inset)* using a crowbar. Pull the nails *(page 107)* with the crowbar *(above, left)* and lift the damaged section out of the post anchor. If the post is embedded in the concrete, saw it off *(page 69)* flush with the top of the footing and remove the damaged wood from the footing *(page 70)*.

To remove the damaged section of post from a joist or beam, remove the fasteners *(page 107)* or hardware; if the post extends beyond the joist or beam to form a railing post, remove the rail *(page 54)* and handrail *(page 53)*. Lower the damaged section from the joist *(above, right)* or beam; if it is stubborn, carefully knock it out from between double joists or from under a beam using a sledgehammer.

REPAIRING A POST (continued)

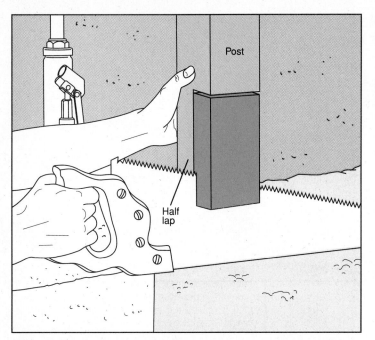

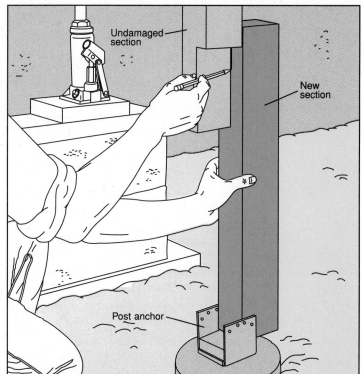

3 **Measuring and sawing for a splice.** At the end of the undamaged section, measure and mark one side of a half-lap joint 6 to 8 inches long: Using a tape measure and a carpenter's square *(page 112)*, mark the length of the half lap along the centers of two opposite sides, then join the ends across one adjacent side. Cut the half lap using a handsaw *(above)* or a power saw *(page 112)*; if required, temporarily nail on a straight-edged wood block as a saw guide.

4 **Marking a half-lap joint.** Purchase lumber for a new section of the same dimensions as the post at a lumber yard. To mark a half lap on the new section, position it against each side of the half lap on the undamaged section. If replacing a piece below the undamaged section, also position the new section against the post anchor *(above)*; if replacing a piece above the undamaged section, also position the bottom of the new section against the bottom of the half lap. Saw the half lap *(page 115)*. Apply preservative or finish *(page 120)*.

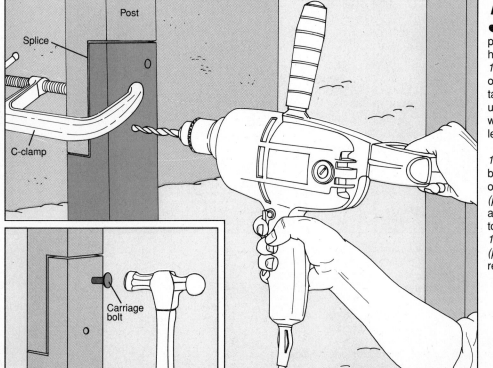

5 **Splicing the new section.** Position the new section; first repour the footing and install a post anchor *(page 70)* if the old post was embedded in concrete. Clamp the half-lap joint *(page 116)*. Bore two holes *(page 117)* through the splice about 2 inches apart, offsetting them *(left)*, and install bolts *(page 108)*; tap each bolt into the hole flush with the post using a ball-peen hammer *(inset)*. Attach washers and nuts, then saw off excess bolt length with a hacksaw *(page 112)*.

Install fasteners *(page 108)* or hardware *(page 110)* on the new section at the footing, joist or beam. If the new section extends beyond a joist or beam to form a railing post, saw it to length *(page 112)*, measuring the height of another post above the decking; apply preservative or finish to the end grain *(page 120)*. Caulk joints *(page 106)* and reinstall any rail *(page 54)* and handrail *(page 53)* removed. Reinstall any deck boards removed *(page 52)*.

REINFORCING OR REPAIRING A FOOTING

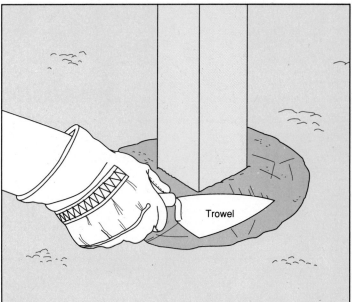

1 **Removing the damage.** To reinforce or repair a footing, break up the damaged area of concrete using a bull-point chisel and sledgehammer *(above)* or a demolition hammer *(page 122)*; wear work gloves and goggles. Clean off loose particles using a wire brush. If the footing is damaged below ground level, dig up the soil around the footing with a spade; working on each side of the post, dig to the depth required to break up and remove the damaged section.

2 **Repouring the footing.** Pour a concrete footing to a height at least 1 inch above the ground; to repair only the surface, use concrete patching compound *(page 122)*. If desired, install a cylindrical form *(page 122)*. Dampen undamaged concrete with water. Wearing work gloves, use a spade to mix and pour the concrete. Shape the top of the footing with a trowel, sloping it away from the post *(above)*. Allow the footing to set; for concrete, wait 48 hours. Caulk the post base after the footing has cured one week *(page 106)*.

REPAIRING A POST AND FOOTING

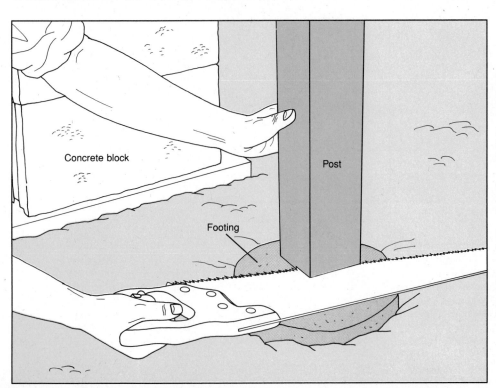

1 **Removing the post.** To repair a post and footing, support each joist or beam attached to the post using a jack *(page 124)*, then replace the damaged section of the post and footing. If there is no room to work under the deck, remove deck boards to work from above *(page 51)*.

Set the jack on a level wood pad or concrete block, directly below the joist or beam and within 2 feet of the post. Temporarily nail a 2-by-6 or 2-by-8 pad on the bottom of the joist or beam. If required, add to the reach of the jack with a 4-by-4 or by stacking concrete blocks under it. Raise the jack until it fits snugly against the joist or beam, supporting it in position but not lifting it.

Use a handsaw to cut off the post flush with the top of the footing *(left)*. To remove the post from a joist or beam, remove the fasteners *(page 107)* or hardware; if the post extends beyond a joist or beam to form a railing post, remove any rail *(page 54)* and handrail *(page 53)* attached to it. Apply preservative or finish to the end grain of the undamaged section *(page 120)*.

REPAIRING A POST AND FOOTING (continued)

2 **Removing the damaged wood.** To remove a damaged section of the post from the footing, bore a series of holes *(page 117)* 6 to 8 inches deep into it. Chisel out the wood using a wood chisel and ball-peen hammer *(above, left)* or mallet *(page 116)*. Repeat this procedure, removing as much of the wood as possible.

Wearing work gloves and goggles, use a bull-point chisel and sledgehammer to chip out a layer of concrete around the wood *(above, right)*. Continue chiseling the wood and chipping the concrete to the depth required to reposition the post or to splice on a new section of post *(page 68)* and install a post anchor.

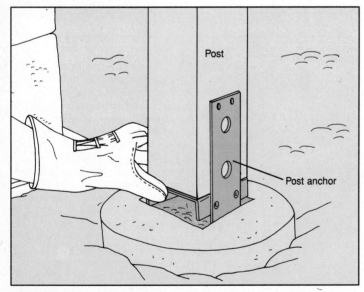

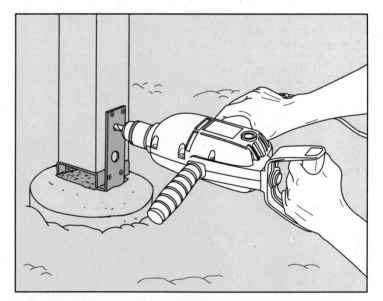

3 **Repouring the footing.** Purchase a post anchor at a building supply center, position it on the bottom of the post and temporarily nail it *(page 108)* in place. Dampen the undamaged concrete and repour the footing to a height at least 1 inch above the ground; use concrete or concrete patching compound *(page 122)*. Wearing work gloves, use a trowel to shape the top of the footing, sloping it away from the center. Position the post, sitting the post anchor in the footing *(above)*. With a helper supporting the post, bore pilot holes *(page 117)* and temporarily nail it to another section or to the joist or beam. Allow the footing to set; for concrete, wait 48 hours.

4 **Reinstalling the post.** To reinstall the post, splice on any new section *(page 68)* and install fasteners *(page 108)* or hardware *(page 110)* to it at the joist or beam. At the footing, install the post anchor *(page 110)*; if required, bore holes *(page 117)* for bolts *(above, right)*. If the new section extends beyond a joist or beam, saw it to length *(page 112)*, measuring the height of another post above the decking. Apply preservative or finish to the end grain *(page 120)*. Fill holes and caulk joints *(page 106)*. Reinstall any rail *(page 54)* and handrail removed *(page 53)*. Reinstall any deck boards removed *(page 52)*.

REPLACING A POST AND FOOTING

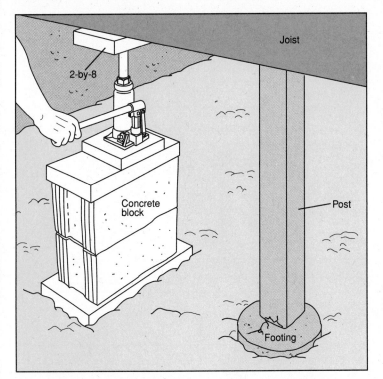

1 **Supporting joists or a beam.** To replace a post and footing, support each joist or beam at the post using a jack *(page 124)*; if required, remove deck boards to work from above *(page 51)*. Set the jack on a level wood pad or concrete block, directly below the joist or beam and within 2 feet of the post. Temporarily nail *(page 108)* a 2-by-6 or 2-by-8 pad on the bottom of the joist or beam. If required, add to the reach of the jack with a 4-by-4, or by stacking concrete blocks under it. Raise the jack until it fits snugly under the joist or beam, supporting it in position but not lifting it *(above)*.

2 **Digging around the footing.** To disconnect the post from a joist or beam, remove the fasteners *(page 107)* or hardware *(page 110)*. If the post extends beyond a joist or beam to form a railing post, remove any rail *(page 54)* and handrail *(page 53)*. If the post is installed on the footing with a post anchor, remove the fasteners from it; if only the post is damaged, purchase wood for a replacement post at a lumber yard, position it in the anchor and install it *(page 70)*. Dig up the soil around a damaged footing using a spade *(above)*. Dig to the depth required to remove the post and footing or to break up the damaged concrete *(page 122)*; if replacing only the footing, prepare the posthole *(step 4)*.

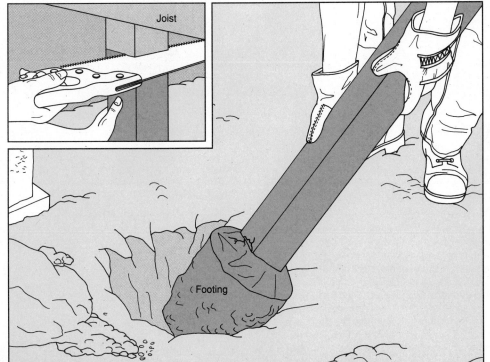

3 **Removing the post and footing.** Loosen the footing by rocking the post back and forth, working on each side of it; if required, first saw off the post *(page 112)* near the joist or beam *(inset)*. Dig deeper and rock the post until it can be pulled out of the ground *(left)*. If required, lift out the post with two helpers using 2-by-4s as levers under the footing.

It may be easier to lift out the post using a car jack *(page 122)*. Position the car jack on one side of the post and two concrete blocks, stacked, on the opposite side, 2 to 3 feet away from the post. Nail a 2-by-4 at least 12 inches long on the post about 18 inches above the ground *(page 108)*. Position the edge of a 2-by-6 or stronger board under it, resting one end on the car jack and the other end on the concrete blocks. Support the car jack firmly, have a helper support the post and raise the car jack to lift out the post.

REPLACING A POST AND FOOTING (continued)

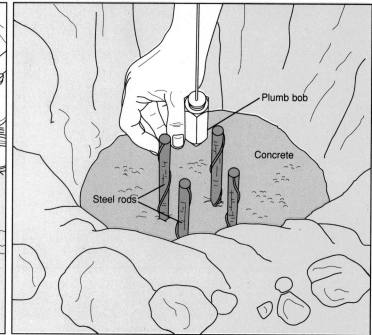

4 **Preparing the posthole.** To locate a posthole, drop a plumb bob *(page 118)* from the post's position on the joist or beam. Using a posthole digger or clamshell digger, dig a posthole at least three times the width of the post and 6 inches deeper than the frostline or than half the height of the tallest post next to the hole—the minimum depth required is usually 24 to 30 inches. Tamp the bottom of the posthole using the end of a 2-by-4.

Use a spade to fill the posthole with 6 inches of gravel *(above, left)* and tamp again. To install a post with a post anchor, pour a concrete footing 6 to 8 inches high at the bottom of the posthole. Wearing work gloves, use a spade to mix concrete in a wheelbarrow or trough and pour it into the posthole. To secure the footing to a pier, set four 1/2 inch steel rods half way into the concrete at the center of the footing *(above, right)*. Allow the concrete to set 48 hours.

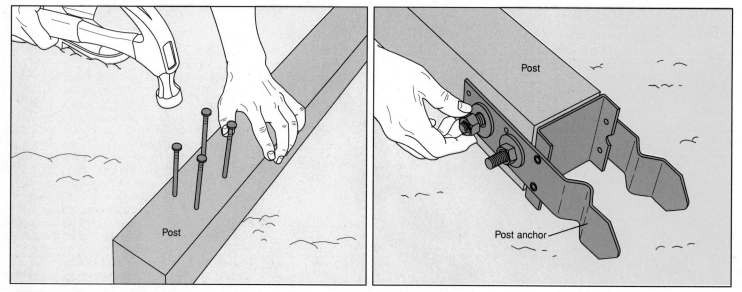

5 **Preparing the post.** If you are not installing a post anchor, install the post on the bottom of the posthole; if installing a post anchor, install the post 2 to 4 inches above the ground. To determine the length of the post, use a plumb bob *(page 118)* and tape measure to measure down from the post's position at the joist or beam; if the post does not end at the joist or beam, add on at least the height of the post's extension above the decking.

Purchase lumber of the same dimensions as the old post at a lumber yard. Saw the new post to length *(page 112)* and apply preservative or finish *(page 120)*. If you are not installing a post anchor, drive long nails *(page 108)* partway into the post 6 to 8 inches from the bottom to reinforce it in the footing *(above, left)*. If installing a post anchor, position it on the bottom of the post, bore pilot holes and install fasteners *(page 108)*; twist a nut onto a bolt by hand *(above, right)* and tighten it using a wrench.

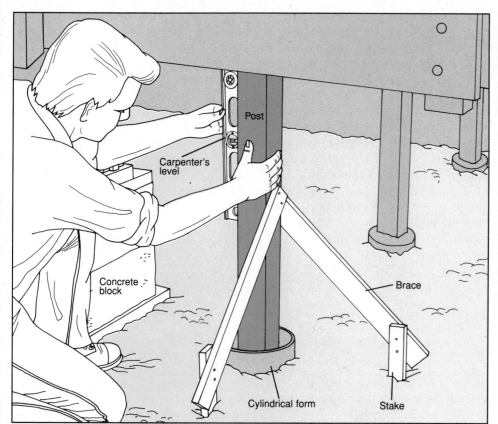

6 **Bracing the post in position.** If desired, install a cylindrical form *(page 122)*. Before backfilling around it, position the post at the joist or beam and temporarily install 2-by-4 braces with stakes on adjacent sides of the post, at a 90-degree angle to each other. Saw the braces to a length about equal to the height of the post from the joist or beam to the ground *(page 112)*. Cut the stakes 12 to 18 inches long, angling the sides to a point at the bottom.

Have a helper support the post in position at the joist or beam, or temporarily nail it in place with only one nail *(page 108)*. Nail a brace about halfway up the post, at a 45-degree angle to the ground, using only one nail. With a sledgehammer, drive a stake into the ground at the other end of the brace, and nail the brace to the stake. Repeat this procedure to install the other brace. Hold a carpenter's level *(page 118)* against two adjacent sides of the post to check whether it is vertical *(left)*. To reposition the post, drive the stakes farther into the ground.

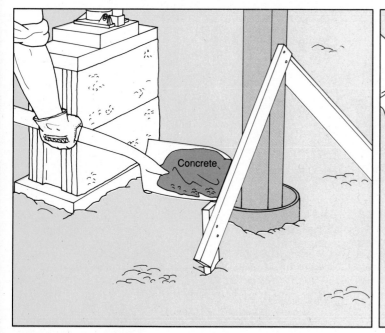

7 **Pouring a footing or pier.** Wearing work gloves, pour a concrete footing or pier to a height at least 1 inch above the ground. Use a spade to mix the concrete in a wheelbarrow or trough and fill the cylindrical form *(above, left)* or the posthole. To settle the concrete, work a 2-by-4 up and down in it, or tap the sides of the form. Check the position of the post using a carpenter's level *(page 118)*; if required, reposition the post with additional braces *(step 6)*. Use a trowel to add concrete around the post base, sloping the top away from the post *(above, right)*. Allow the concrete to set 48 hours.

Install fasteners *(page 108)* or hardware *(page 110)* to connect the post to the joist or beam. If the post does not end at the joist or beam, saw it to length *(page 112)*, measuring the height of another post above the decking. Apply preservative or finish to the end grain *(page 120)*. Caulk joints *(page 106)*; if the post is installed without a post anchor, caulk the base of it after the footing has cured for one week. Reinstall any rail *(page 54)* and handrail *(page 53)* removed. Reinstall any deck boards removed *(page 52)*. To keep the concrete from drying out, dampen it with water until it has cured for one week.

FENCES

Whether it keeps in the children or keeps out the prying eyes of neighbors, your fence provides the backdrop for your family's outdoor activities. A typical wood picket fence is illustrated below; imaginative variations on the classic wood fence are pictured on page 75. A standard chain link fence is shown on page 76. The modular fence on page 76 is prefabricated from metal sections. It may be aluminum, steel or alloy, and is enameled or anodized. Easily assembled with self-tapping screws, it resembles the traditional wrought-iron fence, which can only be repaired using expert welding and metalwork techniques not covered here.

All fences are similar in construction and basic components. Posts set in the ground are supported by footings of soil or concrete. Rails mounted horizontally help keep the posts in position as well as carry the fencing. A gate opens on hinges and shuts with a latch assembly.

Although built for the rigors of the outdoors, a fence cannot withstand such punishment without regular maintenance. Fortunately, fence problems are seldom difficult to spot and remedy, but their causes can easily be overlooked — resulting in repeated or worsening problems. To help in your diagnosis, consult the Troubleshooting Guide appropriate for your type of fence on page 77 or page 78.

For a specific fence problem, there can be several solutions. The best one usually depends on a range of factors that call for individual judgments — the type of fence and its purpose, the nature and severity of the problem, the final appearance desired, your available time, the current weather. For example, you may opt to reinforce a post this year and postpone replacing it until next year; or you may find replacing a rail more eye-pleasing than reinforcing it. Choose the procedure most suited to your present circumstances.

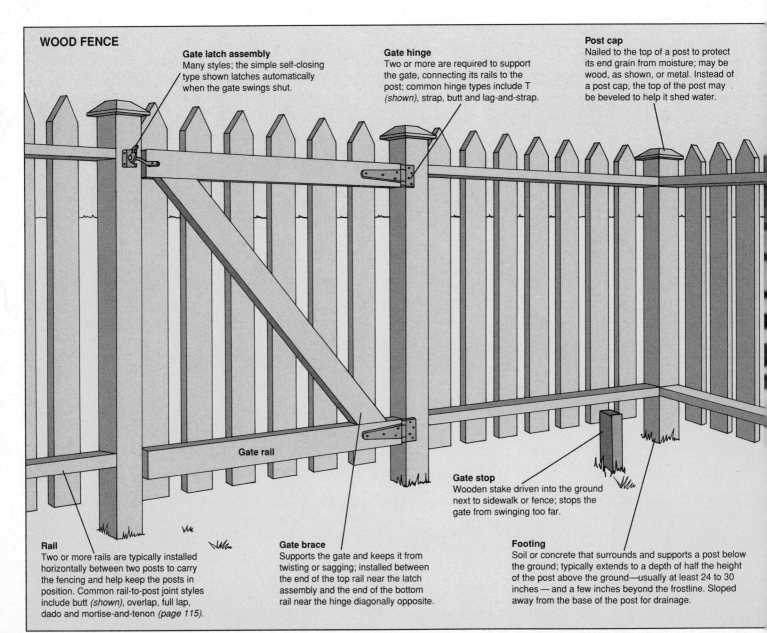

WOOD FENCE

Gate latch assembly
Many styles; the simple self-closing type shown latches automatically when the gate swings shut.

Gate hinge
Two or more are required to support the gate, connecting its rails to the post; common hinge types include T *(shown)*, strap, butt and lag-and-strap.

Post cap
Nailed to the top of a post to protect its end grain from moisture; may be wood, as shown, or metal. Instead of a post cap, the top of the post may be beveled to help it shed water.

Gate rail

Gate stop
Wooden stake driven into the ground next to sidewalk or fence; stops the gate from swinging too far.

Rail
Two or more rails are typically installed horizontally between two posts to carry the fencing and help keep the posts in position. Common rail-to-post joint styles include butt *(shown)*, overlap, full lap, dado and mortise-and-tenon *(page 115)*.

Gate brace
Supports the gate and keeps it from twisting or sagging; installed between the end of the top rail near the latch assembly and the end of the bottom rail near the hinge diagonally opposite.

Footing
Soil or concrete that surrounds and supports a post below the ground; typically extends to a depth of half the height of the post above the ground—usually at least 24 to 30 inches — and a few inches beyond the frostline. Sloped away from the base of the post for drainage.

The only skills called for in tackling fence problems are basic carpentry techniques, including leveling, nailing, drilling and sawing. Most of the tools, materials and supplies required for fence repairs are readily available at a lumber yard or a hardware store; replacement parts for a chain link or modular fence may have to be obtained from the fence supplier. Refer to Tools & Techniques *(page 102)* for guidance before starting work on your fence.

Routinely inspect your fence each spring and fall; the joints and the post bases, in particular, are vulnerable to rot, insect damage or rust. Stop problems from developing further by undertaking repairs as soon as symptoms are detected. Prevent accidents while working on your fence by following the safety advice in Emergencies *(page 8)*; wear the proper clothing and protective equipment for the job. Use caution when working with cleaning and finishing products or preserved lumber.

Post
At least two are required to support each 8-foot length of fencing; usually 4-by-4s or 6-by-6s, with at least one-third their height set into the ground in a footing of soil or concrete. The post at an end or corner of the fence, or supporting the gate, is typically set in a footing of concrete.

Fencing
Most variable fence feature; may be nailed on, board by board, or installed in panels; placed vertically, horizontally or at an angle on the rails or the posts; on one side or both sides of the fence. Pickets, shown here, are usually spaced evenly with their points at a uniform height above the ground.

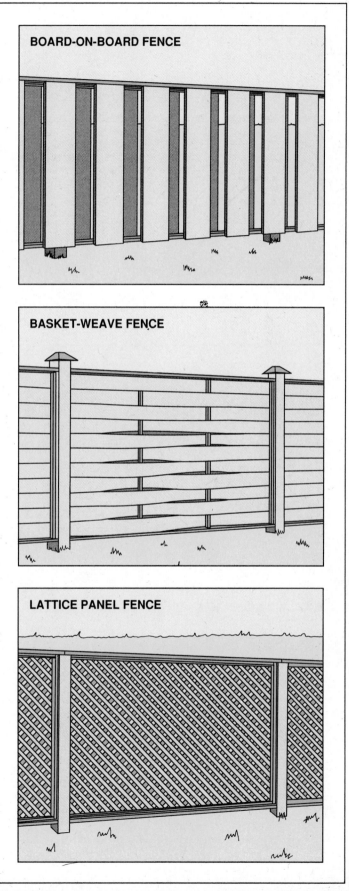

BOARD-ON-BOARD FENCE

BASKET-WEAVE FENCE

LATTICE PANEL FENCE

CHAIN LINK FENCE

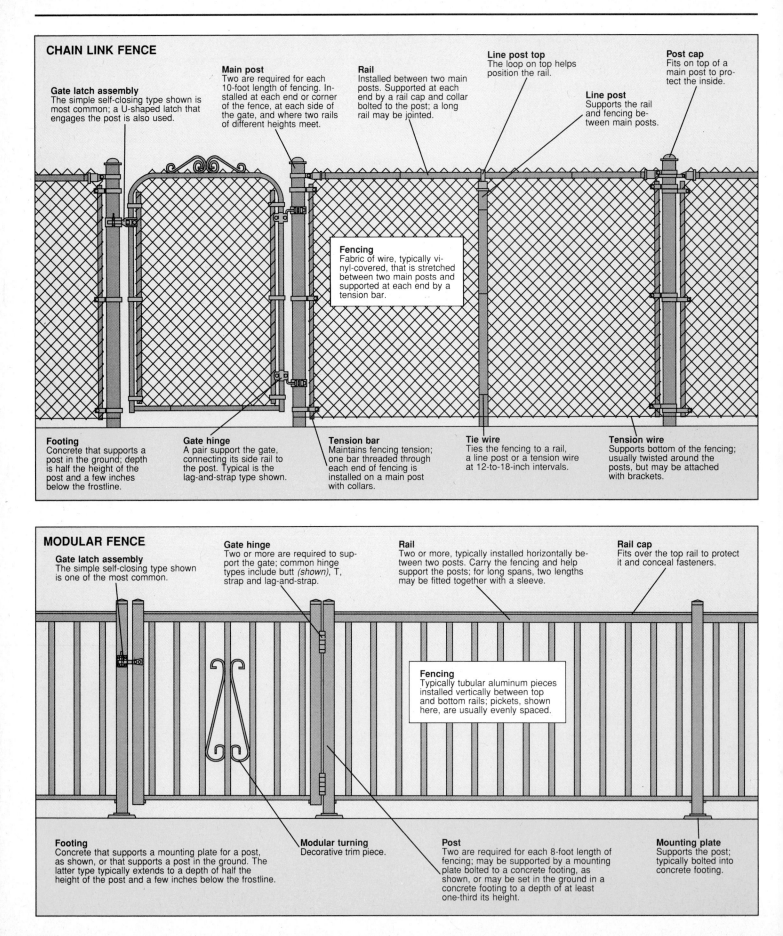

Gate latch assembly
The simple self-closing type shown is most common; a U-shaped latch that engages the post is also used.

Main post
Two are required for each 10-foot length of fencing. Installed at each end or corner of the fence, at each side of the gate, and where two rails of different heights meet.

Rail
Installed between two main posts. Supported at each end by a rail cap and collar bolted to the post; a long rail may be jointed.

Line post top
The loop on top helps position the rail.

Line post
Supports the rail and fencing between main posts.

Post cap
Fits on top of a main post to protect the inside.

Fencing
Fabric of wire, typically vinyl-covered, that is stretched between two main posts and supported at each end by a tension bar.

Footing
Concrete that supports a post in the ground; depth is half the height of the post and a few inches below the frostline.

Gate hinge
A pair support the gate, connecting its side rail to the post. Typical is the lag-and-strap type shown.

Tension bar
Maintains fencing tension; one bar threaded through each end of fencing is installed on a main post with collars.

Tie wire
Ties the fencing to a rail, a line post or a tension wire at 12-to-18-inch intervals.

Tension wire
Supports bottom of the fencing; usually twisted around the posts, but may be attached with brackets.

MODULAR FENCE

Gate latch assembly
The simple self-closing type shown is one of the most common.

Gate hinge
Two or more are required to support the gate; common hinge types include butt *(shown)*, T, strap and lag-and-strap.

Rail
Two or more, typically installed horizontally between two posts. Carry the fencing and help support the posts; for long spans, two lengths may be fitted together with a sleeve.

Rail cap
Fits over the top rail to protect it and conceal fasteners.

Fencing
Typically tubular aluminum pieces installed vertically between top and bottom rails; pickets, shown here, are usually evenly spaced.

Footing
Concrete that supports a mounting plate for a post, as shown, or that supports a post in the ground. The latter type typically extends to a depth of half the height of the post and a few inches below the frostline.

Modular turning
Decorative trim piece.

Post
Two are required for each 8-foot length of fencing; may be supported by a mounting plate bolted to a concrete footing, as shown, or may be set in the ground in a concrete footing to a depth of at least one-third its height.

Mounting plate
Supports the post; typically bolted into concrete footing.

TROUBLESHOOTING GUIDE

continued ►

SYMPTOM	POSSIBLE CAUSE	PROCEDURE
WOOD FENCES		
Surface dirty	Weather, wear, pollution	Clean surfaces (p. 79) □◕
Surface stained or discolored	Fasteners or hardware rusted	Replace fasteners (p. 108) □○ and hardware (p. 110) □◕
	Foliage and resins from trees or plants; black, gray or colored mildew caused by humidity or poor circulation; chalking paint	Clean and refinish surfaces (p. 79) □●
Finish faded, patchy, chipped or lifting	Weather, sun, wear	Clean and refinish surfaces (p. 79) □●
Gate does not stay closed	Latch assembly loose, positioned incorrectly or damaged	Reposition or replace latch assembly (p. 80) □○
Gate squeaks	Hinge lacks lubricant	Lubricate hinges with light machine oil or silicone spray; swing gate back and forth to work in lubricant
Gate sticks	Swelling of wood caused by high humidity	Plane sticking surfaces (p. 117) □○
	Hinge loose, positioned incorrectly or damaged	Reposition or replace hinges (p. 80) □○
Gate crooked, twisted or sagging	Hinge loose, positioned incorrectly or damaged	Reposition or replace hinges (p. 80) □○
	Post or footing damaged	Reinforce (p. 85) □○ or repair (p. 86) ◕◕ post; reinforce or repair footing (p. 87) ◕◕; replace post and footing (p. 88) ■●
	Rail damaged	Replace rail (p. 84) ◕●
	Brace loose, damaged or missing	Reinforce gate (p. 81) □○
Fencing split or cracked; wood spongy	Rot or insect damage	Repair minor rot and insect damage (p. 106) □○
	Wood shrinkage; shifting of wood joints caused by fence settlement	Replace fencing (p. 82) □○
Fencing crooked, twisted or sagging	Fencing fasteners loose	Replace fasteners (p. 108) □○
	Post or footing damaged	Reinforce (p. 85) □○ or repair (p. 86) ◕◕ post; reinforce or repair footing (p. 87) ◕◕; replace post and footing (p. 88) ■●
	Rail damaged	Reinforce (p. 83) □○, repair (p. 83) ◕◕ or replace (p. 84) ◕● rail
	Fencing damaged	Replace fencing (p. 82) □○
Rail split or cracked; wood spongy	Rot or insect damage	Repair minor rot and insect damage (p. 106) □○
	Wood shrinkage; shifting of wood joints caused by fence settlement	Reinforce (p. 83) □○, repair (p. 83) ◕◕ or replace (p. 84) ◕● rail
Rail crooked, twisted or sagging	Rail fasteners or hardware loose	Replace fasteners (p. 108) □○ and hardware (p. 110) □◕
	Post or footing damaged	Reinforce (p. 85) □○ or repair (p. 86) ◕◕ post; reinforce or repair footing (p. 87) ◕◕; replace post and footing (p. 88) ■●
	Rail damaged	Reinforce (p. 83) □○, repair (p. 83) ◕◕ or replace (p. 84) ◕● rail
Post cap split or cracked; wood spongy	Rot or insect damage	Repair minor rot and insect damage (p. 106) □○
	Wood shrinkage; weather	Replace post cap (p. 85) □○
Post split or cracked; wood spongy	Rot or insect damage	Repair minor rot and insect damage (p. 106) □○
	Wood shrinkage; shifting of wood joints caused by fence settlement	Reinforce (p. 85) □○ or repair (p. 86) ◕◕ post; replace post and footing (p. 88) ■●
Post wobbly, twisted or leaning	Post or footing damaged	Reinforce (p. 85) □○ or repair (p. 86) ◕◕ post; reinforce or repair footing (p. 87) ◕◕; replace post and footing (p. 88) ■●
Footing loose, cracked or raised	Moisture; frost heaves; shifting of soil or concrete caused by fence settlement	Reinforce or repair footing (p. 87) ◕◕; replace post and footing (p. 88) ■●
CHAIN LINK FENCES		
Surface dirty	Weather, wear, pollution	Clean surfaces (p. 91) □◕
Surface stained or discolored	Foliage and resins from trees or plants; rust; chalking paint	Clean and repaint surfaces (p. 91) □●
Paint faded, chipped or lifting	Weather, sun, wear	Clean and repaint surfaces (p. 91) □●

DEGREE OF DIFFICULTY: □ Easy ◕ Moderate ■ Complex
ESTIMATED TIME: ○ Less than 1 hour ◕ 1 to 3 hours ● Over 3 hours   ▲ Special tool required

TROUBLESHOOTING GUIDE (continued)

SYMPTOM	POSSIBLE CAUSE	PROCEDURE
CHAIN LINK FENCES (continued)		
Gate does not stay closed	Latch assembly loose, positioned incorrectly or damaged	Reposition or replace latch assembly *(p. 92)* □○
Gate squeaks	Hinge lacks lubricant	Lubricate hinges with light machine oil or silicone spray; swing gate back and forth to work in lubricant
Gate crooked or sagging	Hinge loose, positioned incorrectly or damaged	Reposition or replace hinges *(p. 92)* □○
	Post or footing damaged	Reinforce post *(p. 95)* □○; reinforce or repair footing *(p. 96)* ◨◔; replace post and footing *(p. 96)* ■●▲
Fencing crooked or sagging	Tie wire or tension wire loose or damaged	Reinforce fencing *(p. 93)* □○
	Post or footing damaged	Reinforce post *(p. 95)* □○; reinforce or repair footing *(p. 96)* ◨◔; replace post and footing *(p. 96)* ■●▲
	Rail damaged	Replace rail *(p. 95)* □○
	Tension bar loose; fencing damaged	Repair or replace fencing *(p. 93)* □○▲
Fencing broken	Corrosion; blow by a heavy object	Repair or replace fencing *(p. 93)* □○▲
Rail bent, sagging or broken	Post or footing damaged	Reinforce post *(p. 95)* □○; reinforce or repair footing *(p. 96)* ◨◔; replace post and footing *(p. 96)* ■●▲
	Rail damaged; corrosion	Replace rail *(p. 95)* □○
Post wobbly or leaning	Post or footing damaged	Reinforce post *(p. 95)* □○; reinforce or repair footing *(p. 96)* ◨◔; replace post and footing *(p. 96)* ■●▲
Post bent or broken	Corrosion; blow by a heavy object	Replace post and footing *(p. 96)* ■●▲
Footing loose, cracked or raised	Moisture; frost heaves; shifting of soil or concrete caused by fence settlement	Reinforce or repair footing *(p. 96)* ◨◔; replace post and footing *(p. 96)* ■●▲
MODULAR FENCES		
Surface dirty	Weather, wear, pollution	Clean surfaces *(p. 97)* □◔
Surface stained or discolored	Foliage and resins from trees or plants; rust; chalking paint	Clean and repaint surfaces *(p. 97)* □●
Paint faded, patchy, chipped or lifting	Weather, sun, wear	Clean and repaint surfaces *(p. 97)* □●
Gate does not stay closed	Latch assembly loose, positioned incorrectly or damaged	Reposition or replace latch assembly *(p. 98)* □○
Gate squeaks	Hinge lacks lubricant	Lubricate hinges with light machine oil or silicone spray; swing gate back and forth to work in lubricant
Gate crooked or sagging	Hinge loose, positioned incorrectly or damaged	Reposition or replace hinges *(p. 98)* □○
	Post or footing damaged	Reinforce post and repair footing *(p. 100)* ◨◔; replace post and footing *(p. 101)* ■●
Fencing crooked or sagging	Post or footing damaged	Reinforce post and repair footing *(p. 100)* ◨◔; replace post and footing *(p. 101)* ■●
	Rail damaged	Replace rail *(p. 99)* □◔
	Fencing damaged	Replace fencing *(p. 99)* □○
Fencing bent or broken	Corrosion; blow by a heavy object	Replace fencing *(p. 99)* □○
Rail crooked, sagging, bent or broken	Post or footing damaged	Reinforce post and repair footing *(p. 100)* ◨◔; replace post and footing *(p. 101)* ■●
	Rail damaged; corrosion	Replace rail *(p. 99)* □◔
Post wobbly or leaning	Post or footing damaged	Reinforce post and repair footing *(p. 100)* ◨◔; replace post and footing *(p. 101)* ■●
Post bent or broken	Corrosion; blow by a heavy object	Replace post and footing *(p. 101)* ■●
Footing loose, cracked or raised	Moisture; frost heaves; shifting of soil or concrete caused by fence settlement	Repair footing *(p. 100)* ◨◔; replace post and footing *(p. 101)* ■●

DEGREE OF DIFFICULTY: □ Easy ◨ Moderate ■ Complex
ESTIMATED TIME: ○ Less than 1 hour ◔ 1 to 3 hours ● Over 3 hours   ▲ Special tool required

CLEANING AND REFINISHING SURFACES (Wood)

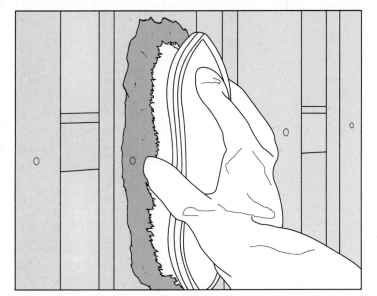

1 **Scrubbing off dirt and stains.** Replace rusted fasteners *(page 108)* and hardware *(page 110)*. Remove peeling, flaking or blistering finish *(step 2)*. To clean off dirt and most stains, use a solution of mild detergent and warm water; wear rubber gloves and scrub with a stiff fiber brush *(above)*. Rinse using fresh water. For tough stains, including mildew or rust, mix 2 to 3 tablespoons of trisodium phosphate or 1 to 2 cups of bleach per gallon of warm water in a plastic bucket and repeat the procedure wearing goggles. A stronger solution may be required but is more likely to harm the finish. Before applying a new finish, let the surface dry, then sand it *(step 3)*.

Paint scraper

2 **Removing the finish.** Repair minor rot and insect damage *(page 106)*. If the finish is well adhered, sand the surface *(step 3)*. To scrape off lifting finish or hardened wood resin, use a paint scraper *(above)*, applying even, moderate pressure along the grain. To loosen thick layers of paint or to reach corners, rub gently with a wire brush. To strip off paint from an entire fence, use a heat gun or a propane torch *(page 120)*. Cut away loose caulk at joints with a utility knife. Brush off debris using a whisk; clean out cracks with a putty knife. Scrub off stains, such as mildew or rust, that penetrated the finish *(step 1)*.

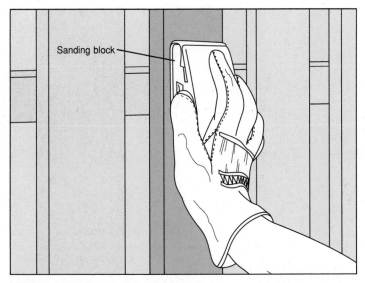

Sanding block

3 **Sanding the surface.** Fill any holes and caulk the joints *(page 106)*. Wearing a dust mask and work gloves, sand along the grain to smooth the surface. On a flat surface, use a sanding block *(above)*, or use a power sander *(page 119)* — especially if smoothing an entire fence. Work by hand to reach corners *(page 119)*. Start with coarse sandpaper if the surface is rough or heavily coated; start with medium sandpaper if the surface is scratched or moderately coated. Use fine sandpaper for final smoothing or if the surface is unfinished. Evenly apply only light or moderate pressure. Brush off sanding dust with a whisk. Wipe with a tack cloth *(page 102)* after sanding.

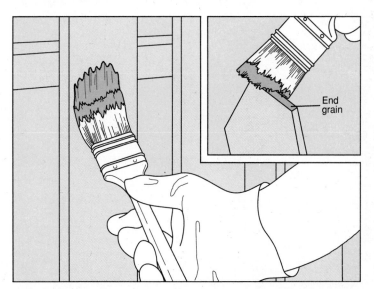

End grain

4 **Applying finish.** Choose a finish *(page 120)* and follow the manufacturer's directions for applying it; a prior coat of preservative or sealer may be required. Protect surfaces not being finished with masking tape or a tarp. In most instances, a finish is best applied using a paintbrush; a synthetic, flagged-bristle type is recommended. For efficiency, use a paintbrush slightly narrower than the surface being coated. Working top to bottom, apply finish evenly along the grain *(above)*. First coat the surfaces hardest to reach; ensure that end grain is adequately coated *(inset)*. Between applications, sand lightly using fine sandpaper *(step 3)*. Finish may also be applied with a roller or sprayer *(page 120)*.

REPOSITIONING OR REPLACING THE GATE LATCH ASSEMBLY (Wood)

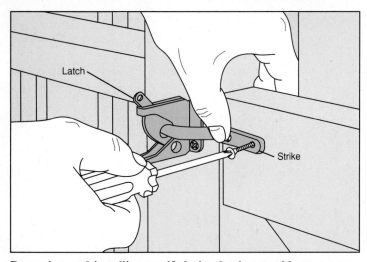

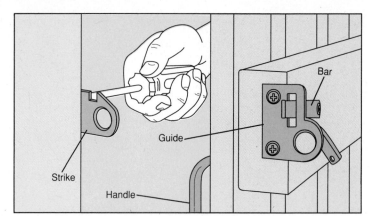

Removing and installing a self-closing latch assembly. To reposition the latch assembly, remove and reinstall the strike; if required, also remove and reinstall the latch. To remove the strike or the latch, unscrew it *(page 107)*. If the latch assembly is damaged, purchase a replacement at a hardware store. Fill the old screw holes *(page 106)*. To install the strike, position it in the latch, mark the screw openings and remove it. Bore pilot holes *(page 117)* and screw *(page 108)* the strike onto the rail *(above)*. To install the latch assembly, use the same procedure, first installing the latch on the post, then the strike. Refinish damaged surfaces *(page 79)*.

Removing and installing a thumb latch assembly. To reposition the latch assembly, unscrew *(page 107)* and reinstall the strike; if required, unscrew and reinstall the entire latch assembly. If the latch assembly is damaged, purchase a replacement at a hardware store. Fill the old screw holes *(page 106)*. Enlarge the thumbpiece's hole in the gate if necessary to reposition it, using a chisel *(page 116)*. To install the strike, position it with the bar in its notch and resting on the bottom of the guide slot. Open the gate to mark the screw openings. Remove the strike, bore pilot holes *(page 117)* and screw the strike *(page 108)* onto the post *(above)*. To install the entire latch assembly, insert the thumbpiece in its hole and use the same procedure, first installing the handle, bar and guide on the rail. Refinish damaged surfaces *(page 79)*.

REPOSITIONING OR REPLACING THE GATE HINGES (Wood)

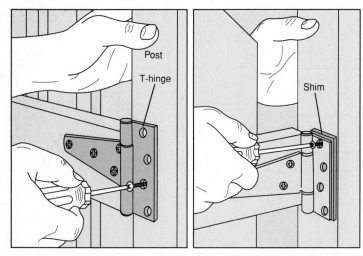

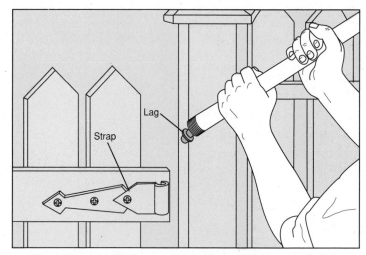

Taking off and rehanging a gate with T, strap or butt hinges. Unscrew the bottom hinge from the post first and the top hinge from the post last *(page 107)*. If a hinge is damaged, remove it from the gate and purchase a replacement at a hardware store. Fill the old screw holes *(page 106)*. To rehang the gate, have a helper support it or prop it on blocks at the correct closed position. Check whether each hinge leaf contacts the post properly; if not, cut a shim from a piece of scrap wood to fit between the hinge leaf and post *(above, right)*. Saw *(page 112)* and chisel *(page 116)* or plane *(page 117)* the shim; apply preservative or finish *(page 120)*. Position the hinge leaves and shims, mark the screw openings and move the leaves. Bore pilot holes *(page 117)* and screw on *(page 108)* the top hinge first and the bottom hinge last *(above, left)*. Refinish damaged surfaces *(page 79)*.

Taking off and rehanging a gate with lag hinges. To reposition or replace a hinge, take off and rehang the gate. To take off the gate, lift the hinge straps off the lags. To reposition a lag, turn it with a length of pipe *(above)* or a pipe wrench; first loosen any nut using a wrench. If a strap or a lag is damaged, remove it and purchase a replacement at a hardware store. Fill the old screw holes *(page 106)*. To replace the strap or the lag, have a helper support the gate or prop it on blocks at the correct closed position. Position the strap or the lag, mark the screw openings or the lag location and remove the strap or lag. Bore pilot holes *(page 117)* and screw on the strap *(page 108)* or install the lag. To rehang the gate, lift the straps onto the lags. If the hinges still need adjustment, take off the gate again and reposition the lags as shown. Refinish damaged surfaces *(page 79)*.

REINFORCING THE GATE (Wood)

Bracing with a turnbuckle. To reinforce the gate, install a turnbuckle assembly, extending from the end of the top rail near the hinge to the end of the bottom rail diagonally opposite. To reinforce the post, install a turnbuckle assembly from the top of it to the bottom of the next post. Purchase a turnbuckle assembly at a hardware store: 1/8-inch woven cable, with a turnbuckle, two U-bolt clips and two eye screws.

Bore pilot holes *(page 117)* and install the eye screws on the rails or the posts; first remove any fencing if required to gain access *(page 82)*. Loosen the turnbuckle and the U-bolt clips. Using diagonal-cutting pliers, cut two lengths of cable, each 5 to 6 inches longer than the distance between the eye screws on the rails or posts. Loop a cable through an eye screw on the rail or post and pull the two ends 5 to 6 inches through a U-bolt clip. Loop the ends through one end of the turnbuckle and double them back through the clip. Tighten the clip using a wrench *(inset)*. Repeat this procedure to install the other length of cable. To tighten the cable, adjust the turnbuckle by turning it; use a screwdriver for leverage *(left)*. Reinstall any fencing removed *(page 82)*. If required, reposition the latch assembly *(page 80)*.

Bracing with wood. To reinforce the gate, install a brace between the end of the top rail near the latch assembly and the end of the bottom rail diagonally opposite; if replacing an old brace, remove its fasteners *(page 107)*. Prop the gate on blocks at the correct closed position. Remove any fencing if required for access *(page 82)* and remove any intermediate rail *(page 84)*. Purchase wood for a brace of the same dimensions as the rails at a lumber yard. Saw the brace to length *(page 112)*, first positioning it against the rails to mark it *(left)*; temporarily nail it *(page 108)*. Apply preservative or finish *(page 120)*.

Position the brace between the rails, bore a pair of pilot holes *(page 117)* an inch from each end and drive screws *(page 108)* into each rail *(inset)*, or install fastening hardware *(page 110)*. For best results, also screw through the rails into the brace if possible; take off and rehang the gate *(page 80)* to make the job easier. Reinstall any intermediate rail *(page 84)* in sections on each side of the brace; saw it into the lengths required, positioning it against the brace to mark it, and apply preservative or finish. Fill any holes and caulk the joints *(page 106)*. Reinstall any fencing removed *(page 82)*. If required, reposition the latch assembly *(page 80)*. Refinish damaged surfaces *(page 79)*.

REPLACING THE FENCING (Wood)

1 **Removing the fencing.** Before removing fencing from a gate, support the gate by nailing lengths of wood between the rails and the posts *(page 108)*, or take off the gate *(page 80)*. To take off an entire fencing panel, remove the rails *(page 84)* from the posts. To remove individual fencing boards, pull the nails *(page 107)*. To loosen the nails, hammer on the back of the fencing near the rail *(above)* or post; cushion the blows with a wood block if you plan to reinstall the fencing. Stopped, channeled or louver fencing may require special procedures *(right)*.

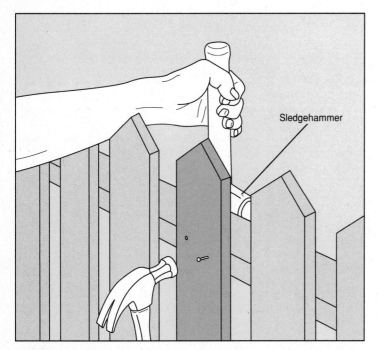

2 **Installing the fencing.** Purchase wood for replacement fencing at a lumber yard and saw it to length *(page 112)*, measuring or tracing the original fencing to mark it. Apply preservative or finish *(page 120)*. Position the fencing and drive in at least two nails at each rail or post, offsetting them *(page 108)*. To steady a rail while hammering, hold a sledgehammer behind it *(above)*. To maintain an even fencing height, run a cord tautly between the posts; to space the fencing evenly, use a piece of wood as a guide. Reinstall the rails *(page 84)* and rehang the gate *(page 80)* if you removed them. Fill holes and caulk joints *(page 106)*. Refinish damaged surfaces *(page 79)*.

REMOVING SPECIAL FENCING

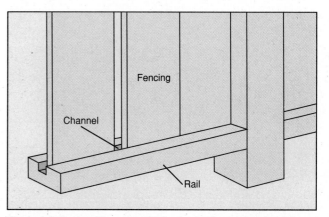

Stopped fencing. To remove the fencing, pull the nails *(page 107)* out of the stop at each end on one side. To loosen the nails, use a pry bar to lift the stop. Note that the fencing may be nailed to the stops. To install the fencing, first position the fencing, nail the stop along one end, then nail the stop along the other end; for best results, drive in nails every 4 to 6 inches *(page 108)*.

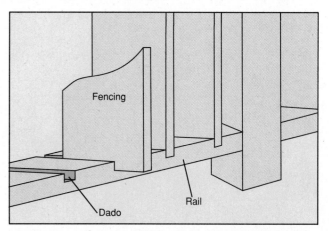

Channeled fencing. To remove the fencing, try bowing it to free it from the channels; if required, saw *(page 112)* and chisel *(page 116)* an opening on one side large enough to pull it out, or remove the top rail *(page 84)*. To install the fencing, bow it to fit it into the channels in the rails or posts, or position it and nail on the block chiseled out *(page 108)*, or install the top rail *(page 84)*.

Louver fencing. To remove the fencing, slide it out of the dadoes on the rails or posts. To loosen it, hammer it on one side, cushioning the blows with a wood block if the fencing will be reinstalled. To install the fencing, slip it into the dadoes and hammer it into position, protecting it with a wood block.

REINFORCING A RAIL (Wood)

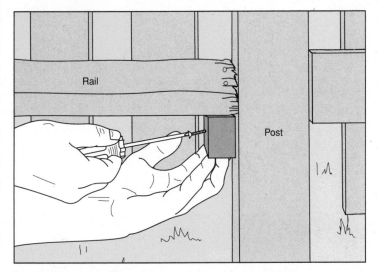

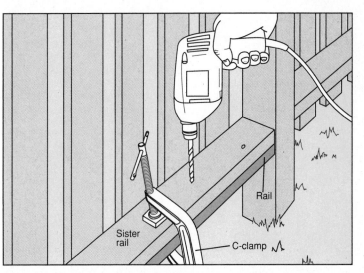

Bracing the end of a rail. To reinforce the end of a rail, install hardware *(page 110)* or a wooden brace. Remove any fencing that is in the way *(page 82)*. To make a brace, use lumber of the same dimensions as the rail and saw it to a length equal to the width of the post *(page 112)*. Apply preservative or finish *(page 120)*. Position the brace under the rail, bore pilot holes *(page 117)* and screw it *(page 108)* onto the post *(above)*, and onto the rail if possible. Fill holes and caulk joints *(page 106)*. Reinstall any fencing removed *(page 82)* and refinish damaged surfaces *(page 79)*.

Bracing the length of a rail with a sister rail. Remove any fencing that is in the way *(page 82)*. Purchase lumber of the same dimensions as the rail at a lumber yard and saw it *(page 112)* to a length equal to the distance between the posts under the rail—or above it, if there is not enough clearance. Apply preservative or finish *(page 120)*. Clamp the sister rail in place *(page 116)* and bore holes every 18 to 24 inches *(page 117)*, offsetting them *(above)*. Install bolts *(page 108)* and saw off excess bolt length *(page 112)*. Drive in nails *(page 108)* or install hardware *(page 110)* at the posts. Fill holes and caulk joints *(page 106)*. Reinstall any fencing removed *(page 82)* and refinish damaged surfaces *(page 79)*.

REPAIRING A RAIL (Wood)

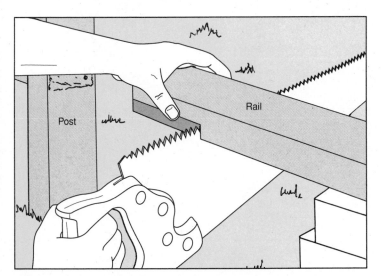

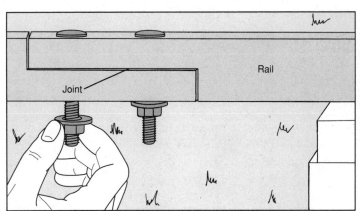

1 **Removing the damage.** Replace a damaged section of rail by splicing in a new section extending to the nearest post. Remove any fencing that is in the way *(page 82)*, as well as any latch assembly or hinges *(page 80)*. Disconnect the damaged end of the rail from the post by removing the fasteners *(page 107)* or hardware *(page 110)*. If the rail extends across the front of the post, saw it in two at the midpoint of the post *(page 112)*. Saw off the damaged section of the rail; have a helper support the rail, brace it with pieces of wood or prop it on blocks. At the cut end of the rail, mark and cut one side of a half-lap joint *(page 115)* 6 to 8 inches long *(above)*.

2 **Splicing a new section.** Purchase lumber for the splice of the same dimensions as the rail at a lumber yard. Position the new section against the cut end of the rail to mark it. Saw the new section to length *(page 112)*, cutting one end for the half-lap joint and cutting the other end to join the post *(page 115)*; if required, rout *(page 118)*, bore *(page 117)* or chisel *(page 116)* it to shape. Apply preservative or finish *(page 120)*. Position the new section and clamp the half-lap joint *(page 116)*. Bore two holes about 2 inches apart for bolts *(page 108)* and install them *(above)*; saw off excess bolt length *(page 112)*. Connect the end of the new section to the post by driving in at least two nails, offsetting them *(page 108)*, or install hardware *(page 110)* at the post or at any adjacent rail or brace. Fill holes and caulk joints *(page 106)*. Reinstall any fencing removed *(page 82)* and any latch assembly or hinges *(page 80)*. Refinish damaged surfaces *(page 79)*.

REPLACING A RAIL (Wood)

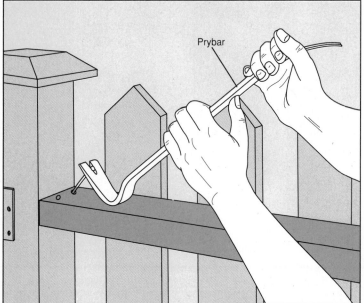

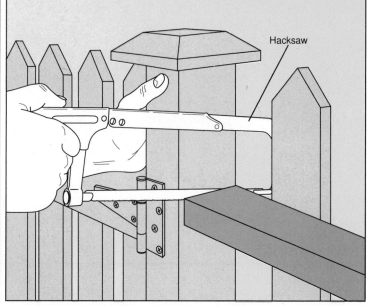

1 **Removing a rail.** Remove any fencing in the way *(page 82)* as well as any latch assembly or hinges *(page 80)*. To take off an entire fencing panel, remove the bottom rail first and the top rail last. Have a helper support the rail, brace it with pieces of wood or prop it on blocks. To take off a rail, pull the nails *(page 107)* using a pry bar *(above, left)* or remove the hardware *(page 110)*.

To loosen the nails, hammer the bottom or side of the rail near the post or near any adjacent rail or brace; cushion the blows with a wood block if the rail will be reinstalled. If the rail extends across the front of a post, saw it in two at the post midpoint *(page 115)*. If the rail is tenoned in a mortise or otherwise difficult to remove, saw through each joint *(above, right)* using a hacksaw *(page 112)*.

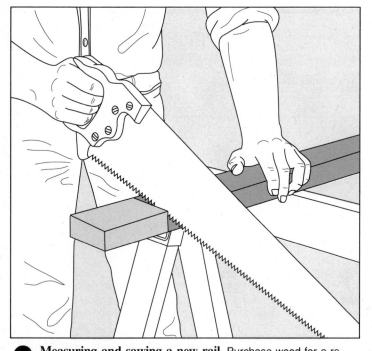

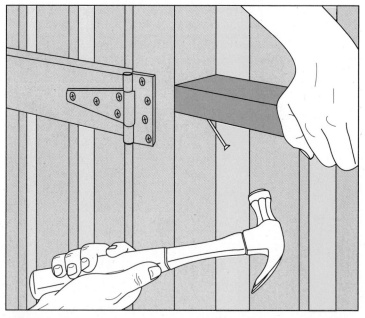

2 **Measuring and sawing a new rail.** Purchase wood for a replacement rail at a lumber yard. Position the new rail against the posts or against the gate to mark it for length; if required, have a helper support one end or temporarily nail it *(page 108)*. Saw the rail *(page 112)* to length *(above)*, cutting the ends to form the necessary joints *(page 115)*. If required, rout *(page 118)*, bore *(page 117)* or chisel *(page 116)* the rail. It may be useful to nail a straight-edged wood block on the rail as a saw guide. Apply preservative or finish *(page 120)*.

3 **Installing a rail.** To put up an entire fencing panel, install the top rail first and the bottom rail last. To install a rail, position it on the gate or the posts; if required, have a helper support it, brace it with pieces of wood or prop it on blocks. Drive at least two nails or screws, offsetting them *(page 108)*, or install hardware *(page 110)* at the post or at any adjacent rail or brace. Fill holes and caulk joints *(page 106)*. Reinstall any fencing removed *(page 82)* and any latch assembly or hinges *(page 80)*. Refinish damaged surfaces *(page 79)*.

REPLACING A POST CAP (Wood)

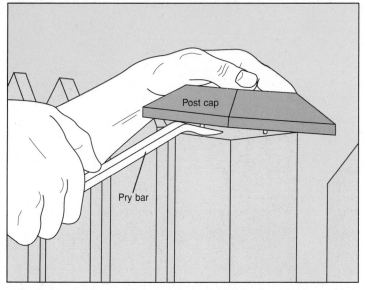

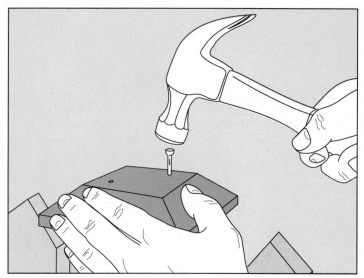

1 **Removing a post cap.** To take off a decorative post cap that is screwed in place, turn it counterclockwise; if required, run a utility knife between it and the post to break any finish or caulk seal. To remove the double-ended screw, twist it counterclockwise using pliers. To take off a standard post cap, pull the nails *(page 107)*. To loosen the nails, lift up the post cap using a pry bar *(above)* or hammer up on the bottom overhanging the post; cushion the blows with a wood block if you intend to reinstall the post cap.

2 **Installing a post cap.** Purchase a replacement post cap or wood for a standard post cap at a lumber yard. Cut a standard post cap *(page 112)*, measuring or tracing the original to mark it; if required, rout *(page 118)*, plane *(page 117)* or chisel *(page 116)* the cap. Apply preservative or finish *(page 120)*. To install a decorative post cap, bore pilot holes *(page 117)* in the cap and post, centering them by marking diagonal lines across opposite corners. Then twist a double-ended screw clockwise into the top of the post using pliers and turn the post cap clockwise onto it. To install a standard post cap, center it and drive in at least two finishing nails *(page 108)*, offsetting them *(above)*. Fill holes and caulk joints *(page 106)*. Refinish damaged surfaces *(page 79)*.

REINFORCING A POST (Wood)

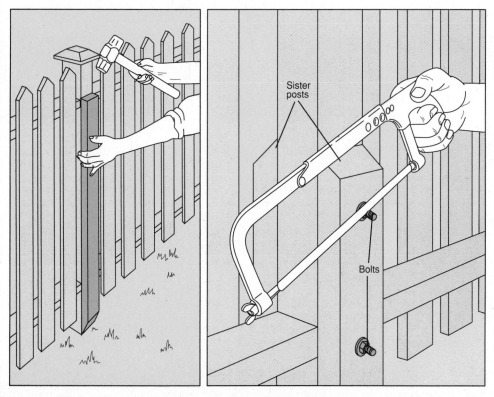

Installing sister posts or shims. To reinforce a post set in soil, install a sister post on each side of it. Purchase 2-by-4s at a lumber yard. Saw them to a length at least half the height of the post, with a 45-degree bevel at one end *(page 112)*, and apply preservative or finish *(page 120)*. Position a sister post, bevel out, against the post and drive it halfway into the ground with a sledgehammer *(far left)*. Saw off its top at a 45-degree angle 18 to 24 inches from the ground. Repeat this procedure to install the other sister post. Bore at least two bolt holes through both sister posts and the fence post *(page 117)* and install bolts *(page 108)*; saw off excess length with a hacksaw *(near left)*. Caulk joints *(page 106)*. Refinish damaged surfaces *(page 79)*.

To reinforce a post set in concrete, force shims into any spaces between the post and the concrete footing. Saw *(page 112)* and chisel *(page 116)* or plane *(page 117)* shims to a length at least a third the height of the post. Apply preservative or finish *(page 120)*. Drive in a shim as far as possible with a rubber mallet, cut it off at ground level using a chisel and caulk around the base of the post *(page 106)*.

REPAIRING A POST (Wood)

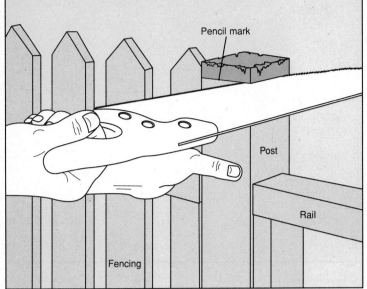

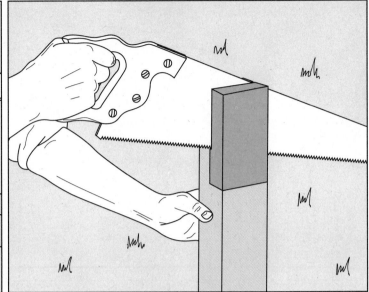

1 **Removing the damage.** To repair a post below the bottom rail or the fencing, reinforce or repair the footing *(page 87)* or replace the post and the footing *(page 88)*. To repair a post above the top rail or the fencing, saw off the damaged section *(page 112)* using a handsaw *(above, left)* and install a post cap *(page 85)*; remove and reinstall any fencing if required *(page 82)*. Cut and cap the other posts to match.

To repair a post between the top and bottom rails or top and bottom of the fencing, replace the damaged section by splicing. Remove any rail *(page 84)* and fencing in the way *(page 82)*. Remove any post cap *(page 85)* and latch assembly or hinges *(page 80)*. Saw off the damaged section *(page 112)*; if required, have a helper support it. At the cut end of the post, saw one side of a half-lap joint *(page 115)* 6 to 8 inches long *(above, right)*.

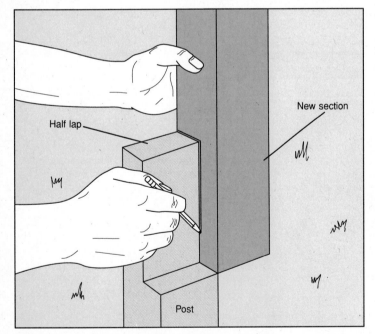

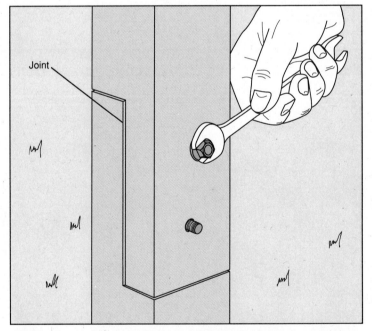

2 **Measuring and cutting a splice.** Purchase lumber for a splice of the same dimensions as the post at a lumber yard. Cut the new section with one side of a half-lap joint to fit the other *(page 115)*. To mark both sides of the half-lap joint, position the new section against the bottom and one side of the joint *(above)*, then against the bottom and the opposite side. Cut the joint as in step 1. To mark its length, position the new section and run a cord tautly between the posts on each side of it, then mark it, remove it and cut it to length. If required, rout *(page 118)*, bore *(page 117)* or chisel *(page 116)* the piece to shape. Apply preservative or finish *(page 120)*.

3 **Splicing the new section.** Position the new section on the post, clamp the half-lap joint *(page 116)*, bore two holes about 2 inches apart *(page 117)* and install bolts *(page 108)*; tighten nuts using a wrench *(above)*. Saw off excess bolt length *(page 112)*. Fill holes and caulk joints *(page 106)*. Reinstall any rail *(page 84)* and fencing removed *(page 82)*. Reinstall any post cap *(page 85)* and latch assembly or hinges *(page 80)*, and refinish damaged surfaces *(page 79)*.

REINFORCING OR REPAIRING A FOOTING (Wood)

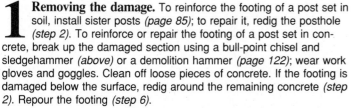

1 **Removing the damage.** To reinforce the footing of a post set in soil, install sister posts *(page 85)*; to repair it, redig the posthole *(step 2)*. To reinforce or repair the footing of a post set in concrete, break up the damaged section using a bull-point chisel and sledgehammer *(above)* or a demolition hammer *(page 122)*; wear work gloves and goggles. Clean off loose pieces of concrete. If the footing is damaged below the surface, redig around the remaining concrete *(step 2)*. Repour the footing *(step 6)*.

2 **Redigging the posthole.** Dig around the post using a spade *(above)*, working on each side of the fence; if required, brace the post with wood *(step 3)*. To reset a post in soil, dig a posthole twice the post width and at least 24 to 30 inches deep; if you are adding concrete, dig the posthole three times the post width and 6 inches deeper than the post. To repair a post below the bottom rail or the fencing, dig a posthole large enough to install a concrete sister footing and post.

3 **Repositioning the post.** To repair a post below the bottom rail or the fencing, saw off the damaged section *(page 112)*. Temporarily install 2-by-4 braces with stakes on opposite sides of the post at a 90-degree angle to the fence; first remove any rail *(page 84)* and fencing *(page 82)* in the way. Saw the braces to a length about 1 1/2 times the height of the post, and cut the stakes 12 to 18 inches long with a point at the bottom. Nail each brace on the post using only one nail *(page 108)*. Drive the stakes with a sledgehammer, have a helper position the post using a carpenter's level, and nail the braces onto the stakes *(above)*.

4 **Backfilling the posthole.** Use a 2-by-4 to tamp the bottom of the posthole *(above)*, fill it with 6 inches of gravel and tamp again. To set the post in concrete, pour a footing *(step 6)*; if you sawed off a damaged section of post, first bolt on a sister post of the same dimensions as the post *(page 108)* and saw it off at a 45-degree angle 18 to 24 inches above the ground *(page 112)*. To reset the post in soil, backfill the posthole, adding and tamping 6-inch layers of soil until reaching 18 inches from the surface; for extra reinforcement, install support cleats *(step 5)*.

REINFORCING OR REPAIRING A FOOTING (Wood, continued)

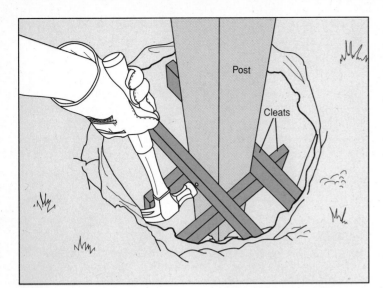

5 **Installing support cleats.** To reinforce a post reset in soil, install four support cleats on the post horizontally at least 12 inches below the surface. Cut the support cleats from 1-by-4s or 2-by-4s to a length about three or four times the post width *(page 112)*. Apply preservative or finish *(page 120)*. Nail the support cleats on the post *(page 108)*, pairing them on opposite sides of it *(above)*. To make nailing easier, drive the nails into the cleats before positioning them, and enlarge the posthole. Backfill the hole with soil *(step 4)*, sloping the surface away from the post. Reinstall any rail *(page 84)* and fencing *(page 82)* removed.

6 **Pouring a concrete footing.** Install a cylindrical form *(page 122)* if desired. Mix concrete *(page 122)* to pour a footing to a height at least 1 inch above ground level; to repair only the top, use concrete patching compound *(page 122)*. Dampen remaining pieces of the old footing. Wearing work gloves, use a spade to mix and pour the concrete. Shape the top of the footing with a trowel, sloping it away from the post *(above)*. Allow the footing to set for 48 hours. Reinstall any rail *(page 84)* and fencing removed *(page 82)*. Refinish damaged surfaces *(page 79)*. Caulk the post base after the footing has cured one week *(page 106)*.

REPLACING A POST AND FOOTING (Wood)

1 **Positioning a replacement post and footing.** Position a replacement post and footing before or after removing the old post and footing *(step 2)*. Run a cord tautly between the posts on each side of the post and footing. For an end post and footing, run a cord tautly from the post next to the post and footing to a stake 3 to 4 feet beyond the post and footing, parallel to the fence; for a corner post and footing, use the same procedure from the post on each side of the post and footing *(inset)*.

Cut stakes from 2-by-4s, angling the sides into a point at the bottom *(page 112)*; drive the stakes into the ground with a sledgehammer. Position the cord on each post or stake at the same distance below the bottom rail or the fencing and temporarily nail the ends *(page 108)*. Tie a marker on the cord at each side of the old post and footing *(left)*; if it has been removed, place the markers by measuring the length of the rails or the fencing on each side of the post position.

REPLACING A POST AND FOOTING (Wood, continued)

2 **Removing the old post and footing.** Remove any rail *(page 84)* and fencing *(page 82)* in the way; remove any post cap *(page 85)* and latch assembly or hinges *(page 80)*. Use a spade to dig around the post or the concrete footing—start with a depth of 12 to 18 inches. Loosen the footing by rocking the post back and forth *(above, left)*, working on each side of it. Dig deeper and rock the post until it can be pulled out of the ground; have a helper pull from one side. Dig to the bottom of the post to break up any concrete footing *(page 122)*. It may be easier to lift out the post using a car jack. Position the car jack on one side of the post and two concrete blocks, stacked, on the opposite side, 2 to 3 feet away from the post. Nail a 2-by-4 at least 12 inches long on the post about 18 inches from the ground *(page 108)* and position the edge of a 2-by-6 board under it, resting one end on the car jack and the other on the concrete blocks; drive one nail through the center of the board for stability. Support the car jack firmly, have a helper support the post and raise the car jack to lift out the post *(above, right)*.

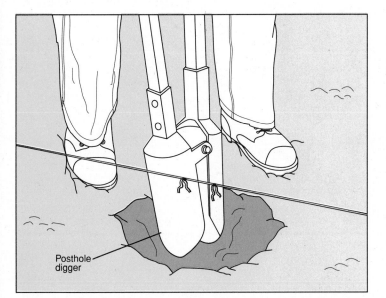

3 **Redigging the posthole.** If you have not done so already, position the post and footing *(step 1)*. Use a posthole digger *(above)* or clamshell digger to dig 6 inches deeper than the frostline, or than half the height of the tallest post next to the hole—the minimum depth required is usually 24 to 30 inches. To set the post in soil, dig twice the post width; to set the post in concrete, dig three times the post width. Tamp the bottom of the posthole with the end of a 2-by-4. Use a spade to fill the posthole with 6 inches of gravel and tamp again.

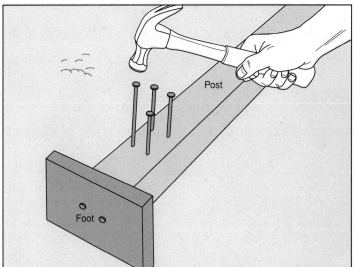

4 **Preparing the post.** Install a new post at least as long as the depth of the posthole plus the height of the tallest post next to it. Purchase wood for a replacement post at a lumber yard; if the old post can be reinstalled, break up any concrete footing *(page 122)*. Saw a foot from a 2-by-6 or 2-by-8 about 4 inches longer than the width of the post *(page 112)*, apply preservative or finish *(page 120)* and nail it onto the bottom *(page 108)*. For extra reinforcement in a concrete footing, drive long nails partway into the post 6 to 8 inches from the bottom *(above)*; if desired, install a cylindrical form for a concrete footing *(page 122)*.

REPLACING A POST AND FOOTING (Wood, continued)

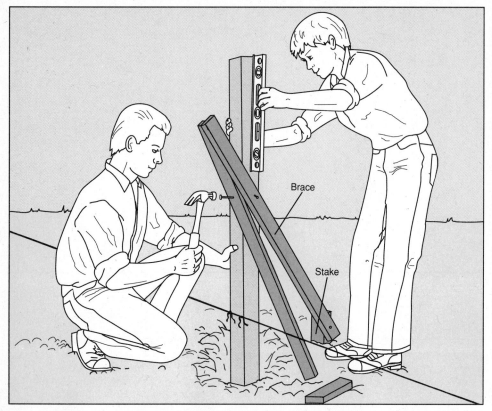

5 **Temporarily bracing the post.** Position the post on the bottom of the posthole and temporarily install 2-by-4 braces with stakes on adjacent sides of the post at a 90-degree angle to each other. Saw the braces to a length about 1 1/2 times the height of the post above the ground and cut the stakes 12 to 18 inches long, angling the sides to a point at the bottom *(page 112)*.

Have a helper position the post against the markers on the cord, using a carpenter's level. Nail a brace near the top of the post at about a 45-degree angle using only one nail *(page 108)*. Drive a stake into the ground at the other end of the brace with a sledgehammer and nail the brace on the stake. Repeat this procedure to install the other brace *(left)*.

To check the location of the post, compare the distance between it and each post next to it using the length of the rails or the fencing; if required, reposition the bottom of the post. To check the vertical position of the post, hold a level against two adjacent sides of it *(page 118)*; to adjust it, reposition the top of the post by driving the stakes farther into the ground.

6 **Backfilling the posthole.** To set the post in concrete, pour a footing *(step 7)*. To set the post in soil, backfill the posthole; use a spade to add 6-inch layers of soil and tamp with a 2-by-4 *(above)* up to about 12 to 18 inches from the surface. For extra reinforcement, especially in sandy soil, install support cleats *(page 88)*. Continue backfilling and tamping, sloping the surface away from the post. Saw the post to height *(step 9)*.

7 **Pouring a concrete footing.** Wearing work gloves, use a spade to mix the concrete in a wheelbarrow or trough and fill the posthole or the cylindrical form to a height at least 1 inch above the ground *(above)*. To settle the concrete, work a 2-by-4 up and down in it. Check the position of the post using a level *(page 118)*; if required, reposition and support it with additional temporary braces *(step 5)*.

REPLACING A POST AND FOOTING (Wood, continued)

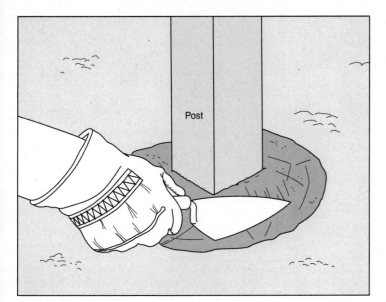

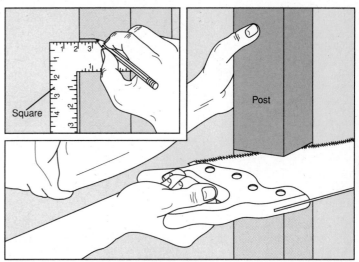

8 **Shaping a concrete footing.** Wearing work gloves, use a trowel to add concrete around the post base, sloping the top of the footing away from the post *(above)*. Allow the footing to set 48 hours before removing the temporary braces or sawing the post to height *(step 9)*. To keep the concrete from drying out, dampen the footing with water until it has cured for one week. Caulk the post base after the footing has cured *(page 106)*.

9 **Sawing the post to height.** Use a carpenter's square to mark the height on the sides of the post *(inset)*, measuring on each post next to it the distance between the cord and the top; if required, use a line level *(page 118)* or reposition the top rail or the fencing and measure up from it. Saw off the top of the post *(page 112)* using a handsaw *(above)*; if required, nail on a straight-edged wood block as a saw guide. Apply preservative or finish *(page 120)*. Reinstall any rail *(page 84)* and fencing *(page 82)* removed. Reinstall any post cap *(page 85)* and latch assembly or hinges *(page 80)*. Refinish damaged surfaces *(page 79)*.

CLEANING AND REPAINTING SURFACES (Chain link)

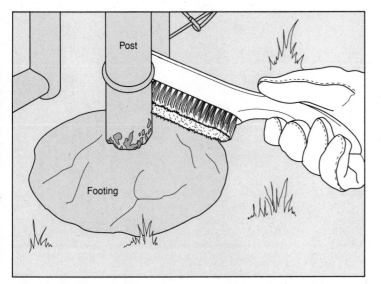

1 **Scrubbing off dirt, stains, rust and loose paint.** Replace rusted fasteners *(page 108)* and hardware *(page 110)*. To clean off dirt and most stains, use a solution of mild detergent and warm water; wear rubber gloves and scrub with a stiff fiber brush. Rinse using fresh water. For tough stains, mix 2 to 3 tablespoons of trisodium phosphate per gallon of warm water in a plastic bucket and repeat the procedure wearing goggles. Higher concentrations may be required but are more likely to harm the finish. To remove rust or loose paint, scrub with a wire brush *(above)* or rub using steel wool; apply a commercial rust remover on stubborn rust spots.

2 **Applying paint.** Choose a paint *(page 120)* and follow the manufacturer's directions for applying it; a coat of primer may be required. Caulk joints *(page 106)*. Protect surfaces not being painted with masking tape or a tarp. In most instances, paint is best applied using a paintbrush; a synthetic, flagged-bristle type is recommended. For efficiency, use a paintbrush slightly narrower than the width of the surface. Working top to bottom, apply paint evenly. Coat first the surfaces hardest to reach; ensure that each post base is adequately coated *(above)*. Between applications, sand lightly using fine sandpaper *(page 119)*. Paint the fencing or other awkward areas with a mitt, sprayer or roller *(page 120)*.

REPOSITIONING OR REPLACING THE GATE LATCH ASSEMBLY (Chain link)

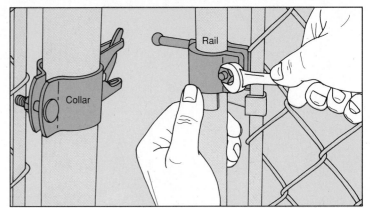

1 **Removing the latch assembly.** To reposition the latch assembly, loosen the collar on the strike; if necessary, also loosen the collar on the latch. Turn the nut with a wrench to loosen the collar. To take off the strike, remove the nut and bolt *(page 107)* and open the collar; if it is stubborn, tap it with a cold chisel and ball-peen hammer *(above)*. To take off the latch, remove the nut and bolt and pry off the collar; use pliers to bend it, if it is tight. If the latch assembly is damaged, replace it.

2 **Installing the latch assembly.** Purchase a replacement latch assembly at a fencing supply store. To replace the latch, close the collar on the post; to replace the strike, close the collar on the rail. Install the bolt on each collar *(page 108)*, turning the nut by hand. To position the strike or the latch, raise, lower or turn the collar until the strike fits in the latch; if it is tight, use a cold chisel and hammer to tap it. Tighten the nut using a wrench. Clean and repaint damaged surfaces *(page 91)*.

REPOSITIONING OR REPLACING THE GATE HINGES (Chain link)

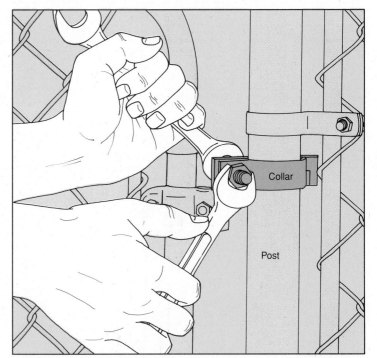

Removing and installing a strap. Have a helper support the gate at the correct closed position. To reposition a strap, use a wrench to loosen the collar nuts, tap it into place using a cold chisel and a hammer *(above)* and retighten it. To take off a strap, remove the nuts and bolts *(page 107)* and release the collar. To take off both straps, remove the gate by lifting the bottom strap off the lag, then lower the top strap off its lag. If a strap is damaged, buy a replacement at a fencing supply store. To put on a strap, position the collar on the rail and install the bolts *(page 108)*. To rehang the gate, push the top strap onto the lag, then lower the bottom strap onto its lag. Clean and repaint damaged surfaces *(page 91)*.

Removing and installing a lag. Have a helper support the gate at the correct closed position. To reposition a lag, loosen the collar by using a wrench on each side to turn the nuts. Tap it into place using a cold chisel and hammer and retighten it *(above)*. To take off a lag, remove the bolt *(page 107)* and release the collar. To take off both lags, remove the gate by lifting the strap off the bottom lag, then lowering the strap off the top lag. If a lag is damaged, buy a replacement at a fencing supply store. To put on a lag, position the collar on the post and install the bolt *(page 108)*. To rehang the gate, push the top strap onto the lag, then lower the bottom strap onto iis lag. Clean and repaint damaged surfaces *(page 91)*.

REINFORCING THE FENCING (Chain link)

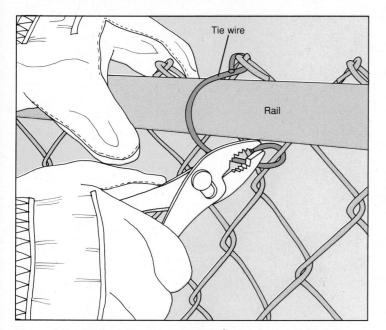

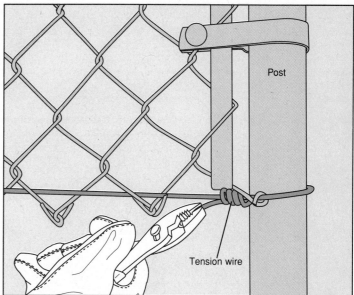

Removing and installing tie wires. Wear work gloves and use pliers. To remove a tie wire, twist open each end and pull it off; if it is stiff, wear goggles and cut it off using diagonal-cutting pliers. Purchase replacement tie wires at a fencing supply store and install them every 12 to 16 inches on the top rail and each line post. To install a tie wire, twist one end closed around the fencing, position the fencing on the rail or the post, and twist the other end closed around the fencing *(above)*.

Removing and installing the tension wire. Wear work gloves and use pliers. To tighten the tension wire, twist open one end, pull it taut around the post and twist it closed *(above)*. To remove the tension wire, twist open and unwrap each end, then unthread the wire; if it is stiff, wear goggles and snip it using diagonal-cutting pliers. Buy replacement tension wire at a fencing supply store. To install it, wrap one end around one post and twist it closed, thread the other end through the bottom of the fencing, pull it taut around the other post and twist it closed. If the fencing has a loose end, as shown, loop it around the tension wire to keep if from unraveling.

REPAIRING OR REPLACING THE FENCING (Chain link)

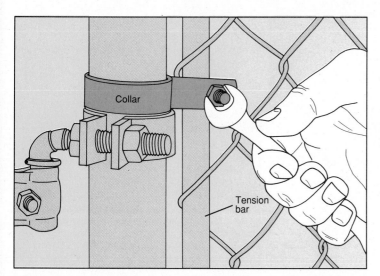

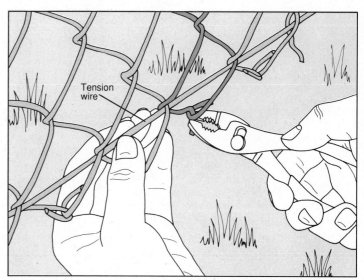

1 Releasing a tension bar. To repair the fencing, release the tension bar at the end nearest the damaged section; to replace the entire length of fencing, release the tension bar at each end. To release a tension bar, use a wrench to turn the nuts *(above)*, remove the bolts *(page 107)* and open the collars. To release a tension bar on the gate, unhook it from the clips by pulling it toward the side rail; if it is stubborn, tap it using a hammer. To repair or replace the fencing on the gate, remove any tie wires *(step above, left)* and install new fencing *(step 3)*.

2 Releasing the tension wire. Release the tension wire from the damaged section by using pliers to twist open the fencing *(above)*; if this is difficult, snip the fencing using diagonal-cutting pliers or remove the tension wire *(step above, right)*. Remove any tie wire on the damaged section *(step above, left)*; to repair the fencing, also remove any tie wires on the undamaged section along any line post between the damaged section and the released tension bar.

REPAIRING OR REPLACING THE FENCING (Chain link, continued)

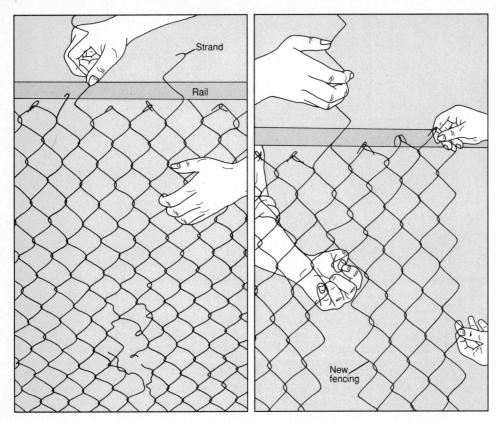

3 **Installing new fencing.** To repair the fencing, unwind one undamaged strand on each side of the damaged section, from the top at the rail *(far left)* to the bottom at the tension wire; keep the strands. To replace the entire length of fencing, unthread the tension bar at each end of it. If a tension bar, collar or clip is damaged, replace it. Buy replacements at a fencing supply store.

To repair the fencing, have a helper position one edge of the new fencing next to the edge of the undamaged fencing and wind an undamaged strand through both pieces, weaving them together *(near left)*. Repeat the procedure to wind the other undamaged strand through the other edges of the new fencing and the undamaged fencing. Bend down the ends of the strands.

To replace the entire length of fencing, position one end of the new fencing next to the post and thread a tension bar through it; fit the tension bar into each collar, close it and install the bolt *(page 108)*. Then tense the fencing *(step 4)*. To install new fencing on the gate, thread a tension bar through each end; hook one tension bar on the clips on one side rail, pull the other tension bar toward the other side rail and hook it on the clips, and install tie wires *(page 93)*.

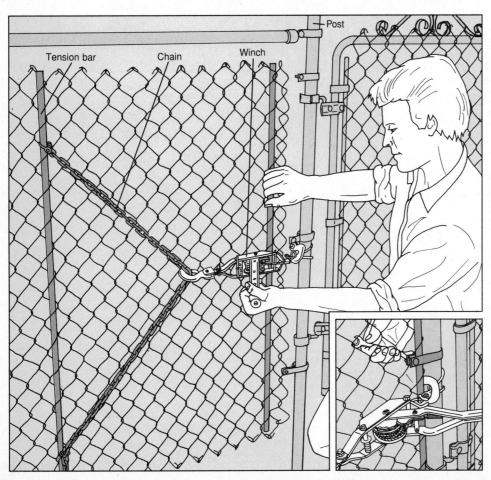

4 **Tensing the fencing.** Use a winch, a length of chain with hooks at each end, and two tension bars; usually these can be rented from a fencing supplier. Pull the fencing tautly toward the post by hand and thread a tension bar through it 5 to 6 feet from the post. Hook each end of the chain to opposite ends of the tension bar. Hook one end of the winch to the middle of the chain and hook the other end of the winch around the post.

Crank the winch handle back and forth to pull the tension bar toward the post, tensing the fencing; continue until the fencing stretches but is not strained. Pull the fencing tautly to the post by hand, thread the other tension bar through it near the collars and fit the tension bar into the collars; if required, pull the tension bar with one hand and crank the winch handle with the other hand *(left)*. Close the collars and install the bolts *(page 108)*, using a wrench to tighten the nuts *(inset)*; if required, have a helper support the tension bar. Unhook the winch and the length of chain, and unthread the tension bar used with them. To remove excess fencing, unwind the strand next to the tension bar, from the top at the rail to the bottom at the tension wire. Install tie wires *(page 93)*. Remove and reinstall the tension wire *(page 93)*, or rethread it by using pliers to twist open the new piece of fencing along the bottom, or install tie wires on the new fencing along it. Clean and repaint damaged surfaces *(page 91)*.

REPLACING A RAIL (Chain link)

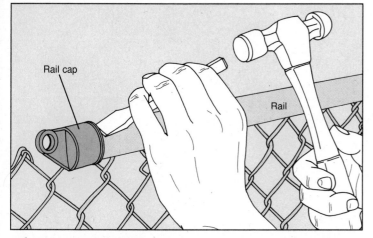

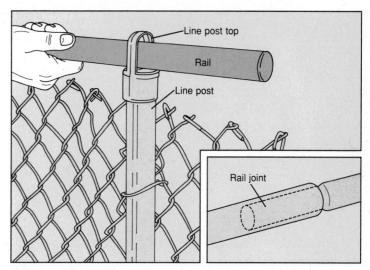

1 **Removing a rail.** Remove any tie wires along the rail *(page 93)*. To take off a rail end supported in a rail cap, use a wrench to turn the nut, remove the bolt *(page 107)* and open the collar. Pull off the rail cap; if it sticks, use a cold chisel and ball-peen hammer to tap it *(above)*. To take off a rail end connected in a joint *(step 2, inset)*, pull it; if it sticks, use a cold chisel and ball-peen hammer to tap it. Slide the rail out of any line post top. If a rail, rail cap, sleeve or collar is damaged, replace it.

2 **Installing a rail.** Purchase replacement rails, rail caps and collars at a fencing supply store. First, slide the rail through any line post top *(above)*. To join a rail end to another rail, slide the narrow end into the wider end *(inset)*. To install a rail end on a post, push on the rail cap and position it in the collar; close the collar and install the bolt *(page 108)*. Install tie wires *(page 93)*, and clean and repaint damaged surfaces *(page 91)*.

REINFORCING A POST (Chain link)

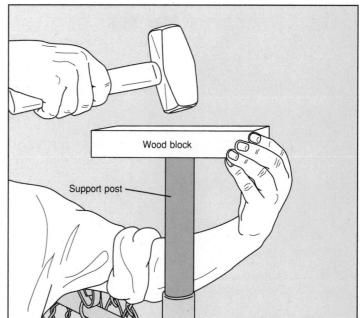

1 **Removing the post cap or the line post top.** To reinforce a post, install a support post inside it. To install a support post in a main post, pull off the post cap; if required, tap it up using a cold chisel and ball-peen hammer *(above)*. To install a support post in a line post, remove the rail *(step above, left)* and pull off the post top. Purchase a support post at a fencing supply store, 2 to 3 feet longer than the height of the post, with an outside diameter equal to the inside diameter of the post; also replace a damaged post cap or post top.

2 **Installing a support post.** Slide the support post into the post and use a sledgehammer to drive it into the ground, cushioning the blows with a wood block *(above)*; if required, position the post using a level *(page 118)* and have a helper support it. Drive the support post slightly below the top of the post by inserting a length of pipe. If the support post protrudes, saw off its top *(page 112)*. Reinstall the post cap or the post top; if it is stubborn, use a ball-peen hammer to tap it, cushioning the blows with a wood block. Reinstall the rail if you removed it *(step above, right)*. Clean and repaint damaged surfaces *(page 91)*.

REINFORCING OR REPAIRING A FOOTING (Chain link)

Bull-point chisel

1 **Removing the damage.** To reinforce or repair the footing, break up the damaged section using a bull-point chisel and sledgehammer *(above)* or a demolition hammer *(page 122)*; wear work gloves and goggles. Clean off loose particles using a wire brush. If the footing is damaged below the surface, redig the posthole with a spade; working on each side of the fence, dig to the depth required to break up and remove the damaged section.

2 **Pouring a concrete footing.** Pour a concrete footing to a height at least 1 inch above the ground; to repair only the surface, use concrete patching compound *(page 122)*. If desired, install a cylindrical form *(page 122)*. Dampen undamaged concrete with water. Wearing work gloves, use a spade to mix and pour the concrete. Shape the top of the footing with a trowel, sloping it away from the post *(above)*. Allow the footing to set; for concrete, wait 48 hours. Caulk the post base after the footing has cured one week *(page 106)*.

REPLACING A POST AND FOOTING (Chain link)

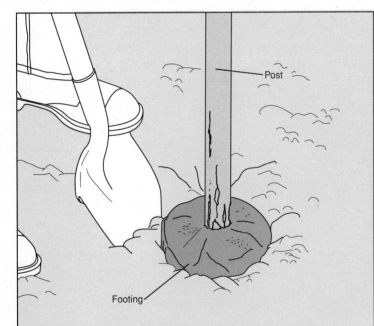

Post

Footing

1 **Removing the post and footing.** To replace a main post and footing, remove the rail *(page 95)*, release the tension bar and remove the tension wire *(page 93)* on each side of the post; also remove any latch assembly or hinges *(page 92)*. To replace a line post and footing, remove the rail *(page 95)* and any tie wires along the post *(page 93)*. Use a spade to dig around the footing *(above, left)*, rock the post to loosen the footing, and pull out the post. If required, lift out the post with two helpers using 2-by-4s as levers under the footing *(above, right)*.

To position a new post and footing, reposition each rail removed on the ground. Use a posthole digger or clamshell digger to dig a posthole 10 to 12 inches wide and 6 inches deeper than the frostline or than half the height of the tallest post next to the posthole—the minimum depth required is usually 24 to 30 inches. Tamp the bottom of the posthole using the end of a 2-by-4. Use a spade to fill it with 6 inches of gravel and tamp again; if desired, install a cylindrical form *(page 122)*. Purchase a replacement post at a fencing supply store; if the old post will be reinstalled, break up the concrete footing *(page 122)*.

REPLACING A POST AND FOOTING (Chain link, continued)

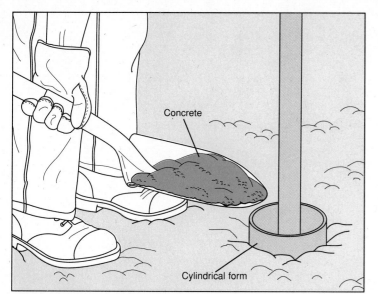

2 **Pouring a concrete footing.** Wearing work gloves, pour a concrete footing to a height at least 1 inch above the ground; have a helper support the post. Use a spade to mix the concrete in a wheelbarrow or trough and fill the cylindrical form *(above)* or the post-hole; to settle the concrete, work a long piece of wood up and down in it or tap the side of the form. If required, reposition the post, checking it with a carpenter's level *(page 118)*, or raise or lower the post in the concrete, measuring and matching the height of the other posts; set a main post 4 inches higher than a line post.

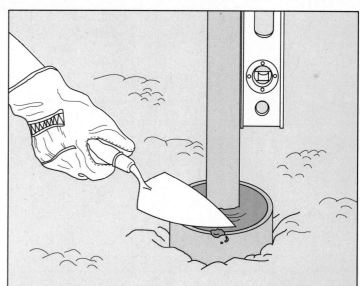

3 **Shaping a concrete footing.** Wearing work gloves, use a trowel to add concrete around the post base, sloping the top of the footing away from the post *(above)*. Allow the footing to set 48 hours; if required, brace the post on opposite sides using sawhorses with boards nailed *(page 108)* across them. Reinstall any rail removed *(page 95)* and any latch assembly or hinges *(page 92)*; if required, tense the fencing *(page 94)*. Install tie wires *(page 93)*. Allow the footing to cure one week, then caulk the post base *(page 106)*. Clean and repaint damaged surfaces *(page 91)*.

CLEANING AND REPAINTING SURFACES (Modular)

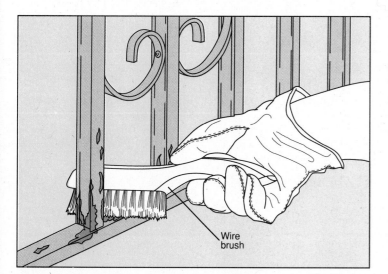

1 **Scrubbing off dirt, stains, rust and loose paint.** Replace rusted fasteners *(page 108)* and hardware *(page 110)*. To clean off dirt and most stains, use a solution of mild detergent or vinegar and warm water; wear rubber gloves and scrub with a non-abrasive scouring pad. Rinse using fresh water. For tough stains, mix 2 to 3 tablespoons of trisodium phosphate per gallon of warm water in a plastic bucket and repeat the procedure wearing goggles. A stronger solution is more likely to harm the finish. To remove rust or loose paint, scrub with a wire brush *(above)* or rub using steel wool; apply a commercial rust remover on stubborn rust spots.

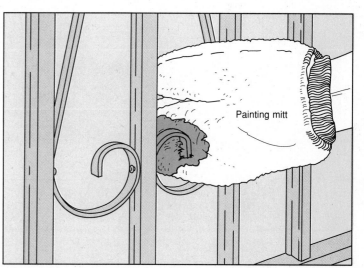

2 **Applying paint.** Choose a paint *(page 120)* and follow the manufacturer's directions for applying it; a coat of primer may be required. Caulk joints *(page 106)*. Protect surfaces not being painted with masking tape or a tarp. In most instances, paint is best applied using a paintbrush; a synthetic, flagged-bristle type is recommended. For efficiency, use a mitt on surfaces awkward to reach *(above)*. Apply paint evenly, working top to bottom. Coat first the surfaces hardest to reach; ensure that each post base is adequately coated. Between applications, sand lightly using fine sandpaper *(page 119)*. Paint may also be applied with a sprayer or roller *(page 120)*.

REPOSITIONING OR REPLACING THE GATE LATCH ASSEMBLY (Modular)

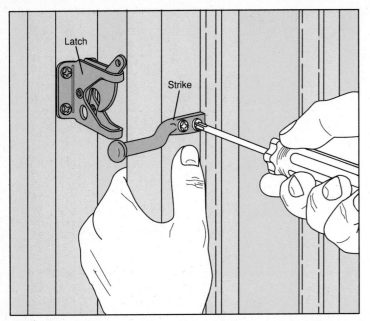

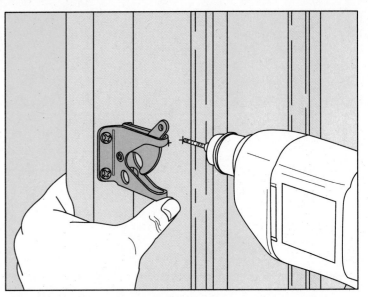

1 **Removing the latch assembly.** To reposition the latch assembly, remove the strike from the rail and reinstall it; if necessary, also remove the latch from the post and reinstall it. To take off the strike *(above)* or the latch, remove the screws *(page 107)*. If the strike or latch is damaged, replace it. Fill holes using epoxy patching compound *(page 106)*.

2 **Installing the latch assembly.** Purchase a replacement latch assembly at a hardware store. To reposition the strike, first insert it in the latch and mark its position on the rail. To reposition the entire latch assembly, insert the strike in the latch, and mark and install first the latch on the post and then the strike on the rail. To install the strike *(above)* or the latch, mark the screw holes, take down the strike or latch, drill holes *(page 117)* and drive in the screws *(page 108)*. Clean and repaint damaged surfaces *(page 97)*.

REPOSITIONING OR REPLACING THE GATE HINGES (Modular)

Removing and installing butt, strap or T hinges. To reposition or remove a hinge, take off the gate: Remove the screws on the post from the bottom hinge first and then the top hinge *(page 107)*; have a helper support the gate or prop it on blocks. If a hinge is damaged, remove it from the gate as well and purchase a replacement at a hardware store. Fill old screw holes using epoxy patching compound *(page 106)*.

To install a hinge, have a helper support the gate or prop it on blocks at the correct closed position. Position the hinges, mark the screw holes *(above, left)*, take down the hinges and drill holes *(page 117)*. Install first the top hinge and then the bottom hinge, using screws *(page 108)*. If required to align the gate, install washers as shims to build up a hinge *(above, right)*. Clean and repaint damaged surfaces *(page 97)*.

REPLACING THE FENCING (Modular)

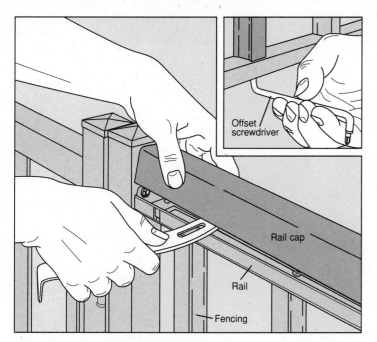

Offset screwdriver

Rail cap

Rail

Fencing

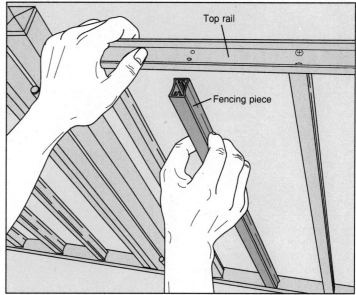

Top rail

Fencing piece

1 **Removing the fencing.** If required for access, first remove the screws from any trim pieces on the fencing *(page 107)*; if a trim piece is damaged, replace it. To remove the rail cap from the top rail, lift up one edge using a pry bar *(above)*. To take off an entire fencing panel, remove the rails *(step 1, below)*. To take off one fencing piece, remove its screws from the top rail and the bottom rail *(inset)*. Slide out the fencing piece; if required, tap it using a hammer, cushioning the blows with a wood block if the piece will be reinstalled. If the fencing is damaged, replace it.

2 **Installing the fencing.** Purchase replacement fencing and trim pieces from a fencing supplier. To install each fencing piece, position it between the rails *(above)*; if required, tap it using a hammer, cushioning the blows with a wood block. Screw the fencing piece on the top rail and the bottom rail *(page 108)*. Reinstall the rails if you removed them *(step 2, below)*. Reposition the rail cap and snap it onto the top rail. Screw on any trim pieces you removed, and clean and repaint damaged surfaces *(page 97)*.

REPLACING A RAIL (Modular)

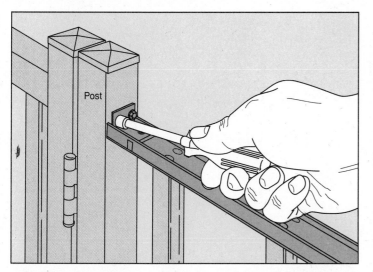

Post

Rail cap

1 **Removing a rail.** To remove the rail cap from the top rail, lift up one edge using a pry bar *(step 2, above)*; if the rail cap is damaged, replace it. To replace a bottom rail, take off the entire fencing panel, removing the bottom rail first and the top rail last. To disconnect a rail end from a post *(above)*, remove the screws *(page 107)*. To disconnect a rail end connected to another rail by a sleeve, pull it. If the rail is damaged, unscrew the fencing from it and replace the rail; also replace any damaged sleeve.

2 **Installing a rail.** Purchase replacement rails, rail caps and sleeves from a fencing supplier. If you removed the fencing, screw it back onto the rail *(page 108)*. To put up an entire fencing panel, install the top rail first and the bottom rail last. To connect a rail end to another rail, position a sleeve between the rails and push the rails together. To install a rail end on a post, position it at predrilled pilot holes and drive in screws *(page 108)*. Snap the rail cap onto the top rail *(above)*. Clean and repaint damaged surfaces *(page 97)*.

REINFORCING A POST OR REPAIRING A FOOTING (Modular)

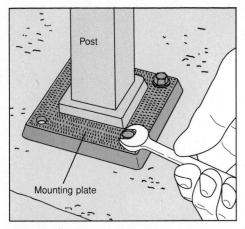

1 **Removing the post.** If the post is set in a concrete footing, break up the damaged area and replace it *(step 2)*. If the post is supported by a mounting plate, remove the rails on each side of the post *(page 99)* and any latch assembly or hinges *(page 98)*. To take off the post, remove the bolts *(page 107)* using a wrench *(above)*. If the expansion shields in the concrete footing are loose, pull them out with long-nose pliers; if they cannot be dislodged, break up the concrete *(step 2)*. Purchase replacement expansion shields and bolts at a hardware store.

2 **Breaking up and replacing concrete.** To break up concrete, use a bull-point chisel and sledgehammer *(above, left)* or a demolition hammer *(page 122)*; wear work gloves and goggles. Clean off loose particles with a wire brush. Dampen the undamaged concrete with water before repairing the footing.

If the post was supported by a mounting plate, break up enough concrete to remove the expansion shields. Use a trowel *(above, right)* to mix and spread concrete patching compound *(page 122)*. Allow the footing to set and reinstall the post *(step 3)*.

If the post is set in a concrete footing, dig around it using a spade to reach below the area of damage. Reposition the post if necessary and pour a footing to a height at least 1 inch above the ground, sloping the top away from the post; if desired, install a cylindrical form *(page 122)*. Caulk the post base after the footing has cured one week *(page 106)*.

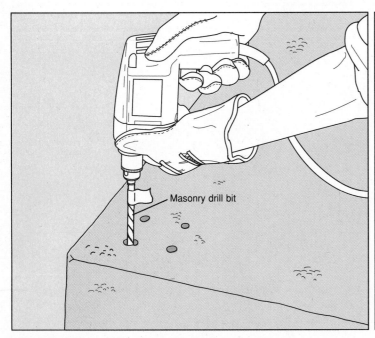

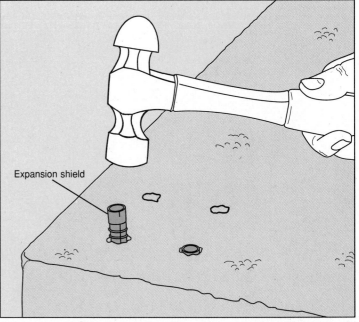

3 **Installing the post.** To install a post supported by a mounting plate, hold it on the footing; have a helper support the rails against the post to position it correctly. Mark the mounting-plate bolt holes on the footing. Drill holes *(page 117)* for the expansion shields using a power drill fitted with a masonry bit *(above, left)*. Fit an expansion shield into each hole, tapping it flush with a ball-peen hammer *(above, right)*. Reposition the post and mounting plate and install the bolts *(page 108)*. Reinstall the rails *(page 99)* and any latch assembly or hinges *(page 98)*. Allow the footing to cure one week, then caulk the post base *(page 106)*. Clean and repaint damaged surfaces *(page 97)*.

REPLACING A POST AND FOOTING (Modular)

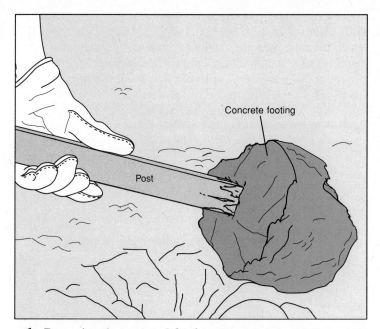

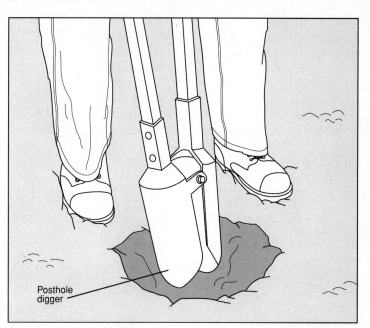

1 **Removing the post and footing.** Disconnect the rails from each side of the post *(page 99)*, as well as any latch assembly or hinges *(page 98)*. Dig around the footing with a spade. Rock the post back and forth to loosen the footing, and pull it out *(above)*; if required, have a helper pull the post while you lift the footing with the spade. Purchase a replacement post at a fencing supply store; if the old post can be reinstalled, break up the concrete footing *(page 122)*.

2 **Redigging the posthole.** To position a new post and footing, align the rails along the ground. Use a posthole digger *(above)* or clamshell digger to dig a posthole 10 to 12 inches wide and 6 inches deeper than the frostline or than half the height of the tallest post next to the posthole—the minimum depth required is usually 24 to 30 inches. Tamp the bottom of the posthole with a board, use a spade to fill it with 6 inches of gravel and tamp again; if desired, install a cylindrical form *(page 122)*.

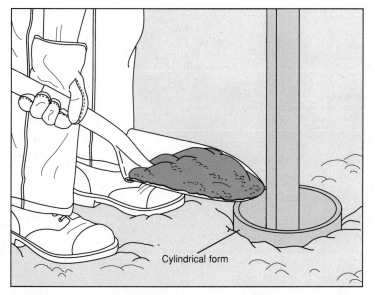

3 **Pouring a concrete footing.** Wearing work gloves, pour a concrete footing to a height at least 1 inch above the ground; have a helper support the post. Use a spade to mix the concrete in a wheelbarrow or trough and fill the cylindrical form *(above)* or the posthole; to settle the concrete, work a long piece of wood up and down in it or tap the side of the form. If required, reposition the post, checking it with a carpenter's level *(page 118)*, or raise or lower the post in the concrete, measuring and matching the height of the other posts.

4 **Shaping a concrete footing.** Wearing work gloves, use a trowel to add concrete around the post base, sloping the top of the footing away from the post. Allow the footing to set for 48 hours; if required, brace the post on opposite sides using sawhorses with boards temporarily nailed *(page 108)* across them. Reinstall the rails *(above)* you removed *(page 99)* and any latch assembly or hinges *(page 98)*. Allow the footing to cure one week, then caulk the post base *(page 106)*. Clean and repaint damaged surfaces *(page 97)*.

TOOLS & TECHNIQUES

This section introduces tools and techniques that are basic to repairing porches, decks and fences, such as replacing fasteners *(page 108)* and hardware *(page 110)*, making saw cuts *(page 112)* and leveling and plumbing *(page 118)*. Also included is information on working with concrete *(page 122)* and using jacks *(page 124)*. Charts on fasteners, hardware, abrasives and finishes are designed for easy reference. Advice on getting help when you need it appears on page 125.

You can handle most repairs to porches, decks and fences with the basic kit of tools and supplies shown below and on pages 104 and 105. Special tools, such as hydraulic and telescoping jacks, a demolition hammer and a paint sprayer, can be obtained at a tool rental agency. For the best results, always use the right tool for the job — and be sure to use the tool correctly. When shopping for new tools, purchase the highest-quality ones you can afford.

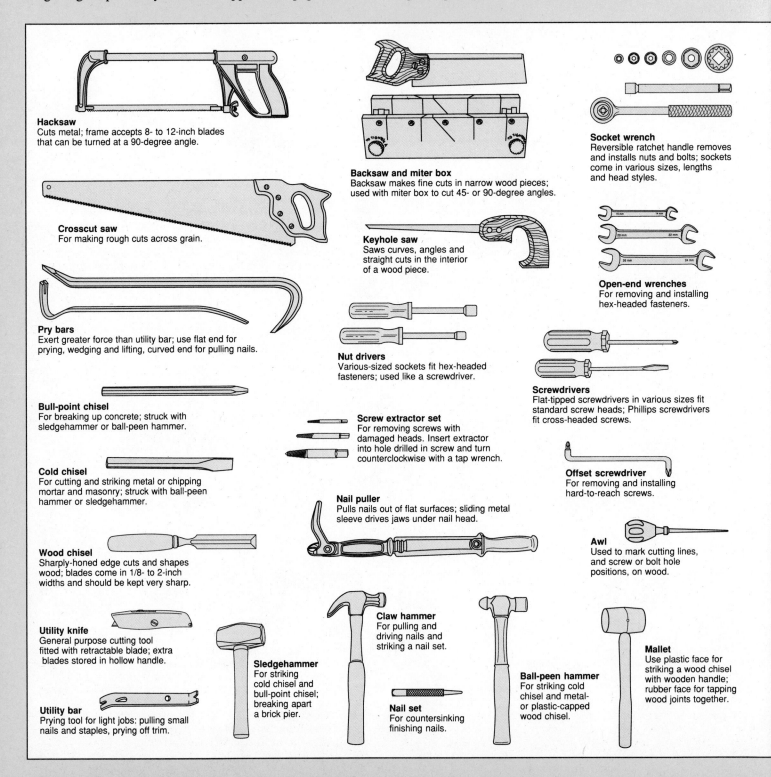

Hacksaw
Cuts metal; frame accepts 8- to 12-inch blades that can be turned at a 90-degree angle.

Crosscut saw
For making rough cuts across grain.

Pry bars
Exert greater force than utility bar; use flat end for prying, wedging and lifting, curved end for pulling nails.

Bull-point chisel
For breaking up concrete; struck with sledgehammer or ball-peen hammer.

Cold chisel
For cutting and striking metal or chipping mortar and masonry; struck with ball-peen hammer or sledgehammer.

Wood chisel
Sharply-honed edge cuts and shapes wood; blades come in 1/8- to 2-inch widths and should be kept very sharp.

Utility knife
General purpose cutting tool fitted with retractable blade; extra blades stored in hollow handle.

Utility bar
Prying tool for light jobs: pulling small nails and staples, prying off trim.

Backsaw and miter box
Backsaw makes fine cuts in narrow wood pieces; used with miter box to cut 45- or 90-degree angles.

Keyhole saw
Saws curves, angles and straight cuts in the interior of a wood piece.

Nut drivers
Various-sized sockets fit hex-headed fasteners; used like a screwdriver.

Screw extractor set
For removing screws with damaged heads. Insert extractor into hole drilled in screw and turn counterclockwise with a tap wrench.

Nail puller
Pulls nails out of flat surfaces; sliding metal sleeve drives jaws under nail head.

Sledgehammer
For striking cold chisel and bull-point chisel; breaking apart a brick pier.

Nail set
For countersinking finishing nails.

Claw hammer
For pulling and driving nails and striking a nail set.

Ball-peen hammer
For striking cold chisel and metal- or plastic-capped wood chisel.

Socket wrench
Reversible ratchet handle removes and installs nuts and bolts; sockets come in various sizes, lengths and head styles.

Open-end wrenches
For removing and installing hex-headed fasteners.

Screwdrivers
Flat-tipped screwdrivers in various sizes fit standard screw heads; Phillips screwdrivers fit cross-headed screws.

Offset screwdriver
For removing and installing hard-to-reach screws.

Awl
Used to mark cutting lines, and screw or bolt hole positions, on wood.

Mallet
Use plastic face for striking a wood chisel with wooden handle; rubber face for tapping wood joints together.

Take the time to care for and store your tools properly. To avoid damaging a cutting tool, for example, check for hidden fasteners before starting a cut. When a saw blade becomes dull, buy a replacement or have it sharpened by a professional. Keep a hand plane on its side when not in use to avoid damage to its blade. Avoid laying tools on the ground unprotected; spread out a drop cloth or tarp for them. Clean and lubricate power tools according to the manufacturer's instructions.

To clean metal hand tools, use a cloth moistened with a few drops of light machine oil — but never oil their handles. Wipe wood resin and dirt off metal tools using a clean cloth dipped in mineral spirits. To remove rust, rub the tool with fine steel wool, then apply a few drops of light machine oil with a soft cloth to keep the tool rust-free. Store tools on a shelf safely away from children, in a locked metal or plastic tool box, or hang them well out of reach.

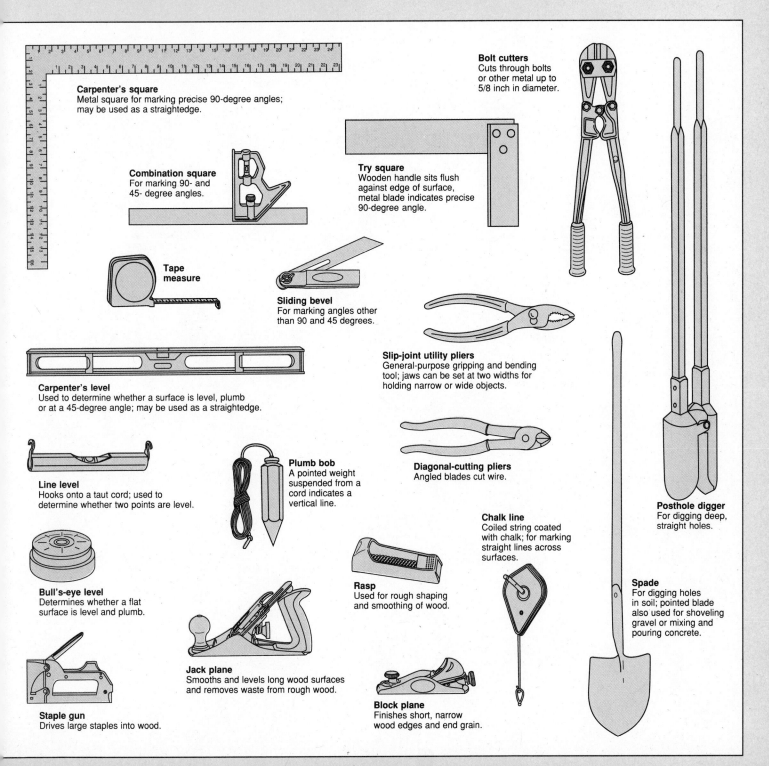

Carpenter's square
Metal square for marking precise 90-degree angles; may be used as a straightedge.

Combination square
For marking 90- and 45- degree angles.

Try square
Wooden handle sits flush against edge of surface, metal blade indicates precise 90-degree angle.

Bolt cutters
Cuts through bolts or other metal up to 5/8 inch in diameter.

Tape measure

Sliding bevel
For marking angles other than 90 and 45 degrees.

Slip-joint utility pliers
General-purpose gripping and bending tool; jaws can be set at two widths for holding narrow or wide objects.

Carpenter's level
Used to determine whether a surface is level, plumb or at a 45-degree angle; may be used as a straightedge.

Line level
Hooks onto a taut cord; used to determine whether two points are level.

Plumb bob
A pointed weight suspended from a cord indicates a vertical line.

Diagonal-cutting pliers
Angled blades cut wire.

Posthole digger
For digging deep, straight holes.

Bull's-eye level
Determines whether a flat surface is level and plumb.

Rasp
Used for rough shaping and smoothing of wood.

Chalk line
Coiled string coated with chalk; for marking straight lines across surfaces.

Spade
For digging holes in soil; pointed blade also used for shoveling gravel or mixing and pouring concrete.

Jack plane
Smooths and levels long wood surfaces and removes waste from rough wood.

Staple gun
Drives large staples into wood.

Block plane
Finishes short, narrow wood edges and end grain.

103

Make a routine check of your outdoor structures each spring and fall. Wood joints, spots where water can collect, and the bases of posts and columns, in particular, are vulnerable to rot and insect damage. Stop problems from developing further by undertaking repairs as soon as symptoms are detected. Inspect carefully for signs of carpenter ants and termites *(page 106),* and consult a pest control professional in case of insect infestation. Throughout this book, various repair options may be presented for each specific problem. A problem can have a number of solutions, the best of which will depend both on external factors and on your individual preference. In many instances, damaged lumber can be reinforced or repaired, but if the wood is badly cracked or warped, or suffering from advanced rot, the piece should be replaced.

Install lumber that is pressure-treated, or naturally decay-resistant redwood or cedar, for outdoor structures. Treat

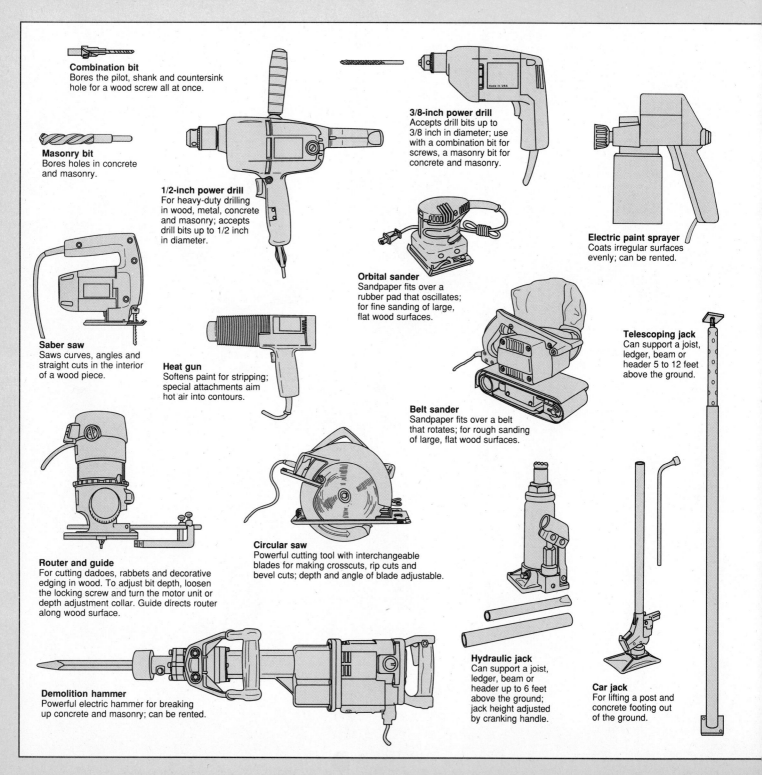

Combination bit
Bores the pilot, shank and countersink hole for a wood screw all at once.

Masonry bit
Bores holes in concrete and masonry.

1/2-inch power drill
For heavy-duty drilling in wood, metal, concrete and masonry; accepts drill bits up to 1/2 inch in diameter.

3/8-inch power drill
Accepts drill bits up to 3/8 inch in diameter; use with a combination bit for screws, a masonry bit for concrete and masonry.

Electric paint sprayer
Coats irregular surfaces evenly; can be rented.

Saber saw
Saws curves, angles and straight cuts in the interior of a wood piece.

Heat gun
Softens paint for stripping; special attachments aim hot air into contours.

Orbital sander
Sandpaper fits over a rubber pad that oscillates; for fine sanding of large, flat wood surfaces.

Belt sander
Sandpaper fits over a belt that rotates; for rough sanding of large, flat wood surfaces.

Telescoping jack
Can support a joist, ledger, beam or header 5 to 12 feet above the ground.

Router and guide
For cutting dadoes, rabbets and decorative edging in wood. To adjust bit depth, loosen the locking screw and turn the motor unit or depth adjustment collar. Guide directs router along wood surface.

Circular saw
Powerful cutting tool with interchangeable blades for making crosscuts, rip cuts and bevel cuts; depth and angle of blade adjustable.

Hydraulic jack
Can support a joist, ledger, beam or header up to 6 feet above the ground; jack height adjusted by cranking handle.

Car jack
For lifting a post and concrete footing out of the ground.

Demolition hammer
Powerful electric hammer for breaking up concrete and masonry; can be rented.

redwood and cedar with a water-repellent preservative. Protect reused and new lumber by applying preservative on exposed grain before installing it. Exercise caution when handling pressure-treated lumber and its sawdust, as well as wood cleaning and refinishing products; the chemicals in them can be toxic. Read and follow the safety information on page 8.

Follow common-sense rules when working outdoors with power tools. Never operate a power tool in wet conditions. Always use grounded or double-insulated power tools and plug them into a grounded outlet or a portable ground-fault circuit interrupter *(page 9)*. Keep an ABC-rated fire extinguisher nearby *(page 10)*, along with a well-stocked first-aid kit. Wear the proper protective clothing and gear for the job, and set up a temporary barrier *(page 11)* to keep others away from the work area. If in doubt about your ability to complete a repair, do not hesitate to consult a professional.

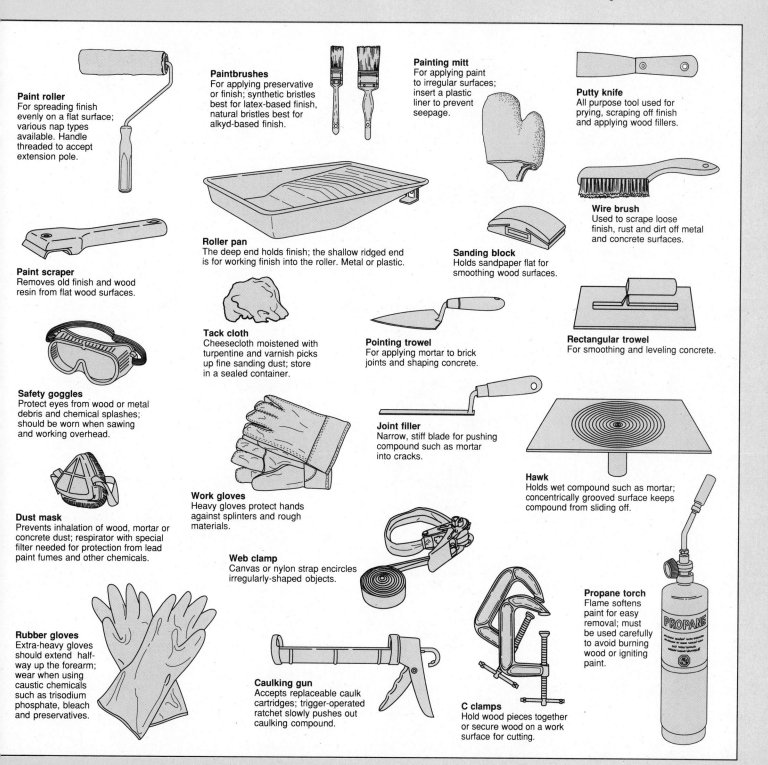

Paint roller
For spreading finish evenly on a flat surface; various nap types available. Handle threaded to accept extension pole.

Paintbrushes
For applying preservative or finish; synthetic bristles best for latex-based finish, natural bristles best for alkyd-based finish.

Painting mitt
For applying paint to irregular surfaces; insert a plastic liner to prevent seepage.

Putty knife
All purpose tool used for prying, scraping off finish and applying wood fillers.

Paint scraper
Removes old finish and wood resin from flat wood surfaces.

Roller pan
The deep end holds finish; the shallow ridged end is for working finish into the roller. Metal or plastic.

Sanding block
Holds sandpaper flat for smoothing wood surfaces.

Wire brush
Used to scrape loose finish, rust and dirt off metal and concrete surfaces.

Tack cloth
Cheesecloth moistened with turpentine and varnish picks up fine sanding dust; store in a sealed container.

Pointing trowel
For applying mortar to brick joints and shaping concrete.

Rectangular trowel
For smoothing and leveling concrete.

Safety goggles
Protect eyes from wood or metal debris and chemical splashes; should be worn when sawing and working overhead.

Joint filler
Narrow, stiff blade for pushing compound such as mortar into cracks.

Dust mask
Prevents inhalation of wood, mortar or concrete dust; respirator with special filter needed for protection from lead paint fumes and other chemicals.

Work gloves
Heavy gloves protect hands against splinters and rough materials.

Hawk
Holds wet compound such as mortar; concentrically grooved surface keeps compound from sliding off.

Web clamp
Canvas or nylon strap encircles irregularly-shaped objects.

Propane torch
Flame softens paint for easy removal; must be used carefully to avoid burning wood or igniting paint.

Rubber gloves
Extra-heavy gloves should extend halfway up the forearm; wear when using caustic chemicals such as trisodium phosphate, bleach and preservatives.

Caulking gun
Accepts replaceable caulk cartridges; trigger-operated ratchet slowly pushes out caulking compound.

C clamps
Hold wood pieces together or secure wood on a work surface for cutting.

REPAIRING MINOR ROT AND INSECT DAMAGE

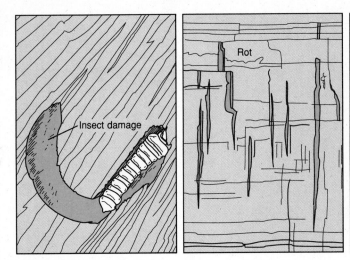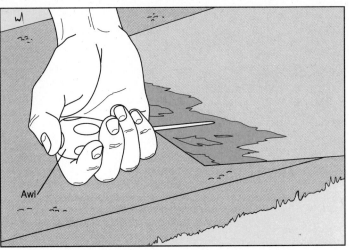

Identifying wood damage. To check for rot and insect damage, closely inspect joints, surfaces where water can collect, and surfaces on or near the ground; the base of a post or a column is especially vulnerable. Chipped, peeling or lifting finish, spongy wood fibers and gray or dark discoloration are telltale signs of rot or insect damage. Remove any loose finish *(page 120)*. If the wood is pitted or powdery, or riddled with tiny holes or tunnels *(above, left)*, suspect insect damage and consult a pest control professional.

Wood suffering from rot may be split or cracked *(above, center)*, but it may also exhibit no visible signs of a problem. To test for rot, poke the wood using an awl, pressing it in as deeply as possible *(above, right)*. If the wood is soft and gives way, crumbling instead of splintering, it is weakened by rot. To repair a small area of rot, use a paint scraper, putty knife or wire brush to remove all the soft, rotted wood down to firm, healthy wood, then fill the damaged area with epoxy patching compound *(step below)*.

APPLYING FILLERS AND CAULKS

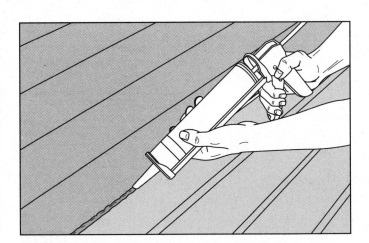

Filling holes and cracks. To fill nail and screw holes or small cracks in wood, apply an exterior-grade wood putty. To fill holes in metal or repair minor rot and insect damage, apply epoxy patching compound. Purchase wood putty or epoxy patching compound at a building supply center and prepare it following the manufacturer's directions. Using a putty knife, pack the putty or compound into the hole or crack, overfilling it slightly; level it with the surrounding surface, scraping off the excess *(above)*. Allow the putty or compound to dry, smooth the surface *(page 119)* and refinish it *(page 120)*.

Caulking joints. To remove old or loosened caulk, cut it using a utility knife and dig it out with a putty knife. To seal wood, metal or concrete joints, purchase an exterior-grade caulk at a building supply center. Load the caulk tube into a caulking gun. Cut off the tip of the tube at a 45-degree angle with a utility knife; make an opening slightly narrower than the joint. Use a long nail or an awl to break the tube seal. Holding the gun at a 45-degree angle to the joint, squeeze the gun trigger to eject a continuous bead of caulk along the joint *(above)*. Wearing a rubber glove, run a wet finger along the caulk to press it into the joint, smoothing and shaping it.

REMOVING FASTENERS

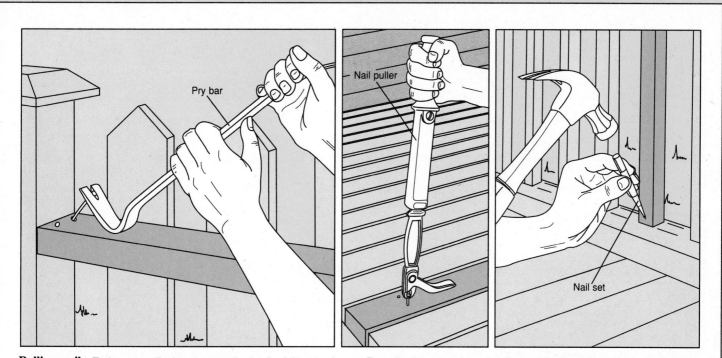

Pulling nails. To loosen nails, hammer on the back of the wood near the joint, or use a pry bar or a crowbar to pull apart the joint. Set a wood block under the head of a hammer, pry bar or crowbar for better leverage and to protect an undamaged surface. To pull most nails, use a claw hammer. For large nails, or nails in awkward corners, use a pry bar or crowbar: Drive the V-shaped notch at the end under the nail head and pull the handle down *(above, left)*.

To pull a large number of nails out of a flat surface, use a nail puller; push down on the sliding metal sleeve to close the jaws around a nail head and pull the handle, using the small lever as a fulcrum, to lift out the nail *(above, center)*. For a countersunk or headless nail, use a nail set or drift punch to drive it through wood *(above, right)*. If a nail cannot be removed, loosen the joint with a pry bar or crowbar and cut through the nail shaft using a hacksaw *(page 112)*.

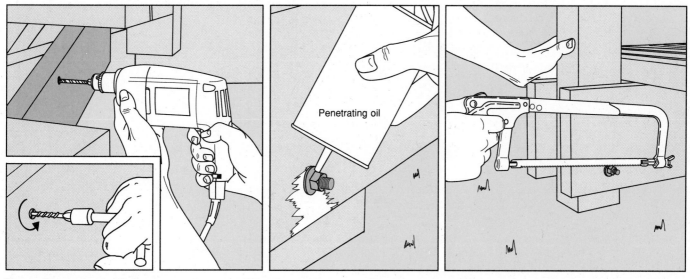

Removing screws or bolts. Remove wood screws with a screwdriver of the same type and size as the screw heads. Remove metal screws, lag bolts or expansion bolts using a wrench or a nut driver of the same type and size as the screw or bolt heads; to pull out a shield, use pliers or chip out around it using a bull-point chisel and a sledgehammer *(page 122)*. To remove a large number of wood or metal screws, lag bolts or expansion bolts, use a reversible drill *(page 117)* and the correct type and size bit. Remove carriage bolts with a wrench of the same type and size as the nuts.

If a screw head or lag bolt head is damaged, use a screw extractor: Drill a pilot hole *(page 117)* in the head *(above, left)*, fit the extractor in the hole and turn the extractor with a tap wrench *(inset)*. To loosen a rusted nut on a carriage bolt, apply penetrating oil on the nut, washer and bolt shaft *(above, center)*; allow the oil to penetrate for 10 to 15 minutes. If a screw or bolt cannot be removed, loosen the joint with a pry bar or crowbar. Then cut through the screw or bolt shaft *(above, right)* using a hacksaw *(page 112)*, or cut off the screw or bolt head using a bolt cutter.

INSTALLING FASTENERS

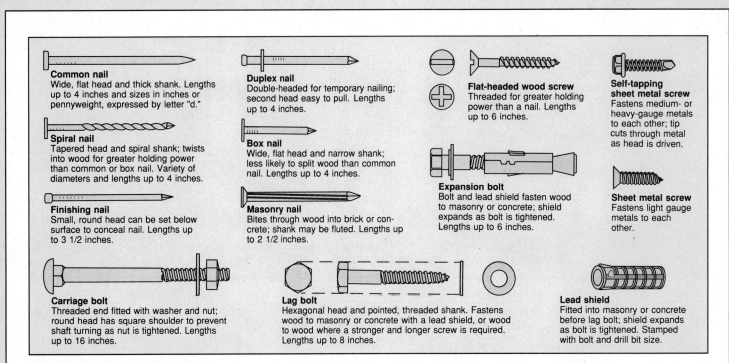

Common nail
Wide, flat head and thick shank. Lengths up to 4 inches and sizes in inches or pennyweight, expressed by letter "d."

Spiral nail
Tapered head and spiral shank; twists into wood for greater holding power than common or box nail. Variety of diameters and lengths up to 4 inches.

Finishing nail
Small, round head can be set below surface to conceal nail. Lengths up to 3 1/2 inches.

Duplex nail
Double-headed for temporary nailing; second head easy to pull. Lengths up to 4 inches.

Box nail
Wide, flat head and narrow shank; less likely to split wood than common nail. Lengths up to 4 inches.

Masonry nail
Bites through wood into brick or concrete; shank may be fluted. Lengths up to 2 1/2 inches.

Flat-headed wood screw
Threaded for greater holding power than a nail. Lengths up to 6 inches.

Expansion bolt
Bolt and lead shield fasten wood to masonry or concrete; shield expands as bolt is tightened. Lengths up to 6 inches.

Self-tapping sheet metal screw
Fastens medium- or heavy-gauge metals to each other; tip cuts through metal as head is driven.

Sheet metal screw
Fastens light gauge metals to each other.

Carriage bolt
Threaded end fitted with washer and nut; round head has square shoulder to prevent shaft turning as nut is tightened. Lengths up to 16 inches.

Lag bolt
Hexagonal head and pointed, threaded shank. Fastens wood to masonry or concrete with a lead shield, or wood to wood where a stronger and longer screw is required. Lengths up to 8 inches.

Lead shield
Fitted into masonry or concrete before lag bolt; shield expands as bolt is tightened. Stamped with bolt and drill bit size.

Choosing fasteners. Most building supply centers stock fasteners of many types and sizes. The chart above shows some common nails, screws, and bolts available for fastening wood or metal to wood, metal, masonry and concrete. The strength of a fastener depends on its length and diameter. Purchase fasteners compatible with the material and dimensions of the pieces being joined; make sure they are galvanized to prevent rust. As a rule of thumb, use a nail, screw or bolt at least one-and-one-half times as long as the thickness of the piece being fastened; use a carriage bolt at least 3/4 inch longer than the combined thicknesses of the pieces.

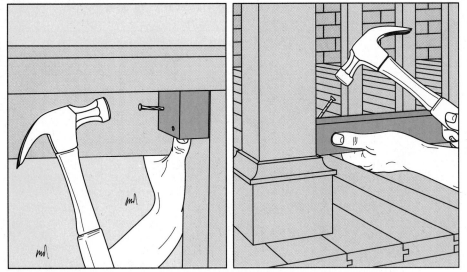

Nail set

1 Driving in nails. To replace a nail, remove the old one *(page 107)* and drive in a new one; if using the same nail hole, choose a new nail longer and thicker than the original. To fasten a joint, install at least two nails. To keep a nail from splitting the wood, punch a starter hole with an awl or bore a pilot hole *(page 117)* with a bit slightly smaller than the diameter of the shaft.

To nail through one piece of wood into a parallel piece, drive in each nail straight —a technique called face-nailing *(above, left)*. For greater holding power, drive in each nail at an opposite angle—called skew-nailing. To drive in a nail at an angle through one piece into a perpendicular piece is called toe-nailing *(above, right)*. Drive in a nail until its head is flush with the surface. Set the head of a finishing nail *(step 2)*. Fill old nail holes *(page 106)*.

2 Setting finishing nail heads. To drive a finishing nail head below the surface, use a nail set with a tip slightly smaller than the head. Position the tip of the nail set on the center of the head and tap sharply on the top of the nail set using a hammer *(above)*, driving the head about 1/16 inch below the surface. Fill holes above set heads and old nail holes *(page 106)*.

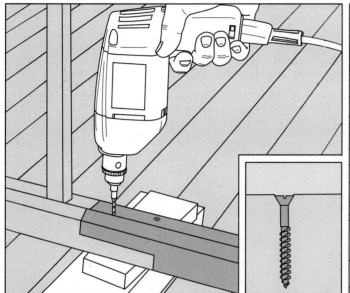

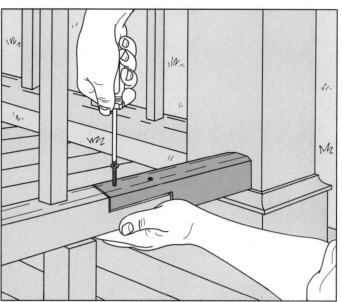

Driving in screws or lag bolts. To replace a wood screw, a metal screw or a lag bolt, remove the old one *(page 107)* and drive in a new one; choose a new wood screw or lag bolt longer and thicker than the original if using the same fastener hole. Install at least two fasteners at a joint. To install a wood screw, bore *(page 117)* a pilot hole *(above, left)*, and then a shank clearance hole into the wood piece being fastened. To set the screw head flush with the surface *(inset)*, use a combination bit; to countersink it, bore an extra 1/16 inch deep. Drive in the screw with a screwdriver of the same type and size as the screw head *(above, right)*.

To install a lag bolt without a shield, use the same procedure to bore holes and drive in the bolt, using a socket wrench or a nut driver of the same type and size as the bolt head. To install a lag bolt with a shield, bore a clearance hole for the shield and tap it into the hole using a ball-peen hammer; then, drive in the bolt. To install a screw in metal, bore a pilot hole and drive in the screw with a socket wrench or a nut driver of the same type and size as the screw head. For a self-tapping metal screw, bore only a shallow pilot hole to get the screw started. Fill old holes, and holes above countersunk heads *(page 106)*.

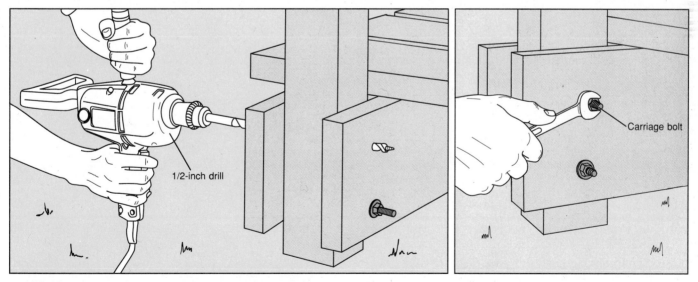

Installing carriage bolts and expansion bolts. To replace a carriage bolt or an expansion bolt, remove the old one *(page 107)* and install a new one, but avoid using the same hole for a new expansion bolt. Install at least two bolts at a joint.

To install a carriage bolt, bore *(page 117)* a clearance hole *(above, left)*. Fit the bolt into the hole, tapping it in place with a ball-peen hammer. Fit the washer on the end of the bolt and twist

on the nut by hand. Tighten the nut using a wrench of the same size as the nut *(above, right)*. Saw off excess bolt length *(page 112)*.

To install an expansion bolt in masonry, bore a clearance hole, starting with a wood bit and then changing to a masonry bit. Fit the expansion bolt into the hole, tapping it in place with a ball-peen hammer. Tighten the expansion bolt using a wrench or a nut driver of the same size as the bolt head. Fill old holes *(page 106)*.

REPLACING HARDWARE

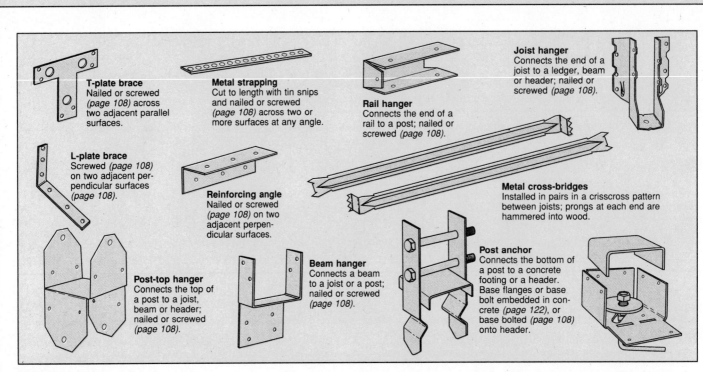

T-plate brace
Nailed or screwed *(page 108)* across two adjacent parallel surfaces.

Metal strapping
Cut to length with tin snips and nailed or screwed *(page 108)* across two or more surfaces at any angle.

Rail hanger
Connects the end of a rail to a post; nailed or screwed *(page 108).*

Joist hanger
Connects the end of a joist to a ledger, beam or header; nailed or screwed *(page 108).*

L-plate brace
Screwed *(page 108)* on two adjacent perpendicular surfaces *(page 108).*

Reinforcing angle
Nailed or screwed *(page 108)* on two adjacent perpendicular surfaces.

Metal cross-bridges
Installed in pairs in a crisscross pattern between joists; prongs at each end are hammered into wood.

Post-top hanger
Connects the top of a post to a joist, beam or header; nailed or screwed *(page 108).*

Beam hanger
Connects a beam to a joist or a post; nailed or screwed *(page 108).*

Post anchor
Connects the bottom of a post to a concrete footing or a header. Base flanges or base bolt embedded in concrete *(page 122),* or base bolted *(page 108)* onto header.

Choosing hardware. Most building supply centers stock a wide range of hardware types and sizes. The chart above shows some typical hardware used to fasten or reinforce joints between rails and posts; joists and ledgers, beams, headers or posts; beams and ledgers or posts; and posts and footings. Usually installed during construction, hardware can also be retrofitted. Purchase hardware compatible with the dimensions of the pieces being joined; install galvanized hardware and fasteners to prevent rust. As a rule of thumb, use nails or screws at least half as long as the thickness of the piece into which they are driven *(page 108).*

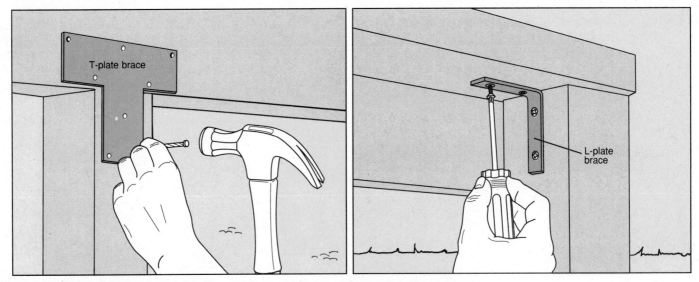

T-plate brace

L-plate brace

Removing and installing metal braces. To replace a brace, remove its fasteners *(page 107)*; to keep the piece it supported from falling, first have a helper support it, or install a jack *(page 124).* If necessary, remove the fasteners from both sides of a brace to take out or put in a new piece of lumber. For maximum reinforcement, install a brace or a hanger *(page 111)* at any joint fastened by toe-nailing and on each side of a joint.

To install a brace, position it on the joint and mark the fastener holes with a pencil or an awl. Remove the brace to bore pilot holes *(page 117)* for fasteners *(page 108)*; reposition the brace to drive in nails *(above, left)* or screws *(above, right).* Fill old holes *(page 106).*

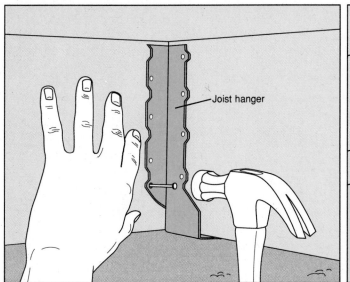

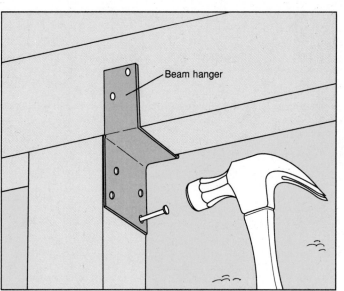

Removing and installing hangers. To replace a hanger, remove the fasteners *(page 107)*; keep the piece it supported from falling by having a helper support it, or install a jack *(page 124)*. If necessary, remove fasteners from both sides of a hanger to take out or put in a new piece of lumber. To loosen nails, pull out the sides of the hanger using a pry bar or a crowbar; if necessary, saw off the hanger *(page 112)*. Install a hanger or a brace *(page 110)* at any joint fastened by toe-nailing, to cover each side of the joint.

Position a new hanger on the joint, mark the fastener holes with a pencil or an awl and remove the hanger. Bore pilot holes *(page 117)*, reposition the hanger and tap in any prongs, then install fasteners *(page 108)*. If retrofitting a joist hanger, install it on one piece of lumber, position the piece, then install the hanger on the other piece *(above, left)*. If retrofitting with a beam hanger, install the hanger on both pieces, driving in fasteners alternately on each side of the hanger *(above, right)*. Fill old holes *(page 106)*.

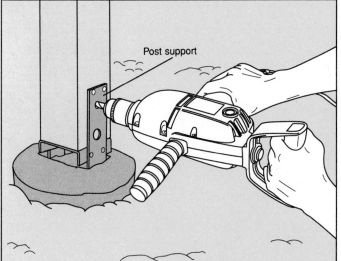

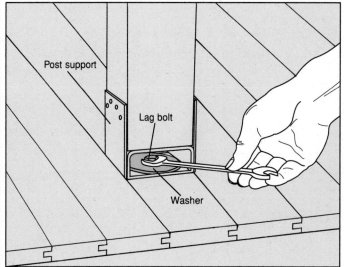

Removing and installing post anchors. To replace a post anchor, support the joist, beam or header above the post on each side using a jack *(page 124)*. To take off the post, remove its fasteners *(page 107)* from the post anchor and from the joist, beam or header. If the anchor base has flanges set in a concrete footing, chip out the concrete around them *(page 122)*. If the anchor base is held by a bolt in a footing, or by a lag bolt in a header, use a wrench to remove the fastener. Take off the washer and lift off the anchor base; pull down one side of the anchor base with a pry bar, if necessary. To remove a bolt set in a footing, chip out the concrete around it.

To install a post anchor in a footing, set its flanges or bolt in concrete *(page 122)*; if retrofitting, first position the post on the post support and nail *(page 108)* it to the post anchor, then install the post at the joist, beam or header with fasteners *(page 108)* or hardware *(page 110)*. To hold the anchor base to a bolt in a footing, fit the washer on the bolt and twist on the nut; to hold the anchor base to a header, install the washer and a lag bolt *(page 108)*: Place the post on the post support and install fasteners or hardware at the joist, beam or header and at the post anchor; bore a clearance hole *(page 117)* for any carriage bolt *(above, left)* or adjust the post and tighten the lag bolt *(above, right)* or nut. Fill old holes *(page 106)*.

MEASURING AND MARKING

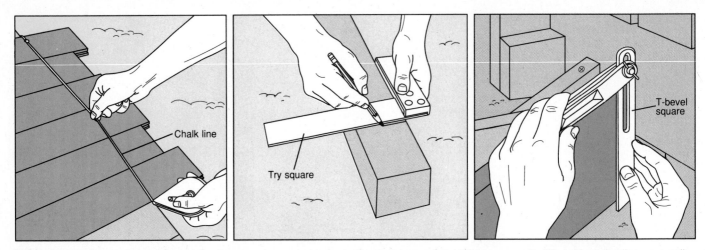

Using measuring and marking tools. Accuracy in measuring and marking is essential when cutting wood. The standard tool for measuring length is a tape measure, which can be used alone or with a carpenter's level or a plumb bob *(page 118)*. Be sure to add the case length when taking an inside measurement. Always measure both sides of an opening rather than presuming corners are square. And while a sawed off piece is an excellent template for tracing awkward angles and patterns, keep in mind that it has been shortened at least 1/8 inch by each cut; do not base measurements for a replacement piece on it. Use a sharp pencil or an awl for marking.

To mark long, straight lines, use a chalkline. Hook the line on a nail or board edge at one end and stretch it tautly to the other end; holding the case firmly, snap the line by lifting it straight up 3 to 4 inches *(above, left)* and letting it go. To mark straight lines and 90-degree angles across a piece, use a try square *(above, center)* or a carpenter's square, holding it flat against the side of the piece. To measure and transfer other than 90-degree angles, use a sliding bevel; loosen the wing nut, adjust the bevel to the angle *(above, right)* and tighten the wing nut. To lay brick courses evenly, use a mason's rule, marked on opposite sides in inches and in courses.

SAWING

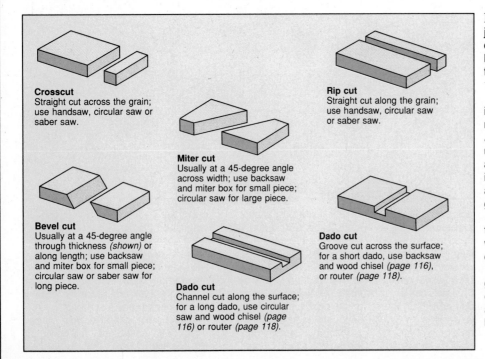

Crosscut
Straight cut across the grain; use handsaw, circular saw or saber saw.

Bevel cut
Usually at a 45-degree angle through thickness *(shown)* or along length; use backsaw and miter box for small piece; circular saw or saber saw for long piece.

Miter cut
Usually at a 45-degree angle across width; use backsaw and miter box for small piece; circular saw for large piece.

Dado cut
Channel cut along the surface; for a long dado, use circular saw and wood chisel *(page 116)* or router *(page 118)*.

Rip cut
Straight cut along the grain; use handsaw, circular saw or saber saw.

Dado cut
Groove cut across the surface; for a short dado, use backsaw and wood chisel *(page 116)*, or router *(page 118)*.

Making saw cuts. The quality of a wood joint is determined in part by the precision cutting of its components. The chart at left lists some common saw cuts and their preferred cutting tools. Consult the chart on page 115 for information on making wood joints.

Choose the best saw for the job and use it properly; make sure its blade is sharp. After measuring and marking the piece *(step above)*, set it on a rigid, flat work surface, unless it is already installed; a workbench or a pair of sawhorses is ideal. Unless a piece is long enough to be held firmly, secure it in a vise or with clamps *(page 116)*. Wear goggles when operating a power saw.

Align the saw blade on the waste side of the saw-cut mark to allow for the kerf—the width of the saw blade removed by a saw cut. For a smooth, even cut, temporarily nail *(page 108)* a straight-edged board as a saw guide along the mark, or along the outer edge of a power saw baseplate. To make a bevel cut along the length of a piece, bevel the saw guide at the desired angle.

SAWING (continued)

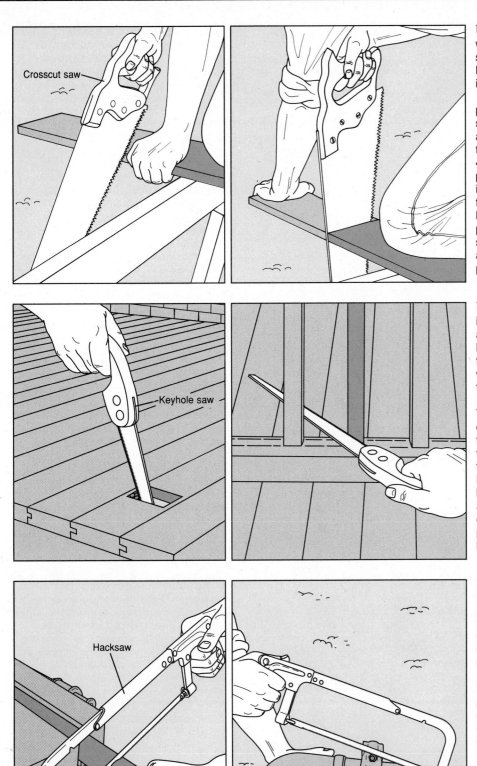

Crosscut saw

Keyhole saw

Hacksaw

Using a crosscut saw. For quick, rough wood cuts across the grain, use a crosscut saw, which has about eight teeth per inch. Measure and mark the piece *(page 112)*; if necessary, secure it with clamps *(page 116)*. To start the cut, hold the saw almost perpendicular to the piece, aligning your shoulder and arm with the sawcut mark, and draw the blade slowly toward you a few times. Lower the angle of the saw to about 45 degrees *(far left)* and cut through the piece on the downstroke until the blade is about 1 inch from the end of the cut. To finish the cut, grip the waste end with one hand, hold the saw perpendicular to the piece *(near left)* and use short up-and-down strokes. Apply preservative or finish on any exposed wood before installing the piece *(page 120)*.

Using a keyhole saw. For cuts within the interior of a piece, in a tight corner or at an awkward angle, use a keyhole saw, which has a long, tapered blade. Measure and mark the piece *(page 112)*; if necessary, secure it with clamps *(page 116)*. If starting in the interior of a piece, bore *(page 116)* and chisel *(page 116)* an opening for the saw blade. To start the cut, hold the saw almost perpendicular to the piece and draw the blade slowly toward you a few times. Lower the angle of the saw to about 45 degrees and cut through the piece on the downstroke *(far left)*; use long, even strokes to keep the blade from buckling. In a tight corner or at an awkward angle, cut with the heel *(near left)* or the toe of the blade using short, rapid strokes. Apply preservative or finish on any exposed wood before installing the piece *(page 120)*.

Using a keyhole saw. For cuts within the interior of a piece, in a tight corner or at an awkward angle, use a keyhole saw, which has a long, tapered blade. Measure and mark the piece *(page 112)*; if necessary, secure it with clamps *(page 116)*. If starting in the interior of a piece, bore *(page 117)* and chisel *(page 116)* an opening for the saw blade. To start the cut, hold the saw almost perpendicular to the piece and draw the blade slowly toward you a few times. Lower the angle of the saw to about 45 degrees and cut through the piece on the downstroke *(far left)*; use long, even strokes to keep the blade from buckling. In a tight corner or at an awkward angle, cut with the heel *(near left)* or the toe of the blade using short, rapid strokes. Apply preservative or finish on any exposed wood before installing the piece *(page 120)*.

SAWING (continued)

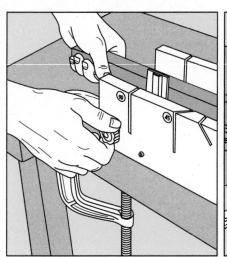

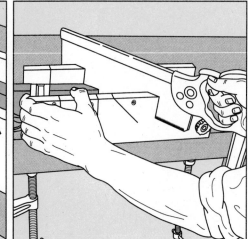

Using a backsaw and miter box. For fine cuts use a backsaw, which has about 13 teeth per inch. To saw a small piece at a 90-degree or 45-degree angle, use a miter box. Measure and mark the piece (page 112). If necessary, secure the piece with clamps (page 116). If using a miter box, protect its interior with a wood block and clamp it to the work surface. Align the mark with the appropriate angled slot and clamp the piece in the miter box (far left). Fit the saw blade into the slot. To start the cut, hold the saw level and draw the blade slowly toward you a few times. Applying light pressure, use long, smooth, back-and-forth strokes to cut through the piece (near left). Apply preservative or finish to exposed wood before installing the piece (page 120).

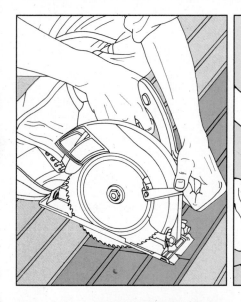

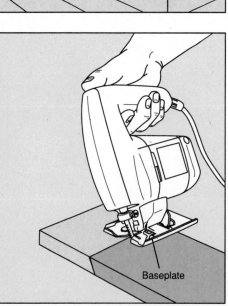

Guard

Saw guide

Using a circular saw. For crosscuts —across the grain, and rip cuts—along the grain, use a circular saw with a combination blade. Measure and mark the piece (page 112); if necessary, secure it with clamps (page 116). Set the blade depth: for a standard cut, about 1/2 inch more than the wood thickness; for a plunge cut, equal to the wood thickness. Set the baseplate to the angle desired. Wear safety goggles. For a standard cut, align the baseplate notch with the mark, turn on the saw and push it forward. For a plunge cut, lift the saw at an angle to the piece and rest the baseplate farther along the mark. Turn on the saw, raise the guard and slowly lower the blade (far left). To make a saw guide, temporarily nail (page 108) a straight-edged board along the outer edge of the baseplate (near left). Apply preservative or finish to exposed wood (page 120).

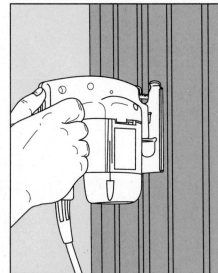

Baseplate

Using a saber saw. For cuts in the interior of a piece, in a tight corner or at an awkward angle, use a saber saw with a blade of 8 to 10 teeth per inch. Measure and mark the piece (page 112); if necessary, secure it with clamps (page 116). Wear safety goggles. For a standard cut, align the baseplate notch with the mark, turn on the saw and push it forward (far left). For a plunge cut, hold the saw at a 45-degree angle above the piece and rest the baseplate farther along the mark; turn on the saw and slowly lower the blade into the piece. For a bevel cut, set the baseplate to the desired angle first and follow the standard procedure (near left). To make a saw guide, temporarily nail (page 108) a straight-edged board along the outer edge of the baseplate. Apply preservative or finish to exposed wood before installing the piece (page 120).

MAKING WOOD JOINTS

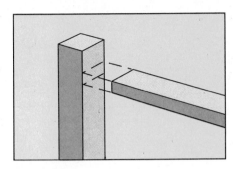

Butt joint
End of first piece fits against side *(shown)* or end of second piece, concealing end grain. To measure and mark angle at end of first piece, use a try square, a carpenter's square or a sliding bevel *(page 112)*. Cut with a crosscut saw or a circular saw *(page 112)*. Nail or screw pieces *(page 108)*; reinforce with hardware *(page 110)*.

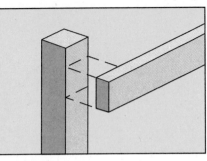

Overlap joint
First piece fits against second piece; end grain of first piece exposed *(shown)* or end of first piece butted against end or side of third piece. To measure and mark angle at piece ends, use a try square, a carpenter's square or a sliding bevel *(page 112)*. Cut with a crosscut saw or a circular saw *(page 112)*. Nail or screw pieces *(page 108)*.

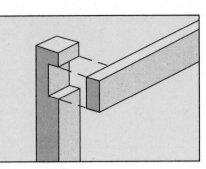

Full-lap joint
Full width and thickness of first piece fits dado in second piece. To measure and mark dado, trace first piece, or use a try square or a carpenter's square *(page 112)*. Cut dado using a backsaw or a circular saw *(page 112)* and a wood chisel *(page 116)*, or use a router *(page 118)*. Nail or screw pieces *(page 108)*.

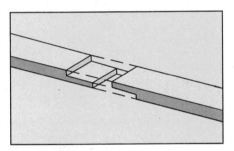

Half-lap joint
Ends of two pieces with opposite half laps fit together. To measure and mark half laps, use a try square or a carpenter's square *(page 112)*. Make both the same length and width and half the piece thickness. Cut with a crosscut saw or a circular saw *(page 112)*. Screw or bolt pieces *(page 108)*.

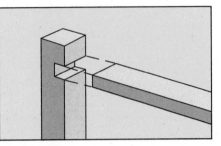

Dado joint
End of first piece fits into dado in second piece, concealing end grain. To measure and mark dado, trace first piece, or use a try square or a carpenter's square *(page 112)*. Cut dado using a backsaw or a circular saw *(page 112)* and a wood chisel *(page 116)*, or use a router *(page 118)*. Nail or screw pieces *(page 108)*.

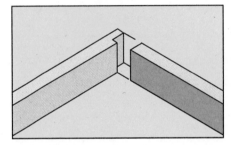

Rabbet joint
End of first piece fits into half lap of the same width and depth on second piece, concealing its end grain. To measure and mark, trace first piece or use a try square or a carpenter's square *(page 112)*. Cut with a crosscut saw, a backsaw or a circular saw *(page 112)*. Nail or screw pieces *(page 108)*.

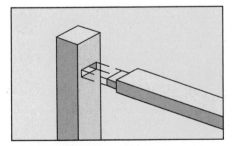

Mortise-and-tenon joint
Tenon on first piece, usually one-third its width and thickness and 2 inches long, fits matching mortise in second piece. To mark tenon, use a try square or a carpenter's square *(page 112)*; to cut, use a backsaw *(page 112)* and a wood chisel *(page 116)*. To make mortise, trace tenon and chisel. Nail pieces *(page 108)*.

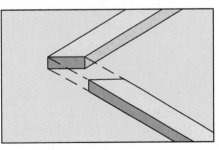

Miter joint
Ends of two pieces fit together at an angle, usually of 45 degrees, concealing end grain. To measure and mark, use a try square or a carpenter's square *(page 112)*. Make miter cuts on small pieces with a backsaw and miter box; on large pieces using a crosscut saw or a circular saw *(page 112)*. Nail or screw pieces *(page 108)*.

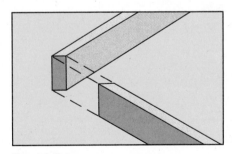

Bevel joint
Ends of two pieces fit together at an angle, usually of 45 degrees, concealing end grain. To measure and mark, use a try square or a carpenter's square *(page 112)*. Make bevel cuts on small pieces with a backsaw and miter box; on large pieces using a crosscut saw or a circular saw *(page 112)*. Nail or screw pieces *(page 108)*.

CLAMPING

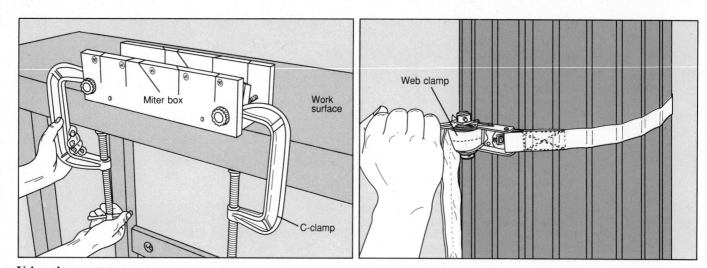

Using clamps. Unless a piece is already installed on the structure, or is long enough to be held firmly, secure it in a vise or with clamps while sawing *(page 112)*, chiseling *(step below)*, planing *(page 117)*, drilling *(page 117)* or routing *(page 118)*. To reinforce a joint, especially when splicing, apply resorcinol or epoxy glue following the manufacturer's directions, then clamp the joint. For most purposes, use a C clamp; for round or irregular wood pieces, use a web clamp.

To install a C clamp, position the jaws around the joint, or around the piece and the work surface. Protect undamaged surfaces from the jaws with pads of wood. Turn the screw *(above, left)* until the jaws grip snugly, then give an extra quarter turn. To install a web clamp, wrap the web around the joint, or around the piece and the work surface. If it is glued, position waxed paper under it to keep it from adhering. Thread the web through the ratchet and tighten the clamp by cranking the handle *(above, right)* or using a screwdriver.

CHISELING

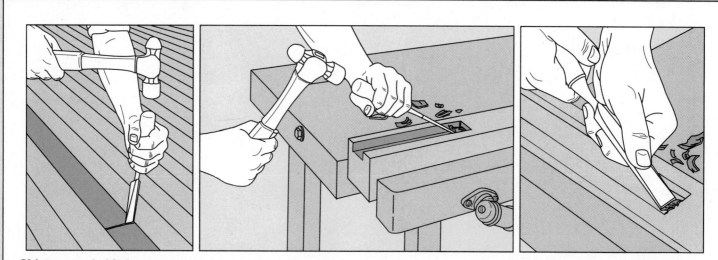

Using a wood chisel. Use a wood chisel to cut all the way or partway through a piece, to clean out a dado or mortise, or to shape and smooth a piece. If necessary, secure the piece with clamps *(step above)*. When working with a chisel, always point the cutting edge away from your body. To make a deep cut across a piece, hold the chisel at a 90-degree angle to it, with the bevel facing the waste. Strike the handle with a ball-peen hammer *(above, left)*; if the chisel handle is wooden and not capped by metal or plastic, use a mallet. To cut a dado or mortise, first saw *(page 112)* its edges or score its outline with a utility knife. Holding the chisel at a 90-degree angle to the piece, make a series of parallel cuts within the cut or scored outline. To remove the wood, hold the chisel bevel down, positioning its tip at a 30-degree angle to the wood surface, and tap the chisel handle *(above, center)*. Repeat the procedure, cutting to the depth desired. To shape or smooth a surface, turn the chisel bevel up; holding it almost horizontal, make light, even strokes using only hand pressure *(above, right)*. Apply preservative or finish on exposed grain before installing the piece *(page 120)*.

PLANING

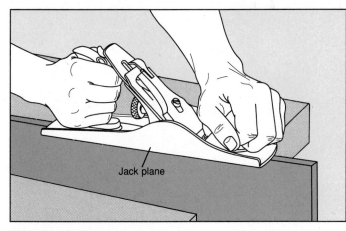

Jack plane

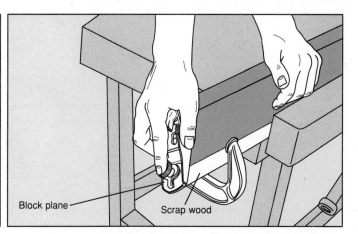

Block plane   Scrap wood

Using hand planes. Use a jack plane to smooth or trim a piece along the wood grain; use a block plane to smooth or trim across its end grain. If necessary, install clamps to secure the piece *(page 116)*. To adjust the blade, or iron, on either a jack plane or a block plane, hold the plane upside down. Turn the depth-adjustment nut until the edge of the iron barely protrudes from the mouth of the plane. Push the lateral-adjustment lever from side to side until the iron edge is aligned squarely within the mouth. Test the plane on scrap wood and readjust the iron until the plane provides the desired cutting depth.

To use a jack plane, hold the knob and the handle firmly. To start the stroke, put pressure on the toe. Push the plane along the grain, shifting pressure to the center *(above, left)*; before the plane passes the end of the piece, transfer pressure to the heel, raising the plane from the surface in a smooth motion. To use a block plane, work across the wood grain; clamp wood blocks on the sides of the piece to avoid splintering the wood. Hold the plane in one hand, with the heel of the lever cap resting in your palm, and push the plane forward, putting pressure on the toe; transfer pressure to the heel *(above, right)* to raise the plane from the surface in a smooth motion.

DRILLING

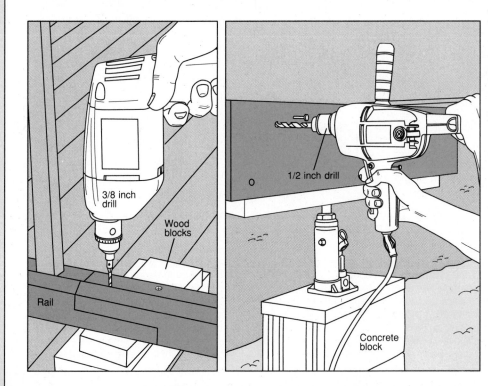

3/8 inch drill

Wood blocks

Rail

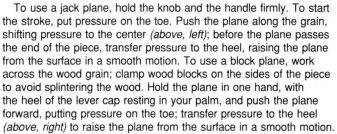

1/2 inch drill

Concrete block

Using a drill. A power drill is sized by the largest diameter bit its chuck can hold. For most drilling purposes, use a 3/8-inch drill; for heavy-duty drilling, use a 1/2-inch drill. Bits are available for boring into wood or drilling into metal or masonry; always use the proper bit for the job. To remove or install screws and lag bolts, use a bit of the same type and size as the screw or bolt head. Unplug the drill when loading and unloading a bit.

When drilling holes, the bit size to use depends on the diameter of the fastener *(page 108)* and the type of hole it requires. Bore or drill a pilot hole equal in depth to the fastener length, using a bit slightly narrower than the fastener. Bore or drill a clearance hole using a bit of the same diameter as the fastener. To mark the hole depth, wrap tape around the bit. Punch a starter hole for the bit using an awl. If necessary, install clamps to secure the piece being drilled *(page 116)*. Wear safety goggles. Position the bit at the starter hole, pull the trigger and push the bit into the wood *(far left)*; steady a 1/2-inch drill with your other hand *(near left)*. When withdrawing the bit, keep the drill running.

ROUTING

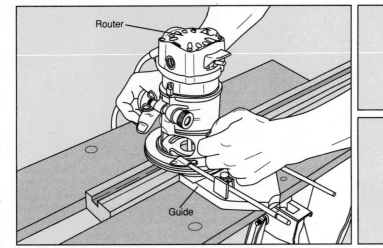

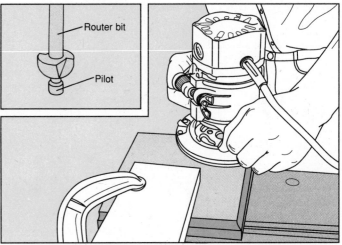

Using a router. Use a router to cut dadoes and rabbets, or to shape a piece. Measure and mark the piece *(page 112)*; if necessary, secure it with clamps *(page 116)*. To keep a router cutting straight, use its guide attachment; if it is not equipped with one, temporarily nail *(page 108)* a straight-edged board along one side of the base as a guide. Or, if cutting along the edge of a piece, use a bit with a built-in pilot. Unplug the router to load and unload the bit. Set the blade depth to remove no more than 3/8 inch of wood in

one pass. Wear safety goggles when operating the router. To rout a dado, turn on the router and feed the bit into the piece at one end. Guide the router slowly to the other end *(above, left)*. To rout along the edge of a piece, start 1 inch from the end, feed the bit straight in until the pilot touches the edge *(inset)* and slide the router steadily to the other end *(above, right)*. To complete the unfinished end, push the router in the other direction. Apply preservative or finish on exposed grain before installing the piece *(page 120)*.

LEVELING AND PLUMBING

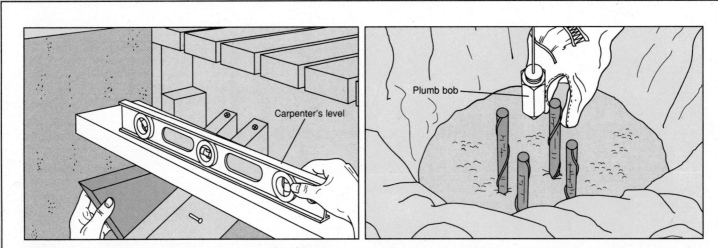

Using leveling tools and a plumb bob. The carpenter's level is the basic tool for determining whether a piece is level, or horizontal, and plumb, or vertical. It can also be used to verify 45-degree angles and to mark a horizontal, vertical or 45-degree-angle line. To use the carpenter's level, place it flat against the surface and check the bubble in the horizontal *(above, left)*, vertical or 45-degree-angle vial; when the bubble is centered between the two lines on the vial, the piece is correctly positioned—or the carpenter's level is correctly positioned on it. Repeat the procedure on two adjacent sides of a piece or in at least two directions on one side of it.

To check surfaces that are short, awkward or hard to reach, use a torpedo level, a small version of the carpenter's level. The line level, another variation of the carpenter's level, can be used to check the height of one piece using a distant piece as a reference. Run a line level tautly between the two pieces. Use a plumb bob to determine whether a piece is vertical, or to locate a point directly below another point. To use the plumb bob, suspend it from a nail or hold it at a reference point at least 1 to 2 feet above the ground and wait for the weighted bob to settle *(above, right)*. The tip of the bob is then at a point directly below the reference point.

USING ABRASIVES

SANDPAPER	GRIT	GRADE	USES
Very coarse	20	3 1/2	Removes heavy coats of paint and rust
	30	2 1/2	stains from wood surfaces
Coarse	40	1 1/2	Removes thick layers of paint and rust
	50	1	from wood and metal surfaces; smooths
	60	1/2	rough surfaces; levels deep depressions
	80	1/0	and scratches
Medium	100	2/0	Removes paint and rust from wood and
	120	3/0	metal surfaces; levels shallow depressions and scratches
Fine	150	4/0	Final sanding of bare wood and metal;
	180	5/0	light sanding of intermediate coats of paint on wood and metal surfaces

STEEL WOOL	GRADE	USES
Very coarse	3	Smooths rough surfaces and removes paint and rust from wood and metal surfaces
Coarse	2	Removes paint and rust from wood and metal surfaces

Choosing an abrasive. Use sandpaper or steel wool as an abrasive to groom surfaces. The chart at left lists appropriate uses for each sandpaper grit or grade and each steel wool grade. When using an abrasive, wear a dust mask to avoid inhaling particles, and wear work gloves. After using an abrasive, brush off dust using a whisk and wipe the surface with a tack cloth *(page 102)*. On the sandpaper backing is listed its grit type and size, and the backing weight —ranging from A, the lightest, to E, the heaviest. Garnet, reddish in color, is best for smoothing rough wood surfaces, although it wears quickly. Aluminum oxide is a tough synthetic, colored light grey to brown; use it to sand rough to medium wood surfaces or to remove rust from metal. Steel wool comes in pads ranging from very coarse to superfine. Use the coarser grades of steel wool to remove rust from fasteners and hardware, to take paint off decorative turnings and to smooth tight corners.

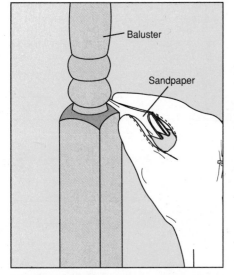

Working by hand. Work by hand using sandpaper or steel wool *(step above)* to remove rust from fasteners and hardware, to remove paint from decorative turnings and to smooth tight corners. Wear a dust mask and work gloves. Stroke along the grain as much as possible, applying even, moderate pressure. To smooth a tight corner, cut a strip of sandpaper, fold it in half and rub using the fold *(above)*. Replace sandpaper or steel wool when it clogs and cannot be cleared by tapping it. Use a whisk to brush off dust. Before applying a finish, wipe the surface with a tack cloth *(page 102)*.

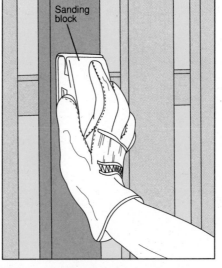

Using a sanding block. Use sandpaper *(step above)* and a sanding block to smooth a small, flat surface. Wear a dust mask and work gloves. Cut a sheet of sandpaper to fit the sanding block, using scissors or a utility knife. Stroke along the grain as much as possible, applying even, moderate pressure *(above)*. Replace the sandpaper when it clogs and cannot be cleared by tapping the sanding block on a hard surface. Use a whisk to brush off dust. Before applying a finish, wipe the surface with a tack cloth *(page 102)*.

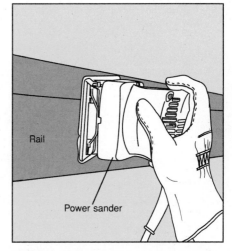

Using a power sander. Use sandpaper *(step above)* and a belt sander or an orbital sander to smooth a large, flat surface. Wear a dust mask and work gloves. A belt sander is best for removing thick layers of paint or for smoothing rough surfaces; an orbital sander is best for final smoothing or for sanding unfinished surfaces. Cut a sheet of sandpaper to fit the sander, using scissors or a utility knife. Applying even, moderate pressure, work along the grain using a belt sander *(above)*; with an orbital sander, keep it moving to prevent gouges. Replace sandpaper when it clogs. Use a whisk to brush off dust. Before applying a finish, wipe the surface with a tack cloth *(page 102)*.

REMOVING FINISHES

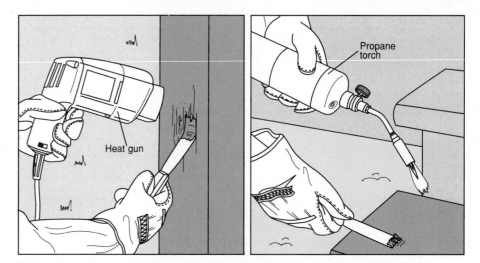

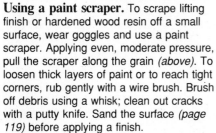

Using a paint scraper. To scrape lifting finish or hardened wood resin off a small surface, wear goggles and use a paint scraper. Applying even, moderate pressure, pull the scraper along the grain *(above)*. To loosen thick layers of paint or to reach tight corners, rub gently with a wire brush. Brush off debris using a whisk; clean out cracks with a putty knife. Sand the surface *(page 119)* before applying a finish.

Using a heat gun or propane torch. To strip thick layers of paint off a large surface or structure, use a heat gun; if there is no flammable material nearby, use a propane torch. Wear work gloves and goggles—as well as a respirator, if you suspect the paint contains lead *(page 9)*. Keep a portable fire extinguisher on hand *(page 10)*. Hold the heat gun or propane torch several inches away from the surface and wait no more than 5 to 10 seconds for the paint to soften or blister—any closer or a longer time may burn the wood or ignite the paint. Move the heat gun or propane torch ahead, along the grain; scrape off the loosened paint behind it with a putty knife *(above, left and right)*. Use improvised tools for hard-to-reach areas. Sand the surface *(page 119)* before applying a finish.

APPLYING PRESERVATIVES AND FINISHES

FINISH	CHARACTERISTICS	REMARKS
Water-repellent preservative	May contain inorganic arsenic, fungicides, wax, solvents; may contain pigment or may temporarily darken wood; eventually weathers to natural color	Apply to bare wood; dip or brush on; can be used under finish in place of primer or for treating end grain on pressure-treated wood; reapply or touch up every 1-2 years
Semi-transparent penetrating stain	Alkyd-based; may contain water repellents, fungicides and mildewcides; contains pigment that tints wood but does not obscure wood grain; penetrates wood	Brush, roll or spray on; must be applied to bare wood or over similar stain; stir frequently to distribute pigment; reapply or touch up every 2-3 years
Opaque stain	Latex- or alkyd-based; colors but does not completely obscure wood grain; forms a thin film on wood surface	Brush, roll or spray on; reapply or touch up every 4-5 years
Enamel paint	Alkyd-based; obscures wood grain; forms a film on wood surface	Brush, roll or spray on; harder and more resistant than other exterior paints; reapply or touch up every 5-6 years
Exterior-grade alkyd paint	Contains synthetic resins; may contain fungicides and mildewcides; forms a film on wood surface	Brush, roll or spray on; apply alkyd primer, then one or two top coats; reapply or touch up every 4-6 years
Exterior-grade latex paint	Contains acrylic or vinyl resins; may contain fungicides and mildewcides; forms a film on wood surface	Brush, roll or spray on; apply latex or alkyd primer, then one or two top coats; reapply or touch up every 4-6 years
Metal paint	Alkyd- or latex-based; contains a rust inhibitor or requires a rust-inhibiting primer; galvanized metal primer available	Brush, roll or spray on; reapply every 5-6 years, touch up rust spots immediately

Choosing a finish. Consult the chart above to select a finish; before applying it, sand the surface *(page 119)*. Pay close attention to the finish manufacturer's instructions concerning surface preparation, primer compatibility, finish application and safety. Finishing products can be toxic; refer to the safety information on page 8. Use tarps and masking tape to protect surfaces around the work area. Wear long pants, a long-sleeved shirt and rubber gloves while applying the finish. Keep product labels for reference when a touch-up or a new finish is necessary. Apply a small test patch of finish on an inconspicuous surface to check its effect before starting work.

APPLYING PRESERVATIVES AND FINISHES (continued)

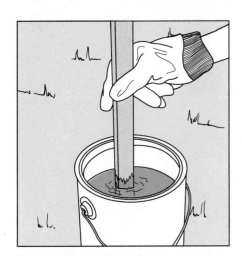

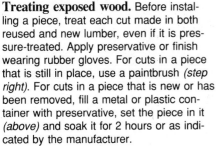

Treating exposed wood. Before instal-ling a piece, treat each cut made in both reused and new lumber, even if it is pres-sure-treated. Apply preservative or finish wearing rubber gloves. For cuts in a piece that is still in place, use a paintbrush *(step right)*. For cuts in a piece that is new or has been removed, fill a metal or plastic con-tainer with preservative, set the piece in it *(above)* and soak it for 2 hours or as indi-cated by the manufacturer.

Using a paintbrush or painting mitt. To apply preservative or finish to most surfaces, use a paintbrush; a synthetic, flagged-bristle type is recommended. To apply finish to dec-orative turnings, on awkward surfaces or in tight corners, use a painting mitt. Apply finish evenly, working top to bottom, coating first the surfaces hardest to reach. Ensure that the end grain is adequately coated. Wear rubber gloves when working with toxic materials.

To use a paintbrush, load about half the bristle length, then brush lightly across the container lip to remove excess. Working along the grain, use short and then long strokes to spread the finish evenly along the surface *(above, left)*. To use a painting mitt, insert a plastic liner to prevent finish from seeping through it. Dip the mitt in the finish, wipe off excess on the container lip and rub the mitt along the surface *(above, right)*. Sand the surface between coats of finish *(page 119)*.

Using a roller. To apply finish to large, flat surfaces, wear rubber gloves and use a roller; to avoid reaching, fit it with an extension pole. Choose the proper roller; most finishes call for a short nap of synthetic fiber. Pour about 1 inch of finish into a roller pan; use the flat, ridged end of the pan to work finish into the roller, without overloading it. Roll on the finish evenly, working on a small area at a time, pushing and pulling the roller along the grain *(above)*. To spread a stain or penetrating finish evenly, backbrush the edges using a dry paintbrush. Sand the surface between coats of finish *(page 119)*.

Using a sprayer. To apply finish to large, irregular surfaces, use a paint sprayer, available at a tool rental agency. Work only on a calm day and wear work gloves, goggles and a respirator. Pour about 8 ounces of finish into the sprayer reservoir; if applying paint, first filter out lumps through a doubled layer of cheesecloth. Screw the reser-voir tightly onto the gun. Test the sprayer on a scrap piece; adjust the nozzle until the sprayer produces an even coating. Working top to bottom, hold the sprayer nozzle 10 to 12 inches from the surface and pull the trigger *(above)*; move the sprayer slowly from side to side. Sand the surface between coats of finish *(page 119)*.

WORKING WITH CONCRETE

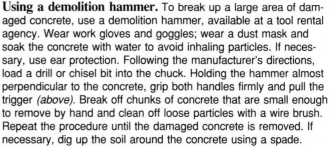

Using a chisel and sledgehammer. To break up a small area of damaged concrete, use a bull-point chisel and a sledgehammer. Wear work gloves and goggles; to avoid inhaling particles, wear a dust mask and soak the concrete with water. Hold the chisel almost perpendicular to the concrete and strike the end of it sharply with the sledgehammer *(above)*. Chip off chunks of concrete that are small enough to remove by hand and clean off loose particles with a wire brush. Repeat the procedure until the damaged concrete is removed. If necessary, dig up the soil around the concrete footing using a spade.

Using a demolition hammer. To break up a large area of damaged concrete, use a demolition hammer, available at a tool rental agency. Wear work gloves and goggles; wear a dust mask and soak the concrete with water to avoid inhaling particles. If necessary, use ear protection. Following the manufacturer's directions, load a drill or chisel bit into the chuck. Holding the hammer almost perpendicular to the concrete, grip both handles firmly and pull the trigger *(above)*. Break off chunks of concrete that are small enough to remove by hand and clean off loose particles with a wire brush. Repeat the procedure until the damaged concrete is removed. If necessary, dig up the soil around the concrete using a spade.

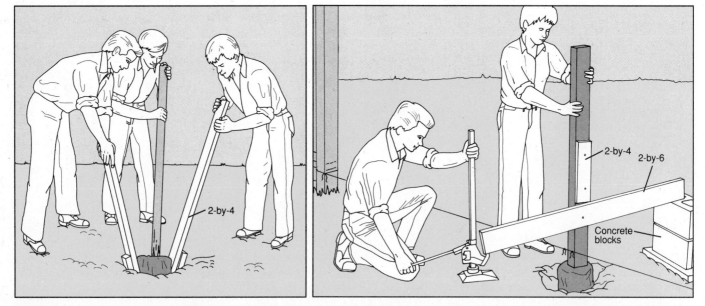

Removing a footing with wooden levers or a car jack. To remove a post and damaged concrete footing, dig up the soil around the footing using a spade. Loosen the footing by rocking the post back and forth. To lift out the post and footing, have two helpers use 2-by-4s as levers under the footing while you pull out the post *(above, left)*. It may be easier to lift out the post and footing using a car jack. Position the car jack on one side of the post and two concrete blocks, stacked, on the opposite side, 2 to 3 feet away from the post. Nail a 2-by-4 at least 12 inches long on the post, about 18 inches from the ground. Position the edge of a 2-by-6 board under it, resting one end on the car jack and the other on the concrete blocks; drive one nail through the center of the board for stability. Support the car jack firmly, have a helper support the post and raise the car jack to lift out the post and footing *(above, right)*.

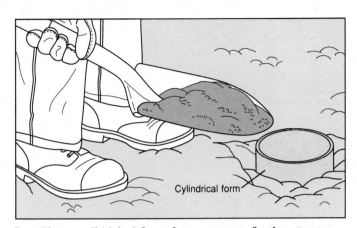

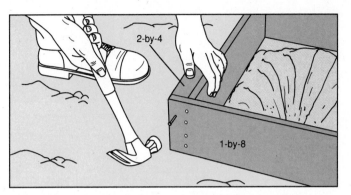

Installing a cylindrical form for a concrete footing. Purchase a form twice the diameter of the post. For a new post and footing, cut the form to length with a crosscut saw *(page 112)* and position it in the posthole. Backfill around it with soil *(above)*, tamping the soil every 6 inches using the end of a 2-by-4. If retrofitting a concrete footing for a post, slit open the side of the form with a utility knife or saber saw, position the form around the post and tie it closed with wire. Cut off the top edge with a utility knife after the concrete has set for 48 hours *(steps below)*.

Installing a wood form for a concrete footing. Purchase 1-by-8s for the sides and 2-by-4s for stakes. Saw two opposite sides to the length required, and two opposite sides 4 inches longer than required *(page 112)*. Saw a stake for each corner. Nail the sides together *(page 108)*, leaving 2 inches at each end of the longer boards. Position the form, drive the stakes into the ground with a sledgehammer, and nail them *(above)*. Using a carpenter's level *(page 118)*, adjust the form by tapping the stakes farther into the ground. Backfill soil around the form to keep it from moving. Take apart the form by pulling the nails *(page 107)* after the concrete has set for 48 hours *(steps below)*.

Mixing concrete, concrete patching compound or mortar. To repair or replace a concrete footing, use premixed concrete, a mixture of cement, sand and coarse aggregate; for a small repair, use concrete patching compound. To repoint or replace bricks, use ready-mix mortar, a mixture of cement and sand. Wearing work gloves, use a spade to mix concrete in a metal container *(above)*, adding clean water according to the manufacturer's directions. Dig out the center of a mound of concrete to add the water, then turn the concrete until it is absorbed. Mix concrete patching compound or mortar the same way. For a small repair, use a trowel to mix a small amount on a mason's hawk or a piece of plywood.

Pouring and shaping a concrete footing. Wearing work gloves, use a spade to pour a concrete footing. To settle the concrete, work a 2-by-4 up and down in it or tap the sides of the form. For a post or wood pier, use a trowel to add concrete around its base, sloping it away from the post or pier *(above, top)*. For a stair assembly or brick pier, level the concrete by pulling a 2-by-4 across the surface, shifting it from side to side to keep the concrete from adhering. Use a trowel to fill in depressions and smooth the surface *(above, bottom)*. Let the concrete set for 48 hours; dampen it with water to keep it from drying out for one week.

USING JACKS

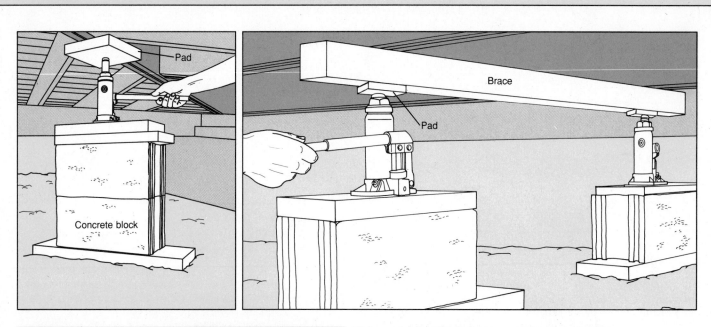

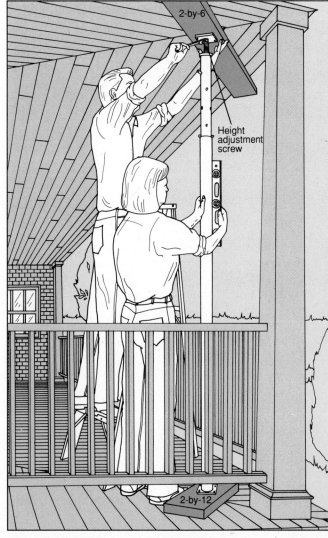

Using a hydraulic jack. Use a hydraulic jack, available at a tool rental agency, to support a joist, ledger, beam or header up to 6 feet above the ground. To set up a jack, position it on a level wood pad or concrete block, directly below the point to be supported. If necessary, add to the reach of the jack with a 4-by-4, or by stacking concrete blocks under it. Position a 2-by-6 or 2-by-8 pad against the part being supported and raise the jack until it fits snugly under the pad, supporting the part in position but not lifting it *(above, left)*. To support two or more parallel points at the same time, use a brace at least 4 inches thick—doubled 2-by-10s work well—supported by jacks every 6 to 8 feet. Having helpers support the brace and pads, use the same procedure to raise each jack under the brace *(above, right)*. While a jack is not being raised, remove its handle.

Using a telescoping jack. A telescoping jack, available at a tool rental agency, can be used to support a joist, ledger, beam or header 5 to 12 feet above the ground. To set up a jack, nail the bottom plate onto a 2-by-10 or 2-by-12 pad, 2 to 3 feet long *(page 108)*. Use a 2-by-6 pad on the top plate; if positioning the jack under a doubled corner joist, use a pad long enough to reach the header on each side of the corner. With a helper supporting the jack, raise the inner tube to within 2 to 3 inches of the point to be supported; insert the pin through the holes to lock it. Have a helper plumb the jack with a level *(page 118)*, and position the pad on the top plate. Turn the height adjustment screw clockwise until the top plate fits snugly under the pad *(left)*, supporting the structure without raising it.

SETTING UP FOR WORK IN AWKWARD AREAS

Working under a low structure. In a cramped space, a little extra planning can make repairs safer and more comfortable. When working under a porch, for example, set up a temporary barrier to keep others off it *(page 11)*. Place a large, light-colored tarp on the ground; it cushions your knees and provides a good backdrop for tools and hardware. Illuminate the area with a portable work light or a freestanding flashlight—not a camping lantern. In hot weather, use a large window fan to ventilate the work area. Wear goggles as eye protection against falling debris; wear a dust mask when working with concrete or mortar *(above)*.

Working safely on a high structure. To work along the length of a high deck, erect a scaffold of 2-by-12s nailed on sawhorses *(page 108)*; support one end on the stair assembly, if possible *(above)*. If the sawhorses are more than 6 feet apart, double the 2-by-12s. Set the feet of a ladder level. Use extension feet on uneven ground, or dig and level the soil. If possible, tie the ladder to the structure. Wear shoes or boots with a well-defined heel for a secure grip. Face a ladder to climb up or down and use both hands to grasp the rungs, not the siderails. Keep your belt buckle between the siderails, and your hips below the top rung.

GETTING HELP WHEN YOU NEED IT

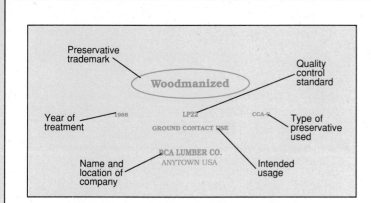

Preparing for the job. Purchase lumber, tools and supplies at a lumber yard or a building supply center. A special tool, such as a telescoping jack or a demolition hammer, is usually available at a tool rental agency. Before starting a repair, make a list of all the materials and supplies required; resist the temptation to improvise.

Wood is given a *grade stamp* at the lumber mill, based on a grading system determined by a regional wood association. Ratings are assigned for size, type, strength and defects in appearance. If in doubt about the information indicated or the grade of wood you should purchase, consult your lumber dealer or local wood products association.

All pressure-treated wood should carry a *quality control stamp (left)*. Only certain woods, notably pine, can be pressure-treated effectively. Pressure-treated wood is guaranteed against damage caused by decay or insects. Request a consumer information sheet from the manufacturer or merchant. It outlines health precautions to take with pressure-treated wood, and the conditions of the guarantee. If you fail to treat cut end grain, for example, the guarantee may be voided.

When purchasing lumber, specify its nominal dimensions; its actual size is somewhat smaller. A nominal 2-by-4, for instance, is actually 1 1/2 inches by 3 1/2 inches after it is milled. Most lumber yards will deliver wood; check the order carefully to ensure you have received the correct amount, lengths and grade.

Regional building codes usually do not apply to repairs on an existing structure. Consult your municipal building authority for information on local codes governing the depth of concrete footings and other specifications, as well as on the proper disposal of rubble. When in doubt about the structural integrity of your porch, deck or fence, have it checked by a professional carpenter or your local building inspector; call a pest-control professional if you suspect insect infestation.

INDEX

Page references in *italics* indicate an illustration of the subject mentioned. Page references in **bold** indicate a Troubleshooting Guide for the subject mentioned.

ACKNOWLEDGMENTS

The editors wish to thank the following:
Brick Institute of America, Reston, Va.; Richard Crutcher, Shelburne Falls, Mass.; Forintek Canada Corp., Ottawa, Ont.; Gamma Tool Rental Inc., Montreal, Que.; Dennis A. Gates, Teco Products, Germantown, Mass.; Seán Gilsenan, Cashway Building Centres, Ajax, Ont.; Andrew Grothé, Montreal, Que.; Hand Tools Institute, Tarrytown, N.Y.; John Hansen, Troy Chemical Co., Livingston, N.J.; Bernie Hamilton, Kango International Inc., Toronto, Ont.; Larry Jones, Robert E. Meadows P.C. Architect, New York, N.Y.; Leonard G. Lee, Lee Valley Tools Ltd., Ottawa, Ont.; John Leeke, Preservation Consultant, Sanford, Maine; R.A. (Skip) Lennox, Glidden Company (Canada) Ltd., Toronto, Ont.; Theo Leonov, Koppers Building Products Ltd., Mississauga, Ont.; Les Portes & Vitraux Anciens Inc., Montreal, Que.; Ren Molnar, Ren Home Consultation, Ottawa, Ont.; Donald L. Osterhout, Southern Building Codes Congress International, Inc., Birmingham, Ala.; Sascho Sealants, Commerce City, Colo.; Andris Vitins, Toronto, Ont.; Dr. David Walker, Division of Emergency Medicine, Queen's University, Kingston, Ont.; Western Wood Products Association, Portland, Oreg.

The following persons also assisted in the preparation of this book:
René Bertrand, Arlene Case, Réjean Coulombe, Cathleen Farrell, Patrick J. Gordon, Normand Guilbeault, Dianne Thomas, Natalie Watanabe and Billy Wisse.